BLACK & WHITE

ROSS TAYLOR

BLACK & WHITE

with PAUL THOMAS

mower

A catalogue record for this book is available from the National Library of New Zealand

ISBN 978-1-990003-44-8

A Mower Book
Published in 2022 by Upstart Press Ltd
26 Greenpark Road, Penrose
Auckland 1061
New Zealand

Designed by Nick Turzynski, redinc. book design, www.redinc.co.nz

Printed by 1010 Printing International Ltd, China

Jacket photographs
Front: Ross during the second test match between Australia and New Zealand at the Mel-
bourne Cricket Ground, 28 December 2019.
Back: Ross on his way out to bat at the MCG on day three of the second test match between
New Zealand and Australia, 28 December 2019.
PHOTOSPORT/GETTY

For Victoria, Mackenzie, Jonty and Adelaide and to all my family and friends, thanks for all your love and support — I couldn't have done it without you.

Fa'amanuia le Atua i la outou ta'aaloga
(God bless this game)

Va'ai lelei mata
(Literally: Use your eyes properly. Metaphorically: Stay focused
and keep your head in the game)

Fa'amanuia i lau ta
(Good luck with your batting)

Fa'apea foi tou au uma
(Good luck to the whole team as well)

Naoupu Taylor's pre-game message to her son, Kelu (Ross)

Inside each of us there are two wolves.
One is evil: it is anger, envy, greed, arrogance, self-pity,
resentment, lies and ego.
One is good: it is love, hope, humility, kindness, empathy,
compassion, truth and faith.
Which wolf wins? The one you feed.

TWO WOLVES: A Cherokee Legend

Contents

Foreword   **11**

Prelude: Redemption at the Rose Bowl   **15**

PART ONE: THE BOY FROM THE BUSH   **29**

1. What's in a Name?   **30**
2. Going Places   **40**
3. Landing on my Feet   **53**
4. Foo (aka Black Cap 234)   **64**

PART TWO: SCAR TISSUE   **79**

5. Be Careful What You Wish For   **80**
6. Captain Cooked?   **95**
7. Blindsided   **108**
8. Forgive but don't Forget   **125**

PART THREE: WELCOME TO MY WORLD   **143**

9. Eyeballs   **144**
10. Mind Game   **158**
11. Yellow Brick Road   **170**
12. Have Bat, Will Travel   **182**
13. Top Guns   **197**
14. Standing in my Shoes   **208**

PART FOUR: THE LONG GOODBYE   **219**

15. A Game of Inches   **220**
16. The Road to the Rose Bowl   **234**
17. Handle with Care   **245**
18. The Boys   **252**
19. Finishing Touches   **265**

Career Record   **277**

Acknowledgement   **279**

Foreword

Written just a few months before Martin Crowe passed away, this message was first read by Ross on the eve of the second test match between New Zealand and Australia at Perth in November 2015. His innings of 290 and 36 not out earned him the man of the match award.

Even if Ross hadn't asked me to pen my feelings about his career, his quest for test centuries and his life in general, I would have done it anyway. Since he first cold-called me to talk about helping him with his game in 2006, I have naturally been inclined to want to offer guidance. Such is the nature of the man . . . I just wanted to be there for him. In a sense, he became the son I never had.

These words will hopefully enlighten those who are interested in knowing the deeper truth about Ross. It also gives me a chance to share my final words with him, to give him one last nudge, to thank him in the most grateful way for the experience of watching his maturity blossom.

What perhaps struck me most about Ross was his shyness — a characteristic that had sprung from his humble beginnings. That reserve, though, was accompanied by a warm smile and a genuine care for others around him. His loving upbringing was obvious.

Not so obvious, though, was how quickly and how badly his calm world would become flipped upside down. The depths of despair he would endure following his mean-spirited removal as the national cricket captain in late 2012 cut deeper than most people would have ever imagined.

For the first time in his life, he experienced overwhelming anger, resentment and mistrust. Trust had never been a problem for Ross. But, in a flash, all that was gone — such was the rotten odour that permeated his gunning down.

Three years on, Ross responded earnestly and proudly. He kept his head up and achieved more extraordinary feats with bat in hand, all for the team cause. Alas, all that came with a heavy toll. The effort to stay positive and to try to believe again in the meaning of trust exhausted his reserves. During the 2015 Cricket World Cup he was desperately trying to ignite another burner, to get the fire in the belly once more, but it never quite came.

As I write this, Ross is on the wrong side of thirty. He will have had to decide whether he wants to carve out one further rich period, one more fitting chapter to finish his days as one of our finest batsmen. Part of that will have involved remaining disciplined in his physical conditioning, his speed of foot and his endurance — all to enable him to push on and cement his name consistently among the top ten test batsmen in the world.

Perhaps to truly do so, Ross needs to chip off the remaining barnacles of an incident that must never be allowed to define him or steer him from his commitment and deep love of the game. All this so he can finish with a satisfied heart.

And yet, this is not so important. The centuries aren't the aim any more, for he will at some stage own, or be close to owning, the record for most international centuries for his country. No, the fundamental truth is to find a balance that will carry his love of playing the game through to the end. There is a big picture at play.

It is just sport. And while it's a privilege and luxury to be able to flirt with this great game, it's nothing like the realities of life. It is as a loving and protective husband, father, son and friend that Ross's peace and fulfilment will ultimately lie. Balancing the real with the lure to chase a game will be his challenge, and the making of him. His beautiful, naturally constructed home life will always be his foundation. No longer will he be rocked and shocked by the frenzied ego on tour. His humble upbringing will ensure he always heads back to the core of who he really is.

Essentially, Ross reveals his deepest truth when reaching a century. He stands modestly still, with arms aloft and tongue sticking out. It is done as a symbol of thanks to his family, friends and fans. It shows his gratefulness for the role he played in entertaining them . . . In that symbolic moment, his grace of character is on display. He has the respect, admiration and love of New Zealanders and many others around the globe.

As I write these final words, I wonder, with so much of his journey still to come, how it will all end up for him.

My sense is that he will pace himself, lifting massively at times, and all the while carve out that legacy he has longed for since day one. This will allow his true worth, as a New Zealander with strong values, to define him. Deep down, that will please Ross.

I trust in him.

Martin Crowe,
Auckland, 12 November 2015

Prelude: Redemption at the Rose Bowl

At dinner the night before the World Test Championship (WTC) final against India at the Rose Bowl in Southampton, I shared a Covid-protocol table for two with Kane Williamson. He asked me how I was going. Usually, when people ask that question, they don't want or expect a detailed analysis of your mental, physical and emotional state. They're really just saying "G'day". And we respond in kind with something like, "Oh, not too bad. Yourself?" But on the eve of what was probably the biggest game of our lives, neither of us was in the mood for idle chitchat.

I'd played 442 games for New Zealand, including 107 test matches. I'd been through form troughs and pressure periods and a traumatic episode that reverberated for years afterwards. I was a highly experienced, resilient campaigner who'd learned how to get through the tough times. Experience is an asset, but there's a downside: some of it is experience of failure. You know things can go wrong; indeed, you know things can go wrong in ways you never imagined. That sort of experience can instil a fear of failure which is inhibiting, whereas youthful naivety can be liberating. That's why selectors in team sports talk about that desirable mix of youth and experience.

I said, "Well, not great, but I'm trying to hang in there."

And Kane said, "I was just asking to initiate a conversation, because I feel like I'm going to get out every ball."

We were coming off a test series win in England, our first since 1999. I'd gone into that series not in the best of form, head space or shape — I had a calf muscle injury. I was 37 years old and some in the media were starting to question my place in the team. More to the point, I'd been dropped from the Black Caps Twenty20 team and sensed that those who'd made that decision weren't necessarily inclined to stop there.

Kane asked how I'd approached facing England's world-class seam and swing bowling combination Jimmy Anderson and Stuart Broad, in overcast conditions and armed with the bowler-friendly Duke ball, in the second test at Edgbaston. I said, "Do you really want to know?" He did, so I told him what was going through my mind as I waited to bat.

To put it bluntly, I was crapping myself. Head coach Gary Stead was on the other side of the room. I was looking at him, thinking, 'He wants me gone but doesn't want to get crucified in the media for dropping me.' I was looking at batting coach Luke Ronchi, thinking, 'He doesn't know how I'm going to score my next run.'

Even my wife Victoria had had a go at me, telling me to pull myself together and front up. She had a gut feeling we were going to win the WTC final but could see this scenario unfolding: I don't perform against England; I don't get picked for the final; we win; I never get over it. Victoria doesn't tell me what to do very often, but this time she didn't hold back. I didn't enjoy it one little bit, but maybe I needed it.

Devon Conway had made 200 on debut in the first test at Lord's, compelling evidence that he had the game and the mind for test cricket. Will Young had come in from scoring runs in county cricket and was out in the middle playing well. Generation Next was becoming Generation Now in front of our eyes. The clouds were rolling in. In that series the older ball swung more than the new one so the best time to bat was at the start of the innings. The innings and the ball were 40 overs old.

Kane didn't play at Edgbaston because of injury. I told him, "When you walked past me as I was waiting to bat, I seriously contemplated tapping you on the shoulder and asking, 'Kane, if I don't get any runs here, are you still going pick me for the final?'" (In international cricket, the captain tends to have a big say in selection. As it was, I ended up getting 80.)

He pissed himself. I'd never seen him laugh so much.

We spent 40 minutes talking about our form, our issues, what we were thinking and feeling. We went through the things you do to overcome self-doubt, to get yourself through bad patches, to find a way to survive and prosper. I suspect Kiwi cricket fans would have been aghast if they'd known that, on the eve of the WTC final, their number three and four, their most experienced batters and highest run-scorers, were telling each other how insecure they were. But it was a fantastic conversation that set the stage for what was about to unfold.

We'd had the better preparation. India were a little underdone but, the way we looked at it, they were in the same position as we'd been going into the Lord's test in which we performed pretty well. In the build-up, Indian coach Ravi Shastri and captain Virat Kohli argued that the WTC should be decided by a three-match series, rather than a one-off final. When I saw them saying that, I thought, 'We're a chance here.' Putting that message out into the media came across to us as getting your excuses in early.

With the Duke ball, overhead conditions have more of a bearing on proceedings than the surface. The long-range weather forecast was for rain. We'd spent 10 days in Southampton leading into the England series and the forecast had been spot on every day. A spinner plays more of a holding role than an attacking one in damp, overcast conditions, whereas a fourth seamer or seam-bowling all-rounder aren't bowling dead overs. Steady asked me, "What's your team?" I said, "Four seamers and Colin [de Grandhomme]." He said, "Yeah, that's our thinking too." If the sun came out, there would've been a case for playing Ajaz Patel, but I didn't think Kyle Jamieson was quite good enough at that stage to bat at seven, which he would have done had Ajaz played.

So, we were happily surprised that India picked two spinners. As it turned out, we took runs off Ravichandran Ashwin and Ravindra Jadeja, then Kyle [Jamieson] and Tim Southee smacked their seamers around. It wasn't that conditions were easier, but their three quicks had bowled a lot of overs. With a fourth seamer, you lessen the load so guys come back fresher for their third and fourth spells. No doubt about it, batting would have been harder work for us if they'd taken in another quick. They didn't make the same mistake in their subsequent series against England.

The first day was completely washed out, as was the fourth. The toss was a big deal: the batters were mighty pleased that Kane won it and we were bowling first. I'd never heard a New Zealand cricket team sing the national anthem the way we did before that game — we sounded like a team that was well and truly up for the battle. I'm not sure we would have sung quite so lustily if we'd been going out to bat.

But I thought Tim Southee and Trent Boult were nervous and didn't bowl particularly well to begin with. It wasn't what we'd become used to from them. I put it down to a combination of the occasion, the Duke ball and the pressure of expectation from the team. In the first 20 overs, Rohit Sharma and Shubman Gill put on 62 at three runs an over, which was well over par in the conditions. Kyle and Neil Wagner gained a measure of control and Tim and Boulty settled down in their second spells, concentrating on line and length rather than trying to bowl miracle balls. India's total of 217 was too many; we should have held them to 150-odd given the wicket and conditions.

There were times during that game when we would have been off the field if it had been just another test match: the outfield was too wet and the light wasn't good enough. But it was the inaugural World Test Championship final and there was a lot at stake, not just for the two teams taking part.

At stumps on day two, the first day of play, India were 146/3 with Kohli 44 not out. The next morning the outfield was really wet and wasn't going to dry in a hurry: there was no wind, no sun and the lights were on. We would have been happy to have walked off. Kane went up to Kohli and said, "Mate, this is wet, what do you reckon? Do you think we should be out here?" Virat just shrugged and said, "It is what it is." I have no idea what his mindset was: maybe he was thinking 'If we can get the ball into this wet outfield, it's going be hard to bowl with it.' Or maybe, 'I want to bat and I don't need the opposition captain talking to me about the conditions.'

Or maybe he knew what the powers that be were thinking. The umpires told Kane that they were getting directions 'from above' — presumably the International Cricket Council (ICC) — along the lines of, 'If it's not raining, you're playing, regardless of how wet the outfield is.' Once it became clear that the umpires weren't calling the shots, we knew we just had to get on with it. You could see it from the ICC's perspective: it had taken two years to get to the first-ever test championship final so not to have a winner would have been a major anticlimax. It didn't work for Kohli though — he was out without adding to his overnight score.

Like Twickenham, the Rose Bowl complex includes a hotel. It was the first time I'd ever stayed at the ground for the duration of a test match. It was quite nice to be able to switch off when it was raining, especially because I was nought not out for two days. When you're not out during a weather break that might last half an hour or half the day, it's hard to switch off sitting in a changing room. Being in my hotel room watching TV was much more relaxing.

Michael Gough, one of the umpires, was in the next room. I'd open my curtains in the morning, see him out on his balcony and say, "Any chance?" He'd say, "Go back to bed, Ross." Even if you're staying only a few kilometres from the venue, you can't be sure that what you see out your hotel room window is what's happening at the ground. When the texts came in from my family asking when play was likely to start, I could tell them to go to bed — no play today.

BJ Watling, who was playing his last game, and I had our own changing room — the geriatric ward. Because of Covid and the restrictions on spectator numbers, we had the whole side of the building to ourselves but, being superstitious and having scored an ODI century at the Rose Bowl, I had to sit in the same seat. So, it was just BJ and me up in the normal changing room; everyone else was down in a makeshift changing room in the hospitality area. But then our bowlers can't sit still during run-of-the-mill games so they'd come up to watch with us.

In our first innings, Kane and I batted together for 14 overs, advancing the score by 16 runs. He was struggling and I probably let our painfully slow progress get to me. After drinks I tried to get things moving but played a loose shot and Gill took a good catch at mid-off. In the 2015 ODI World Cup final, I got out nicking a slower ball from James Faulkner — to this day I don't know how I did it. In the 2019 final I was given out lbw when it was going over the top of the stumps but we'd lost our referral. On both occasions I walked off knowing that was it: I wouldn't get a second chance. This time I walked off thinking, 'I'm going to get another bat; I'd better make the most of it.' That was how I dealt with it: I was disappointed but didn't beat myself up too much.

We were 100 behind and going at less than two runs an over. I was thinking that if India had a good spell and knocked a couple more over, we'd be under the pump. Which is pretty much what happened. I said to Steady, "We need to play some shots here; we can't die in a hole." "Yeah," he said, "we'll suss something at the break." First ball after lunch, Colin smacked a cover drive for four. That set the tone. It sent a message that we were going to be positive and it took a bit of pressure off Kane.

The shackles loosened. Kyle and Kane put on 30 as did Tim and Kane, with the bowlers throwing the bat. Then Tim and Boulty put on 15 for the last wicket, valuable runs in a low-scoring game. The change of approach was the key: if we'd kept blocking it, we'd have been bowled out for 180 which would have put us behind the eight ball. Instead, we led by 32. Kane batted almost five hours for 49 but, crucially, he was still there for those partnerships with the lower order.

The game was extended to six days. Late on day five Tim got the big wicket of Rohit. It was quite dark, with less than 20 minutes till stumps, so we assumed they'd send out a nightwatchman. But out came the big gun: Kohli. In the slip cordon we were saying, "Is this a good idea? Is it an ego play or what?" Straightaway, Tim hit him on the helmet. I chased it to the boundary, the first time I'd really stretched out since injuring my calf. I was thinking, 'One more day to go, surely the calf is up to it.'

I was intrigued that Virat had opted to come out to bat. Most top-order batters would have a nightwatchman in less challenging conditions and when the stakes were nowhere near as high. I know Virat pretty well, having played with him at Bangalore in the Indian Premier League, so I thought, 'Bugger it, I'm going to ask.' I went up to him and said, "Virat, no nightwatchman?" He was amped up, feeling the heat of battle. He snarled, "I'm better than the f----n nightwatchman." It came out like, "I'm better than the **F----N** nightwatchman."

I started laughing, thinking, 'Fair play to you, mate, fair play to you.' He realised it was me, and that it had been a genuine question rather than a sledge, and started laughing too. I got into the slip cordon and told the boys what he'd said. It was hilarious but also an insight into his mindset. I'd have a nightwatchman every day of the week but, if I ever become a coach, I'll tell anyone who wants one, "No way. In the WTC final Virat Kohli said, 'I'm better than the f---n nightwatchman,' so get out there." He survived till stumps, but KJ picked him up, for the second time in the game, early the next morning,

A few months earlier in Australia we'd seen what Rishabh Pant could do with the bat so my heart sank when Tim dropped him just as he was starting to look threatening. When we were in Sri Lanka in August 2019, Tim had poked fun at Boulty for standing on the boundary rope when he'd caught Ben Stokes in the World Cup final. Tom Latham had been gobbling them up at second slip but Tim, who has a great pair of hands and has taken some terrific catches in the cordon, prefers fielding in the slips to boundary riding, especially when he's bowling. No slip catch is easy, and this one came pretty fast, but I couldn't help thinking, 'You want to take those in a World Cup final.' We've all been there and it's not a great place: the last thing you want is another catch coming to you. Tim started edging closer to me. We got so tight that I said, "Don't worry about it, mate — just catch the next one." But every two or three balls he'd edge a fraction closer.

I was running scenarios in my head. If they got a lead of 180 or 200, then both sides would be in the game: it's the WTC final so you're going to go for it, but that would give them a better chance of winning than if we put up the shutters. Pant charged Boulty, looking to smash it over mid-on. The bat turned in his hands, he sliced it and the ball went sky high square of the wicket on the off side. I didn't register that Henry Nicholls had called for it; I just saw Devon running the other way and thought, 'Oh no, it's going to drop in no-man's-land.' Henry, running back from gully, took an amazing catch. The TV footage simply doesn't capture the degree of difficulty.

The umpires called drinks and a few of us ran off for a toilet break. Henry and Tom overtook me. I thought, 'Fair enough, their need must be greater than mine.' There were three toilets; the middle one — the most convenient — was vacant. Nice of them to leave it for the old boy. I had sunglasses on but could still see things weren't proceeding the way that nature and Thomas Crapper, the English engineer who played a significant role in the development of the modern toilet, intended: my pee was coming straight back at me. Someone had put Glad Wrap over the bowl and I was getting serious splashback. "Oh f--k," I yelled, "who did this?"

Henry and Tom were cracking up in the other cubicles. When I emerged, the support staff eyed me warily, wondering how I'd react. I said, "Who was it?" Someone said, "I think it was Riaan," meaning high performance logistics manager Riaan Muller. I said, "Riaan, was it you?" He said, "Maybe." "All good, mate," I said. "A bit of a laugh." But manager Mike 'Roman' Sandle was sensible enough to deactivate the little booby trap before it claimed another victim. I very much doubt Kane would have seen the funny side of it if it had happened to him just before he went into bat. For that matter, I probably wouldn't have seen the funny side if I'd just taken a catch.

Which I did immediately after the resumption — a straightforward one, off Ashwin. I was the only one in the cordon so I was probably at one and a half and it came at a nice height, just on my inside. In the huddle there was no talk about the game situation: it was all about my wee misadventure. A bit of light relief probably wasn't a bad thing because the game had reached squeaky-bum time.

We bowled India out for 170 which meant we were 139 runs away from being crowned the first-ever world champions of test cricket. I went in to join Kane at 44/2 in the 17th over. We chipped away at the target; Kane was much more fluent than in the first innings which helped me out because I was hanging in there. I got hit on the head by Jasprit Bumrah. Getting 'sconed' by a bouncer isn't an unexpected outcome. After all, the bowler intended to get the ball head high or, to put it another way, the bowler was aiming for your head. But when you get hit there by a ball that wasn't that short, you're left wondering: did it take off or did I get it wrong? When Kane came down to check on me, I said I'd felt I needed to get forward to it. He assured me I'd read it right — the ball had just taken off.

Our physio, Tommy, came out to take me through the

concussion procedure: Do you know what ground this is? The
Rose Bowl. Do you know who you are playing? India. What's the
score? We're not far away from winning. I told him it felt exactly
like when I got hit by England's Liam Plunkett in Cardiff in 2017.
"Well, if you can remember that," Tommy said, "there's nothing
wrong with you."

People must wonder what physios say to batters in that
situation. Tommy was probably supposed to get me to recite the
months of the year backwards, which some people couldn't do
at the best of times, let alone when they've been nailed on the
melon. But the fact that I could remember getting hit at the 2017
Champion's Trophy was good enough for him.

On that occasion, my focus was on getting as far forward as
possible to the next one. I wasn't going to act scared and hang
on the back foot. Better to get out than look scared and feel like
you'd bottled it. Given the circumstances, I wasn't quite so gung-
ho this time, but Bumrah's follow-up was another back of a length
delivery. If he'd bounced me, he probably would have pinned
me again and I'd have had Tommy out there asking me the same
questions. Or maybe not.

Partnerships are the key to chasing down a modest total. The
bowling team needs to take wickets at regular intervals to maintain
belief, build momentum and create a bit of panic in the batting
team's dressing room. Conversely, a productive partnership erodes
the bowling team's belief that they really have a chance of pulling it
off. The longer the partnership lasts, the more the arithmetic shifts
in the batting team's favour. Then the finish line comes into view
and, suddenly, you're coming home with a wet sail. Kane and I put
on 96, including 14 boundaries, which was as many as India hit in
their entire second innings.

It's hard to express how rewarding it was to hit the winning
runs and for the two of us to be there at the end and walk off
together. That iconic photo captures us savouring the moment
in a typically Kiwi way: down to earth but heartfelt. I said, "Well,

we're bloody world champions and no one can take that away." Kane grabbed me and said, "F--k, yeah." That's as emotional as he ever gets.

There was a good contingent of New Zealand fans in the Rose Bowl. They were singing the Cranberries song, "Zombie" with slightly different words: "He's in your hea-ead, in your hea-ead, Conway, Conway, Conway." Or: "We're in your hea-ead, in your hea-ead, Kohli, Kohli, Kohli." I was doing media in the changing room; the boys were in a huddle, singing along with the Kiwi supporters. When I joined the huddle, they broke into, "Ooh, aah, Ross Taylor." Kane and I performed a duet of "Islands in the Stream": "And the message is clear: this could be the year — for the real thing." (Just for the record, I was Kenny and he was Dolly.)

I've never seen the Black Caps drink as much gin as on that trip — Colin has a mate who's the boss of a big distillery. But despite being inundated with quality New Zealand product, it was a comparatively subdued celebration: I sat next to Kane drinking chardonnay, talking to home — Victoria, Mum and Dad and my long-time manager Leanne McGoldrick — and just letting it sink in. It was equal parts elation and relief: to have lost a third World Cup final would have been unbearable.

It wasn't a messy night. I definitely had a sorer head after the 2019 World Cup final after-party down in the Long Room. The fact that there weren't many partners or family there because of Covid probably had something to do with it. KJ and Devon were staying on to play county cricket so their partners were there, as was Kane's wife Sarah, who's English. That was about it.

For the first time I didn't make a point of responding to messages. I just decided to enjoy the moment. Previously, when I'd made runs or we'd won big games, I'd felt duty-bound to reply promptly. I had over 600 messages. When we got home, I ploughed through them in MIQ (quarantine), but apologies if all you got by way of a reply was "Thank you."

I didn't feel physically tired but mentally I was shot. About

2.30 in the morning I fell asleep talking to my best cricketing mate Martin Guptill. I said, "Mate, I've got to go to bed, I'm cooked." I pulled the sheets over me and went out like a light. I was still in my whites.

We got all our shirts signed but two of mine went missing. I told Mike Sandle who said, "Oh, funny that Kane's missing two shirts as well." For both of us to have a couple of shirts go missing suggests it wasn't a coincidence — maybe they'll turn up on eBay or Trade Me one day. I was and still am annoyed, not because I wanted mementoes, but they could have gone to a good cause. Tim sold one for over $40,000 to help a young cancer sufferer. At least I've still got the shirt I fell asleep in.

I'd signed to play for Derbyshire after the final. Victoria had encouraged me to do so on the reasonable grounds that I was getting towards the end of my career and there wouldn't be many more of those opportunities. But there was to-ing and fro-ing over getting an MIQ spot. After the first day got rained off, we pulled the pin on the Derbyshire gig: I needed to focus on the final and the uncertainty around MIQ was a distraction. In hindsight, I'm very glad we made that call. With the final going to a sixth day, I would've been playing for Derbyshire in Birmingham the day after winning the World Test Championship. That would have been a challenge.

(During the home series against the West Indies in 2017, I was having a drink with their coach, Stuart Law, the former Australian batsman. We got onto the subject of English county cricket. Stuart, who'd played for a few counties, said, "You always go to Derbyshire when your career is on the wane; that's the last club you go to." I thought, 'Oh, that's handy: if I ever get to Derbyshire, I'll know the end is nigh.'

A month or so later I found myself sitting next to Tom Harrison, the chief executive of the England and Wales Cricket Board, on a flight out of Dunedin. When I realised that he'd played county cricket, I passed on what Stuart Law had said. Tom seemed to find that interesting. Then I asked the question I should have asked *before* I thought of sharing Stuart's theory: "Where did you play your county cricket?" The answer, of course, was Derbyshire. I was very apologetic, but he just laughed.)

I had a few champagnes in the lounge at Heathrow and a few more on the plane. I'm not a big champagne drinker, but it seemed appropriate. It was a strange state of mind to be in: on a high but not ecstatic because you know you're heading for MIQ. Roman must have got sick of being asked, "Do we know what hotel we're in?" We had business class to ourselves so I had the speakers out, but it was as if the pilot was determined to keep a lid on things: every time we congregated in one area, we'd hit turbulence. In Singapore we found out we were going to the Sebel in Manukau. Roman allocated the two available suites to me and Tim on the grounds of seniority. Age has its consolations.

Two hours out of Auckland the pace battery — Boulty, Wags and Tim — woke everybody up and started pouring Baileys. It was like, "Morning, boys, get this down you and enjoy quarantine." It was decided that BJ would look after the trophy for two weeks. He didn't get much say in the matter.

It wasn't until we left MIQ and got out among the public that the significance of what we'd achieved really hit home. There was the same sort of thing after the 2019 World Cup and beating the Aussies in Hobart in 2011 — people shaking your hand in the supermarket and cafés — but this time it was still happening six months later. I think for players and fans alike there was a sense of karma, a feeling that winning the test championship made up for 2019. We had our share of luck in the WTC, but the cricketing gods did us no favours at Lord's.

I felt for Martin Guptill, who'd played in the 2015 and 2019 finals, and Mitchell Santner. Mitch played at Lord's, got a duck and didn't bowl particularly well. He had a finger injury so was rested for the Edgbaston test; Ajaz Patel took his place and bowled beautifully. We were restricted to a squad of 15 for the

Rose Bowl so Mitch missed out on being part of the final and sharing that historic moment, despite playing an important role in getting us there.

As we were soaking it up in the dressing room afterwards, I told Kane that I'd loved the conversation we'd had the night before the game. He said, "Yeah, mate." That was our sign-off. One week from that conversation to walking off together as world champions. How strange and sometimes wonderful this game of cricket is.

PART ONE:
THE BOY
FROM THE BUSH

Chapter 1.
What's in a Name?

My full name is Luteru Ross Poutoa Lote Taylor. My mother Naoupu — also known as Ann — is Samoan. She had 13 brothers and sisters and, when she was 15, her widowed and slightly overwhelmed mother sent her down here to live with one of her brothers. My father Neil is a Pakeha New Zealander. I'm half and half: black and white. I grew up equally comfortable with both parts of my identity, equally at home in both cultures.

My sisters Rebecca, Elianna and Maria also have multiple names and Mum made sure we understood the significance of all of them. In my case, Luteru — the Samoan equivalent of Luther — was the name of the minister at the Samoan church in Wainuiomata. Ross is my paternal grandmother's maiden name; her family came from Scotland. Poutoa refers to our connection to the old Samoan royal family and Lote is a diminutive of my maternal grandfather's name.

The first leg of the flight home from the Caribbean is from Port of Spain, Trinidad to Houston, Texas. I'm always a bit nervous going through an American airport. You feel guilty, even though there's no reason you should. The officials and cops look at you with an expression that seems to say, 'You may think you've got no reason to be worried, but we know better.' One immigration officer studied my passport for a while. "That's a long name," he said. "I can see this is a New Zealand passport but are you an Aborigine?" "No," I said, "my mother is from Samoa." "Oh," he said, "so you're Samonian." Once he remembered that Dwayne "The Rock" Johnson is also Samonian we were all good.

At home, I was called Luteru or "Kelu", the familiar variation. Mum and my grandmother went with me on my first day of school. The principal struggled to pronounce Luteru — this was 1989 when there probably weren't many Pacific Islanders in Masterton — so Grandma Sylvia said, "Just call him Ross." I'd never been called Ross, but I've been Ross ever since. Sports writer Dylan Cleaver once wrote on *espncricinfo*: "Ross Taylor. Three clipped syllables. So very Anglo. So very middle New Zealand, but that's not who Taylor is. That person is a figment."

(New Zealand Cricket made all my bookings in the name of Luteru Taylor because that's what appears on my passport and various other forms of documentation and ID. It confused more than a few taxi drivers and hotel staff over the years.)

Mum reckons I could've been called "Wainui". There wasn't a Samoan church in Masterton, so we often went down to Wellington, where some of Mum's brothers and sisters lived, to attend services. (We also went to my grandparents' church in Masterton; between them, the two sides of my family ensured I had a religious upbringing.) Mum went to Wainuiomata for a weekend and I arrived early. I was scheduled for April but born in Lower Hutt on 8 March 1984. The umbilical cord got wrapped around my neck three times but, luckily, there was an experienced nurse on duty.

Dad's a true-blue Masterton/Wairarapa man: to this day, he gets annoyed whenever a journalist or commentator mentions that I was born in Lower Hutt. My sisters were all born in Masterton.

We often spoke Samoan at home. Mum wanted us to speak and understand the language so that we remained connected to our Samoan heritage and identity. Every time a Samoan made the All Blacks, Mum would come up with a family connection, no matter how tenuous. It was like she was trying to prove the proposition that all Samoans are related. Whenever it happened, we'd ask, "So how are we related to this guy, Mum?" It never failed to crack us up.

However, Mum and Eroni Clarke actually are cousins. When Eroni — in just his first year in the All Blacks — played against Ireland at Athletic Park in 1992, Mum's sister Aunty Tu — short for Tualupetu — asked him for tickets to the game, but he'd already given his allocation away. He managed to get a couple of tickets off Michael Jones and Aunty Tu suggested to Mum and Dad that they should send me down to Wellington for the game. So, eight-year-old me caught the train from Masterton to Wellington by myself. It was a journey I'd made many times and Mum and Dad knew the conductor who kept an eye on me. But how times have changed: nowadays, most parents — and Victoria and I are in this category — wouldn't let their eight-year-olds go to the dairy by themselves.

I watched my first All Blacks test sitting next to Zinzan Brooke, who was very nice. His brother Robin played his first game for the All Blacks that day. It was the last test with four-point tries, but that didn't stop the All Blacks rattling up 59 points to Ireland's six. Those were the days when the All Blacks simply didn't lose to Ireland.

Togi Lote and her sister Upu, who played for the New Zealand softball team for years, were probably our closest cousins. When I was 10 and they were 16 or 17, their older brother Norman Lote decided I was soft and set about hardening me up, basically by using me as a tackling bag. "We're just hardening you up for cricket, mate," they'd say. Eventually, for self-preservation, I'd put my knee up just before I was tackled. You'd get red-carded for that now. Fast forward a couple of decades and they're telling me that facing Brett Lee bowling 155 kph is a piece of cake compared to being steamrollered by them in the backyard. I've never needed to worry about getting too big for my boots because my family, immediate and extended, would have brought me down a peg or two in a big hurry.

Dad was a factory worker while Mum worked at the New Zealand Housing Corporation. When she was made redundant things started to change. Money had always been an issue but after that it got really tight. Mum's second job was cleaning the Work and Income premises. I'd go there after school to help her by cleaning toilets and sinks and getting rid of rubbish. I used to clean 10 or 15 toilets a day. As I got older, I came to understand what Mum and Dad had to do to make ends meet and the sacrifices they were making for their children. Later, whenever cricket wasn't much fun, I always tried to put things in perspective by thinking back to those days.

Mum was the disciplinarian; if Dad got involved it meant you'd done something pretty bad. His parenting rules were: no drugs, no motorbikes and take your time when batting. He had a cousin who was left paralysed after falling off a motorbike, which affected Dad profoundly.

Mum says I was "a real boy" by which I think she means a real handful. She tells a story about looking for the belt when I'd been naughty and me saying, "It died so I buried it." They found it when they dug up the potato garden. Maria, on the other hand, reckons I was a "Mama's boy" and got away with stuff my sisters wouldn't have dreamed of trying.

I got bullied on my first day at school. When I told Mum about it, she said that, if it happened again, I should hit back with whatever was at hand. As it turned out, it happened again after I'd been playing tennis so I grabbed a racquet and whacked my tormentor on the nose.

The principal rang Mum at work to say I was in his office and in hot water, could she come in? When she arrived, she asked me, "What have you done, Ross?" I said, "I hit him, just like you told me to." Some mothers might've taken exception to being thrown under a bus. Not mine: she told the principal that, yes, she had instructed me to stick up for myself; if the teachers couldn't protect little kids from being bullied, what choice did they have?

Apparently, the mother of the kid who wore my cross-court forehand wasn't happy.

Mum taught me the rudiments of cooking, just like her father had taught her. She and Dad worked long hours so Rebecca and I often had to feed ourselves, which meant making do with whatever was in the cupboard: bread, eggs, spaghetti and, occasionally, corned beef. When cheese became an option, we got a bit more ambitious and creative. That's probably where my love of cooking comes from.

I had three hugely influential relatives on Dad's side: his mum, Grandma Sylvia, her husband, Grandad Jack, and my great-aunty who we called Aunty Mary. They were our babysitters when Mum and Dad were at work — there was always shortbread in their cupboards — and they funded a lot of the trips to hockey and cricket tournaments that my parents couldn't afford. I was really close to Grandma Sylvia who was a very special person and a big part of my life. She died when I was on the fateful tour of Sri Lanka in 2012, making it a doubly devastating blow. Aunty Mary died during the equally grim West Indies tour earlier that year.

Grandma Sylvia loved cricket. She was my biggest supporter. She drummed two things into me: be humble and, at the start of an innings, look for a single down the ground to get under way. Towards the end of their lives, she and Jack struggled to see the ball when they watched live cricket so they'd listen to the radio commentary.

In December 2006, Grandma Sylvia and Dad were watching an ODI against Sri Lanka at McLean Park in Napier. My run a ball 128 not out was overshadowed by Sanath Jayasuriya's 111 off 83 deliveries. One of his five sixes was heading straight for Sylvia but fortunately a guy sitting in front of her jumped up and caught it. She hadn't seen it coming so was blissfully unaware that she was in harm's way.

Grandad Jack, whose name was actually Raymond, had been a chicken farmer and still kept chickens. He'd enter his best birds in the various Wairarapa competitions in my name: he did the work; I got the glory in the form of ribbons and certificates. Of course, I claimed I'd made a crucial contribution but in fact I did next to nothing.

Grandad Jack hadn't been much of a sportsman — my uncles reckoned he scored one try in his life and that was only because his teammates pushed him onto the ball in goal. Grandma Sylvia, though, had an impressive sporting pedigree: her father, my great-grandfather, played rugby league for Australia. He was a Canterbury farmer and a good enough rugby player to actually represent the union. He later went to North Queensland on a working holiday. The family knew he'd played league for Queensland but had no idea that he'd played one game for Australia — against New Zealand Māori — until a rugby league historian discovered it.

The story broke in the *Sydney Morning Herald* when we were playing a test at the Sydney Cricket Ground. My Uncle John was at the game and there wasn't anyone at the SCG more surprised than him. I walked past Nathan Lyon when he was batting. "I always knew you were a good bugger, Ross," he said. "Now it all makes sense — you're one of us." Talking to Dad and my uncles, I still find it amazing that their grandfather never told them he played for Australia. Whether he was being humble or just didn't think it was a big deal, no one knows.

In a sense, Nathan's call wasn't entirely fanciful. Growing up, I loved watching the cricket from Australia; in fact, I probably preferred the cricket across the ditch given that a golden era in Australian cricket was unfolding before our eyes. I can remember watching that famous one-day international in Hobart in 1990 when Chris Pringle bowled a maiden with Australia needing two runs off the last over. I dreamt of playing at those fabled grounds — the Gabba, the SCG, the MCG, the Adelaide Oval. (My favourite Aussie ground would be the "old" Adelaide Oval; I don't like it as much now with the big new stands.)

I don't know whether I would have played cricket if Dad

hadn't been keen on it. He was a decent cricketer, good enough to be picked in a North Island junior school team with future internationals Bruce Edgar and, coincidentally given our future relationship, Ian Smith. I loved watching him play for the Lansdowne Club.

I can remember being five or six and counting down the hours till my first game of cricket. I'd been to practice and turned up keen as mustard on the Saturday, only to find the rest of the team were no-shows. Tears were shed. I ended up playing with older kids, as often happens in small towns and rural areas. In terms of my development, I firmly believe that playing as much as I did against kids who were older and better than me was a massive help. Dad claims to remember the very first ball I bowled. Apparently, I came off the long run thinking I was Richard Hadlee and rattled the stumps.

The problem was my sisters weren't that interested in cricket. The solution was a hockey ball in a hockey sock on a string suspended from a branch of the kowhai tree in front of our house. As an 11– or 12-year-old, I would hit that ball for three or four hours a day. One night I was still hitting at 9.30; the guy across the road, fortunately a good mate of Dad's, yelled, "That's enough, Ross — go to bed." Without knowing it, I was teaching myself how to bat. If I hit the ball too hard, it would swing up and get stuck in the tree so I had to develop a bit of touch. I did it partly to pass time — we didn't have Sky TV at that stage and had to go to Aunty Mary's to watch the Hurricanes or any big sports event — and partly because I enjoyed it. It absorbed me. When the kowhai lost its main branches in the big winds that hit Masterton in 2021, Mum and Dad rang to deliver the bad news. They were quite upset because of the fond memories attached to that tree.

I also played kilikiti in inter-church games in Newtown with my cousins and uncle. English missionaries introduced cricket to Samoa in the early nineteenth century and kilikiti evolved into Samoa's distinctive take on the game. There's no limit to the size of teams — basically whoever turns up, regardless of age or gender, plays — and the rules are pretty flexible. Supposedly, the only hard and fast rule is that the host team forfeits the game if they can't provide enough food.

In the Newtown games they lobbed under-arms to the little kids. I stood right in front of the wickets and smashed it, which caused mutterings among the elders. My cousins had to tell them, "He plays palagi cricket." They stopped lobbing it to me and started bowling fast, but I blocked it, which was also frowned upon. The core principle of kilikiti is that you try to slog everything; my attitude was that, if the ball wasn't in my hitting area, I'd block it. I also made a nuisance of myself with the ball, to the point where someone asked the minister of Mum's church, "Why did you bring that little boy?"

The Lansdowne club had several third-grade teams. When I was nine, I was drafted in to play for one of them, who were short-handed, against Dad's team. The batting order was literally a lucky dip — you stuck your hand in a bag and pulled out a number. I picked two so I opened the batting. I was given out caught behind when I was on not many — I didn't get anywhere near it — but they let me have another go. I ended up getting 40. They definitely went easy on me, but you've still got to get them. As they say, look in the book. There it was in black and white — Taylor, R: 40.

When I was about 10, Mum took me to the Warehouse to buy some rubber-soled sports shoes, as opposed to cricket shoes. I was a size 9 then, but Mum got size 12s on the basis that I'd grow into them and it would save money. I'm sure some parents must have watched me flopping around in them like a clown and thought, 'Jeepers, this kid's got big hooves.' Within a few years I was a size 12 but those rubber-soled shoes were long gone.

Dad had played rugby and wanted me to do so, but Mum wouldn't have it: I was quite small at seven or eight and around that time my Uncle Tumua suffered a broken neck playing rugby in Samoa and died, aged 23. So, I played hockey. It kept me fit, although I wouldn't say it improved my aerobic capacity. I was a striker who didn't do a lot of back tackling. And when I did back tackle, it was usually because someone had tackled me and I'd gone after them to get even. That, in turn, usually led to me being penalised, so I rationalised it was better in big-picture terms if I just flagged back tackling. I wasn't all that skilful, but I was fast and I smacked it. I definitely made life interesting for defenders and goalkeepers.

I enjoyed hockey and made it into various rep teams. I think it helped my cricket in terms of hand–eye coordination. Then again, if I hadn't played hockey, I might have played straighter — as it was, my natural arc became cow corner. That mightn't have endeared me to the purists, but it actually made sense back then because teams rarely put fielders at cow — at least, not until the penny dropped that I didn't give a hoot what it said in the MCC Coaching Manual.

At one stage I asked Mum whether I should focus on hockey or cricket. She said she'd prefer me play cricket because it was a family game and lots of our relatives in Samoa played kilikiti. Back then, of course, not much thought was given to the career prospects. When I was 10, I had a church/cricket clash with Mum: I was in my whites, all set for a Sunday morning rep game, but she told me to get ready for church instead. One of her arguments was that I could never make a living from playing cricket.

Being a mixed-race family in the heartland almost four decades ago meant we had to put up with a certain amount of what's now called casual racism — and some not so casual. When Mum was at Housing Corporation, a woman asked her, "How did you get this job?" Mum just laughed and said, "My father sent me to school."

A lot of the time I was the only non-white in my cricket and hockey teams. Before one rep hockey game, I was in the changing room with the other players and some parents when someone started squawking that their wallet was missing. Every pair of eyes swivelled to me. Maybe it wasn't solely about race; Mum and

Dad's financial circumstances might have been a factor in their automatic assumption. Whatever, it wasn't a great feeling. But what do you do? Back then you had no choice but to suck it up. You learned to deal with it; you did what you had to do to get by. Don't get me wrong, I loved playing in those teams, but casual racism was part and parcel of it. Was it prevalent? No. But I'd be kidding myself if I said I wasn't subjected to it. And I'd be lying to you if I said it didn't leave its mark on me.

It turned out the wallet wasn't missing at all — the guy had left it at the motel. There was no apology, not even a "Ha-ha, just having you on."

Chapter 2.
Going Places

My first proper bat was a Slazenger V100 Waugh Zone — after Mark Waugh — that Grandad Jack bought me when I was 12. I was stoked: Waugh was one of my two favourite players, the other being Sachin Tendulkar, and the bat was a beauty. And, of course, it meant I no longer had to borrow my teammates' bats.

I made a few runs with the V100 at an Under 15 tournament at the Hutt Recreation ground. There were two Central Districts teams, CD Green and CD Gold, plus Hutt Valley and Wellington. During the 2019 World Cup, I met National MP Chris Bishop, who was in the UK with a parliamentary cricket team. He'd played for Hutt Valley as a youngster and claimed that once when they played against Wairarapa, Jesse Ryder and I amassed a grand total of two runs between us. I was sceptical but Chris found the scorecard and put it out there on Twitter. Just for the record, Jesse made zero contribution to our combined tally.

My Uncle Max told me to watch out for this guy in the Wellington team, Stephen Murdoch — "He'll play for New Zealand one day." Many is the time I've had him on about it: "You kept raving on about Murdoch, but you didn't seem to notice your own nephew wasn't too bad." No disrespect to Stephen, a very good batter who played first-class cricket for Wellington and Canterbury, and was arguably a bit unlucky not to get a crack at international cricket. Ged Robinson, who later played hooker for the Hurricanes and three other Super Rugby franchises, was also in that Wellington team.

Graham Sherlock, one of the CD selectors, must have noticed me borrowing kit because he told me to sing out if there was anything he could do to help. I asked if he could get me some gear. Just before Christmas, Gunn & Moore sent me some pads and gloves. At the following year's tournament, I made a couple of centuries, a 99 and a half-century. Two days before my fourteenth birthday, I received a full contract from Gunn & Moore, thus formalising a relationship that lasted my entire career.

My tie-up with GM would have to be one of the longer continuous athlete-kit supplier relationships in professional sport. It was based on loyalty: at various times I've had big offers to switch to another supplier. Equally, I'm sure that, now and again, people got in the ear of Chris Brittain, GM's New Zealand agent, suggesting it was time to move on to the next big thing. But Chris and I have stuck together through thick and thin. I'd like to think the relationship has been as rewarding for him and GM as it has been for me.

I'd gone from being the kid who annoyed the hell out of the owner of Trev's Sportswear in Masterton to having a full kit sponsorship. It was pretty cool being 14 and able to say I had a sponsor. More to the point, I no longer had to worry about where my next pair of batting gloves was coming from. Later, GM started numbering my bats. I got RT1 when I was 19 and at the New Zealand Cricket Academy and was up to RT158 when they discontinued the practice. With RT1, GM began making my bats to my specifications — Taylor-Made, so to speak. They were around 2 lb 10 oz, slightly heavier for white ball cricket.

In 2010, I played county cricket for Durham. They wore navy blue kit in one-day cricket so GM sent me some dark blue pads. For some perverse reason, though, Durham wore black in Twenty20. I noticed Albie Morkel, the other overseas player, spray-

painting his pads black and followed suit. Having just secured
a sponsorship from Emirates, Durham had laid the famous red
carpet in the changing room and on the viewing balcony. I spray-
painted my pads on the carpet, let them dry and removed them
without realising I'd left a black outline of a pair of pads on the
sponsor's brand-new carpet. Next thing, the manager was going
ape: "Who's the effin' idiot who spray-painted their pads on the
new carpet?" And I wasn't even playing in that game. The Durham
boys absolutely shredded me.

In January 1998, Central Districts played Northern Districts
in a Shell Trophy game at Queen Elizabeth Park in Masterton. I
talked Dad into taking me down to watch them train. I was 13
and had just become a CD rep, so I stood behind the nets proudly
wearing my CD cap. What happened next is a matter of dispute.

Mark Greatbatch's international career had just drawn to a
close, but he was still heavily involved with CD — as provincial
captain, scout and development officer and age-group coach.
In Batchy's version of events, related in many an after-dinner
speech, I marched up to him during the net practice and asked
if I could be their twelfth man, drinks boy and dressing room
dogsbody. Bear in mind Batchy had represented New Zealand
with distinction, starred at the 1992 World Cup and was the most
famous Central Districts player of the era: no way in the world
would I have had the nerve to do that. He usually mentions in
passing that I was very polite, which does have the ring of truth.

What really happened was that Batchy noticed my cap and
came over. We had a chat and he said, "Why don't you ask your
Mum and Dad if you can come down and help out during the
game?" My most vivid memory is of being sent to get him a coffee.
It cost five bucks. In Masterton. In 1998. I thought, 'Holy moley,
that's daylight robbery.'

Mark Greatbatch: Ross loved being involved and did all
the right things. I recall giving him some throwdowns at

the end of the day's play. He was quite a big lad and, after a few underarms, I decided to retreat two or three metres because he was hitting it rather hard and I was concerned for my safety. At the end of the game, I rang my boss, Blair Furlong, a former All Black and Central Districts cricketer who was the CD CEO. I said, "Mate, I've just met a young kid and had three days with him; we need to get him involved with our rep programme."

I used to call him "Ijaz Ahmed", after the Pakistani batsman who was known as "The Axe Cutter" because he had a very strong bottom-hand grip. Ross was like that because he'd played hockey. My first observations were that he was very strong, he hit it very hard and was very much a leg-side player.

There was definitely something about him. He was well ahead of his age in regard to skill and quality. He had a bit of a rawness, but he had some power and was passionate about the game — loved it, lived for it. I mean, what boy would spend three days working his butt off and getting kicked up the bum by first-class cricketers in the dressing room telling him, "Get this, get that."?

CD got thumped, rolled for 142 in their second innings — Batchy got 53 — with Dan Vettori taking 5/28. My first actual appearance for the CD Shell Trophy team had a happier outcome.

I was drinks boy again the following year when Central Districts played Auckland at Queen Elizabeth Park. When twelfth man Lance Hamilton sprigged himself, I was next cab off the rank. As Jacob Oram was warming up to have a bowl, Andrew Penn left the field to change his boots or go to the loo. I went on, 14 years old and desperate not to make a mess of it. I was at mid-off so Jake bowled his warm-ups to me. Next over I was stationed on the square leg boundary. Brooke Walker swept Campbell Furlong (son of Blair); the ball was barely moving when it got to me, but I gave it the long barrier — turn side on and get your knee on the ground so you've got something in the way if you don't field it cleanly — to make absolutely sure I didn't stuff up. The boys gave me heaps: "Mate, you don't need the long barrier when it's going that slow."

It wasn't totally daunting because I'd been playing with and against men in club cricket — albeit not senior grade — since I was nine. Plus, I started playing first XI cricket for Wairarapa College — alma mater of Sir Bob Charles, the first Kiwi to win a major golf tournament, and Sir Brian Lochore, an All Blacks captain and World Cup-winning coach — in the third form and we often played against men.

I would have been a real pain, always asking questions. Dipak Patel, the coach, turned the air blue in the team meetings; I thought 'Oh, so this is how it is, this is how cricketers talk.' Lou Vincent, not long back from Australia, was in the Auckland team and the CD boys wanted to get into this hotshot from Aussie so that was another eye-opener. Mathew "Skippy" Sinclair got a century which partly explains why I've always rated him so highly. In fact, he got 166 off 448 balls — take your time, mate. To put that in perspective, I used up 374 balls getting to 290 against the Aussies in Perth in 2015.

CD won by 101 runs so my first-class career was off to a winning start. All in all, it was a huge thrill; I knew that this was what I wanted to do. Obviously, playing for New Zealand was the ultimate goal, but Central Districts was my first love. I guess playing for CD seemed more attainable and, besides, I knew I'd have to play for CD to have any hope of playing for New Zealand.

When I was 14, the newly minted New Zealand Cricket Academy introduced a mentor programme. My mentor was Dermot Payton, a local farmer, former CD player, notable coach and all-round Wairarapa cricketing luminary. He picked me up at 5.30 one morning to drive to Palmerston North for a flight to Christchurch to meet Dayle Hadlee who headed up the Academy.

In those days, they served wine on domestic flights. On the

flight home, Dermot gave me a taste of his white wine, which, to my uneducated palate, didn't seem to taste too bad. Then he let me try some red, probably cabernet sauvignon or cabernet merlot rather than pinot noir back then. That was much more like it. I learnt more about wine than cricket on that little jaunt.

(Mum and Dad never drank alcohol at home. Dad would have a beer at the cricket club which had this rule: if you got a century, you bought a round — six jugs — which set you back $18. I can remember Dad not having the money to pay for it and having to give them an IOU to tide him over till payday. Somehow, though, he always had enough money on him to get an ice cream for me and a can of Coke for himself. Mum and Dad still don't have a drop of booze in their house whereas their son is usually spoilt for choice when he feels like a glass of wine.)

I loved playing in the annual age-group tournaments in Hawke's Bay, involving teams from Wairarapa, Horowhenua, Wellington, Hutt Valley, Mana, Manawatu, Hawke's Bay, and Taranaki. We stayed at Riverbend, a youth camp just outside Havelock North. It was always hot — 30 degrees — but no sunscreen or sunglasses. No wonder I had eye issues later.

Years later, I was in the Bay on Black Caps duty. Campbell Furlong's sons were playing in the tournament so I went along for a catch-up. Some parents told me they'd been coming to the tournament for years and kept hearing this story: when Jesse and I had played in the tournament, we'd gone eeling at the local creek, caught some eels and decided it would be a hoot to put them in people's pillowcases. The upshot was that Riverbend stank to high heaven. I said, "I don't want to burst your bubble, but I've never caught an eel in my life." It probably happened at some point, but we certainly didn't do it. I guess it makes a better story if the perpetrators were Jesse Ryder and Ross Taylor.

Jesse and I go back a long way. We had similar upbringings, but I had the crucial benefit of a tight, supportive, settled family network. In a small town the kids with extra ability stand out and

get talked about; I'd heard a lot about this gun left-hander before
our paths ever crossed. Jesse and I are only six months apart but,
because of when our birthdays fall, I was a year ahead at school
so I didn't run into him or play in the same team until he started
intermediate. Jesse would open the batting; I'd bat four or five.
We had some great partnerships and, even then, he made batting
look ridiculously easy. Greg Todd was another young star. With all
due modesty, all the way through to Under-19s our age group rep
teams' fortunes depended heavily on one or more of the three of us
scoring runs.

I started putting on a bit of size at about 12. There were kids
who were taller than Jesse and me but none who hit the ball
harder. Plenty of self-appointed experts, a lot of them coaches,
warned us we'd get found out as we got older — "You can't play
that way at Under 15s." What they failed to recognise was that it
wasn't just our size: sure, we were stronger than most, but we were
also better than most.

A constant refrain throughout my career, from Under 9s to
Black Caps, has been "You can't do that." Or the extended version:
"You won't get away with that at secondary school/first-class/
international level." But I had enough confidence in my ability
to keep doing what came naturally. From the outset, my natural
instinct was to hit the ball for four. That never changed, although
I had to develop and adapt my technique and approach as I
progressed in the game.

I didn't spend a lot of time with Jesse and Greg away
from cricket. We were friends, but didn't hang out, except at
tournaments where the Masterton boys stuck together. Going on
rep team trips as a 15-year-old I just tagged along, which meant
going to pubs and nightclubs. The boys would get you in. My
roommate, who was usually years older than me, would be down
to Pak'n Save to get two dozen beers, so there I was: 15, drinking
Tui beer in a motel room with a big, hairy quick bowler the night
before a game.

We always had a chip on our shoulder. We knew we had to fight because we were the underdogs, the little boys from the Bush. (Our provincial rugby team, Wairarapa Bush, was an amalgamation, Bush being a small province centred on Pahiatua. As kids, we used to refer to our region as "the Bush". I still do.) As a rule, Wairarapa players struggled to make Central Districts teams: the players tended to come from Hawke's Bay, Manawatu, Taranaki or Nelson. It often had a fair bit to do with where the coach was from. I was the only Wairarapa kid in my first Central Districts team — that was in my form two year — and I felt like a bit of a token. I went from batting four for Wairarapa to batting nine for CD, who obviously saw me as more of a bowler. By the end of the tournament, though, I was batting five.

Greg was one of the best players going around but didn't even make the Central Districts Under-15 team; two years later he was playing first-class cricket. It was hugely encouraging that a young guy from Wairarapa, someone I'd played a lot of cricket with, could make the senior CD team.

When I was 15, I made the tournament team at the national Under-17 tournament. I rolled up the next year thinking I was a bit of a gun but didn't make any really big scores and missed out on the tournament team. That brought me down to earth with a thump. After Christmas, I went to the Under-19 tournament, got 80 and 100 in my first two games, and made the New Zealand Under-19s, along with Jesse and Greg. In the space of a couple of months I'd gone from failing to make the Under-17 tournament team to being vice-captain of the New Zealand Under-19s. (Brendon McCullum was the skipper.) The highs and lows of sport.

Jesse and I were shockers in age-group cricket because we'd had men, some of whom were first-class players, sledging us for years. In club cricket it was always "Who are these little pricks?" (It was a rhetorical question; they knew the answer.)

When I was 14, I played for Wairarapa B against Hawke's Bay B and the verbal barrage was relentless. One of the most vociferous sledgers was the All Black Richard Turner's brother. I got 20-odd not out and, as we were walking off the field, he came over and said, "Mate, I only gave it to you because I was trying to put you off. Well done for not letting it affect you."

Players from the traditional cricket schools, the likes of King's College and Auckland Grammar, might have traded a bit of lip in first XI cricket but that wasn't much of a preparation for what we dished up. Jesse certainly didn't hold back. I suppose we were pretty intimidating, but we never won a national tournament. We always seemed to come second because we'd lose a game we should never have lost, usually against Wellington. And, as we got older, we started coming up against the likes of Neil Broom and Rob Nicol, good players and strong personalities who didn't take a backward step.

But we probably beat England at the 2002 Under-19 Cricket World Cup because Jesse and I sledged the bejesus out of them. Those English private school boys would never have experienced anything like the gobfuls they got from these ruffians from Masterton. I was a saint off the field but very much a product of my cricketing environment on it. (Some of our teammates at that tournament thought Mum was Jesse's mother. There actually is a family connection: Jesse's grandfather married one of Mum's cousins.)

Jesse's dad lived in Napier so he was up there a lot and ended up going to Napier Boys'. Greg went to Rathkeale and would have played traditional cricket schools like Whanganui Collegiate whereas Wairarapa College played the likes of Dannevirke High. Not quite in the same league. Enter, once again, Batchy.

Mark Greatbatch: It would be fair to say Wairarapa College wasn't a traditional cricket school. Dave Syms, who'd taught me at Auckland Grammar, was Rector of Palmerston North Boys' High School. I told him there was a lad over in Wairarapa who was pretty handy. Would he be interested in having him for his last couple of years to help with his sport and education?

The long and short of it was that Ross made the move. I got a lot of shit for taking the prodigy away from Wairarapa. Back then there wasn't really a scholarship system, but we somehow found the funding. I had a lot of contacts who helped out and we ran raffles at a pub in Havelock North on Friday nights.

So, in my sixth-form year, I went off to board at Palmerston North Boys' High. I'm not sure Dad was overjoyed about being the sole male in a house full of females but, for me, it was the right move at the right time. While I'd enjoyed Wairarapa College, I loved Palmy Boys. It probably helped that I missed the first three years when a boarder's life can be a bit tough. I was playing traditional cricket and hockey fixtures and learning a work ethic and life skills that put me in good stead for a career in professional sport.

I didn't know anyone there apart from guys I'd played cricket with. The only hostel boy I knew was Jarrod Smith, Ian's son. To this day, Ian blames me for Jarrod not being head boy and having to go back for a second year in the seventh form — apparently, he was a top student until I turned up. But if Jarrod hadn't had that extra year — at Havelock North High School — he wouldn't have made the New Zealand secondary schools soccer team, wouldn't have got a scholarship to West Virginia University, wouldn't have played Major League Soccer against David Beckham and alongside Freddie Ljungberg. But that was when I first encountered Smithy.

Ian Smith: Jarrod was never destined to be head boy, but he might have just taken a step backward when Ross arrived. I know one thing for sure: I used to have to pay double because Ross had quite a healthy appetite. There was a dairy/takeaway place about 50 metres from the hostel and I realised after a little while that the allowance

Jarrod was wanting, and normally getting, wasn't going as far as it used to.

I have two standing jokes with Ross Taylor. One was that when he started playing for Central Districts, I asked him how things were going and he went on at some length about how he was doing it tough because he wasn't making a lot of money. I said, "Mate, you're only ever going to earn my tax so don't worry about it." Then, for a long time, his highest test score was 154 while mine sat at 173 so I was always telling him, "Mate, you're no chance, I'll always have the highest score between you and me." Of course, he cruised past 173 with ease and now he can buy and sell me 95 times over.

Against India at Eden Park in 1990, Smithy came in with New Zealand 131 for 7 and made 173 off 136 balls. So, for a while, Smithy's go-to was, "Oh Ross, remind me, what's your highest test score?" That 173 is still the highest score by a number nine batter in test cricket so once I'd passed it, the chirp became "Well, Ross, I've still got the world record. Have you got a batting world record?" I always fire back with, "It's a disgrace that you were batting nine."

Paul Gibbs, the PNBHS First XI coach at the time, has told journalists that he didn't intend to put me straight into the team because he'd never seen me play and wasn't going to pick me sight unseen. But I'd played Under-17s with a couple of first XI guys who got in the coach's ear, telling him I was a gun. Someone got injured so I played the first game: I made 20-odd, took three wickets and a couple of smart catches at first slip and got sledged by CD player Dave Cooper. Years later Dave, who went on to become chief executive of Northern Districts and also worked for New Zealand Cricket, messaged me to say he was pleased to see his sledging had had a good effect.

The protocol with player-umpires was that, if you nicked it, you walked, so your teammate umpiring didn't have to make a decision. But what if you're not sure whether you nicked it or not? My mate Luke Toynbee was umpiring; he wasn't sure either so he gave me not out. The senior club side we were playing went feral to no avail: I got a century in both innings.

I got a big hundred against Napier Boys' and also had the satisfaction of claiming Jesse's wicket. He had the last laugh though: they chased down our 290 with ease with Matt Berquist, who would play Super Rugby for the Highlanders and Crusaders, getting an even bigger hundred. The other noteworthy aspect of that game was Smithy bustling onto the field to apply Voltaren when my back played up.

I became very good mates with Luke and Marcus Emery, who I played hockey with and who played for the New Zealand indoor hockey team. That pair and Jarrod were my closest friends at school and are my closest friends today.

Marcus, Jarrod and I were prefects. I never liked "gating" kids: it just didn't seem right to stop them going home to their families for the weekend for some trivial offence. So, if a third or fourth former did something wrong, we'd give them a choice between being gated or spinning the wheel. Most of them were cashed up farmers' sons so it was a no-brainer — you'd happily cough up $2 rather than miss out on going home for a weekend. Even then we didn't play by the book: if we were thirsty and it landed on a cheeseburger or chips, we'd insist on a two-litre bottle of Coke.

It was all pretty tame compared to some of the stuff that has gone on at boarding schools over the years. You certainly heard some hair-raising stories. Marcus, who started boarding in the third form, reckoned there was a prefect who was a squash player: he'd make boys line up against a wall and drop their trousers, then blast a squash ball at them from 10 metres away.

My first overseas tour was to South Africa with the PNBHS First XI. I didn't play the game in Singapore en route — we had a big squad — but I can't use that as an excuse for getting a bit carried away at the hotel buffet. As people who know me will attest, I tend to eat the most whatever the circumstances and whoever the competition. My only plea in mitigation was that I wasn't used to being in an "all-you-can-eat" dining environment. I did notice the eggs had a slight green tinge but figured that was the Singaporean way with eggs. About 8 o'clock that night, I started throwing up and having diarrhoea. The parents who were travelling with us didn't want to ruin my trip by leaving me in Singapore — besides, someone would have had to stay with me — so it was a matter of putting on a brave face and steeling myself for what promised to be a deeply unpleasant flight.

By the time we got to Singapore Airport, three other players were "presenting with symptoms", as they say. By the time we landed, 22 of the 34-strong party were crook, which meant our games in Cape Town had to be cancelled. I'd spewed all the way across the Indian Ocean. Craig Clare, who also played Super Rugby and was still playing footy for Whanganui in 2021, and I disembarked in wheelchairs. I didn't need my new passport: they whisked us straight through Customs into an ambulance.

I glimpsed Table Mountain through the ambulance window on the way to hospital where I spent four nights and had the confronting experience seeing one of my teachers erupt from both ends simultaneously. The doctors never established what triggered the outbreak. The buffet scrambled eggs were the prime suspect for the simple but compelling reason that everyone who had them got sick.

Chapter 3.
Landing on my Feet

I first played with Brendon "Baz" McCullum in 2001, for the New Zealand Under-19s against the touring South African Under-19s. He was captain and Mark Greatbatch was coach. I was 16, the youngest in the team, and vice-captain, but not on merit. The idea was to give me experience because a number of our players weren't eligible for the following year's World Cup.

South Africa had a pretty good side — the likes of Hashim Amla, Johan Botha and the other Imran Khan. He later played for South Africa and now coaches the Dolphins, formerly Kwa-Zulu Natal. (I was billeted with Imran's family in Durban on the Palmerston Boys' High tour and remember going into my bedroom to find a strange woman picking my clothes up off the floor. Domestic help was a foreign concept to me, as it would be to most Kiwis.)

We were a decent side too, with Ian Butler, Rob Nicol, Shanan Stewart and Luke Woodcock. But Baz was the difference between the teams: he was way better than anyone else, really a man among boys. He was confident, bordering on brash, a very good wicketkeeper and a fantastic batter. He got centuries in all three games.

The first test was in Alexandra. We got a $30 a day meal allowance which, for a 16-year-old at boarding school, was a windfall. Rather than eat out or get takeaways, my roommate Luke Woodcock and I decided to do a shopping run to the New World over the road from the motel and cook for ourselves. Sweet and sour pork was the dish of the day. I diced the pork and was heating the oil when my girlfriend rang. The oil went on the back burner, in both senses.

I don't know where Luke had got to — maybe I'd volunteered to cook and he'd left me to it — but, as I chatted away, the gauze on the window above the stove caught fire. I was far from a model student, but I must've paid some attention in Home Economics because I grabbed a towel, soaked it and smothered the fire. I went to tell the motel manager, thinking, 'So much for saving money — I'm going to end up out of pocket here.' He was pretty relaxed about it, though, and didn't make me pay for the damage. That still left the daunting prospect of explaining what had happened and why to our manager Dayle Hadlee, a former school principal.

Fortunately, the game went well. We made over 400 — I got 50-odd — and bowled them out twice for not much. The subsequent celebration at a local pub was a learning experience: there were semi-naked haka and an introduction to sambuca. How I made it back to the motel is one of life's great unsolved mysteries. The drive to Queenstown the next day was an ordeal for which I could only blame my teammates. I haven't been back to Alexandra since.

After that debacle, it was takeaways every night. I still saved some money — $5 or $10 a day adds up — so back at boarding school, I was the one with cash for a change. I was able to pay back the lads who'd shouted me a $2 fried rice from the local takeaway whenever the hostel food left something to be desired.

New Zealand Cricket (NZC) had sent Rob Nicol to Lord's to be on the MCC ground staff. He made it sound like a great experience, so I set my sights on doing the same, figuring I could always go to the NZC Academy at Lincoln when I came back. So, 2002 found me in London on the MCC ground staff. I wasn't setting the Thames on fire by any stretch, but head coach Clive Radley asked me if I'd like to go on a tour of Croatia, Slovenia and Austria. A bowling all-rounder had gone down and the cupboard was obviously pretty bare, although I was still bowling a bit. I'd heard of those countries but couldn't have pointed them out on a map, not that that deterred me in the slightest.

The other tourists were playing members of the MCC, mostly well-heeled professionals — doctors, lawyers, accountants, finance industry guys — who paid their own way. They drank a lot of wine. I'd had a taste for it for a while but very little access to it; that unsatisfactory state of affairs was about to end.

We flew into Zagreb in our MCC number ones to find a nation in mourning: Croatia had just lost to Ecuador at the FIFA World Cup in Japan, meaning they failed to qualify for the knockout stages. The highlight of my tour was getting a five-for against the Slovenian national team in Ljubljana, especially as it followed a golden duck. Being an all-rounder means you always have the chance to redeem yourself. I was theoretically an off-spinner; in practice, I bowled a mix of undercutters and arm balls.

When I came back from London, I lived in Luke Toynbee's mother's house in Palmerston North — Luke was at university in Dunedin. Robyn spent a lot of time at Waimarama in Hawke's Bay and needed someone to feed the cat. It was a really good arrangement for me when I started playing for Central Districts, especially since Robyn often left me a car.

Luke's father Matt was a part-owner of EziBuy so during the players' strike I worked there as an intimate apparel auditor. Well, that's what it says on my CV. I counted undergarments. Boxes of underwear or bras would arrive and I had to count the contents to ensure there were 200, as advertised. Inevitably, when you got up to 150 or so, one of your workmates would say something to make you lose count and you'd have to start again. I was 18 and didn't really know what the strike was about so I just listened to the senior CD players like Jake Oram and Glen Sulzberger. Without their guidance it would've been easy to have taken one of the contracts that were being waved around.

Robyn was dating a bloke called — believe it or not — Ross Taylor. When they were in residence there were two Ross Taylors in the house. Whenever there was a call on the landline for Ross Taylor, the question was, "Which one: the blue-eyed blond or the dark-haired guy?" It was a situation replete with potential for confusion and embarrassment; amazingly enough, very little eventuated. To this day, he's Ross Senior and I'm Rosco.

Ross senior played rugby league for New Zealand. In fact, he scored a try in the famous upset victory over the Kangaroos at Lang Park in 1987. We were watching the game on DVD, with him explaining that the Aussies were targeting Clayton Friend, the Kiwis' playmaker, with late hits. His job was to stop the Aussies bashing Friend by getting them to bash someone else, i.e., him. (He was a 92-kg prop.) So, he arrived at a tackle half an hour late and speared an elbow into the back of some Aussie's head. The Aussies reacted like Pavlov's dogs and went after him, with Wally Lewis leading the charge. I was going, "You were a dirty prick" and RT senior was running the "I was only following orders" defence. These days he'd be suspended for 10 weeks.

It was a great environment for me. Ross had been a professional athlete — he went to the UK to play for Hull Kingston Rovers — while Robyn had umpired netball at national level. They were knowledgeable and supportive, but they also pushed me. Ross would ask me what I was going to do if cricket didn't work out. That just reinforced my desire to make it as a professional cricketer and the need to work even harder because there was no Plan B. As I tell people, I did go to university but only to pick up my mate Marcus after lectures. Once I became established, Ross's stock question became, "Are you having fun?" Given the nature of professional sport and the vagaries of cricket, that's not always easy to do.

I got a century in an ODI against Sri Lanka in Napier after

Robyn had lent me her car. Over time, a pattern emerged: whenever we played in Napier and Robyn didn't lend me her car, I didn't get any runs. Therefore, it became a rule that when I played in Napier, she had to lend me her car. Robyn and Ross senior have a place in Kinloch so there have been times when she has driven from Kinloch to drop off her car. (Not only was I quite superstitious, I was also surrounded by superstitious people.) This arrangement backfired spectacularly when Robyn gave me a crayfish along with lending me her car, which was brand new. It was a bit like the incident in Alexandra: I didn't give the crayfish another thought until it became impossible to ignore. Robyn was left with a choice between getting rid of the smell or getting rid of the car. It was easier to do the latter.

I met my wife Victoria at the New Zealand Cricket Academy in 2003. She was studying at Waikato University to be a PE teacher and playing for Northern Districts. The late Mike Shrimpton, who'd coached the 2000 World Cup-winning White Ferns, talked her into going down to Lincoln for the year.

Victoria Taylor: There were four girls and eight guys. The boys rolled in after the domestic season and we had a session at which we all had to stand up and introduce ourselves. I'd never heard of Ross Taylor. When he spoke, I thought, 'Oh wow, this guy speaks really well, he can capture a room.' This is a massive stereotype, I know, but I just assumed he came from a well-to-do family or had been a head boy, something along those lines.

You know the old saying that if they're mean to you, they like you? He was a bit like that to start with. I was like, 'Who the hell is this guy? Who does he think he is?' He kept hanging around the girls, but I was so focused on my uni stuff and keeping fit and cricket — trying to make the year worthwhile and become a really good cricketer — that I didn't dwell on it.

We had to partner up for fielding drills and batting drills and he and I kept getting paired up. He might've said something one day; the penny dropped and he sort of just grew on me. Early on, we'd all been sat down by Dayle Hadlee who told us we were there to play cricket, there were to be no shenanigans. I was like, "Of course not — we're here to learn." We tried to keep it a secret but that didn't last long.

When I was 21, Victoria's father, Peter, my future father-in-law, put me on a contract. I'd had a poor season for CD, so he decided to incentivise me to bat time. The premise was that the longer I batted, the more runs I'd get. Peter had watched me play some New Zealand A games in Brisbane. His assessment was that I just wanted to smack it as hard as I could, and I'd never play test cricket if I carried on like that. He put his mind to getting me to knuckle down and face a lot of balls.

The contract was structured to reward runs scored and balls faced up to a maximum of $2500 in both the first-class and one-day competitions. My first-class performances didn't cost him much, but he had to fork out the full monty for the one-day stuff — I was the top run-scorer in the competition. It was a bit of a eureka moment for me: while the game situation often dictates how you play, sometimes you need personal goals to motivate you when the game doesn't.

Victoria Taylor: Obviously, Ross didn't grow up with a lot of money, so money motivated him a bit. Dad picked up on that quite early on — he and Ross had quite similar upbringings. It didn't happen again, by the way. That was the only contract because Ross went out and scored a ton of runs.

Because there were only eight of us at the Academy that year, Jesse came back to help make up the numbers. He was on a CD contract so he had money and therefore led a pretty social life. We were playing Canterbury on a Sunday; Jesse went out the night before. On Sunday morning I walked over to the hall for breakfast and there was Jesse spreadeagled in a bush, sound asleep. One of his shoes was missing. Okay, boys will be boys. But then I noticed something truly disgraceful: an untouched box of KFC in the nearby rubbish bin.

I woke him up. "Come on, mate," I said. "We haven't got much time, we're playing soon." He went to his room for a quick kip. When he reappeared, his main concern was the whereabouts of his other shoe. It was a shambles: Peter Fulton was crook; Neil Broom had gone out with Jesse, been hit in the face with a bottle and ended up in A&E; and the wicket was green, prompting ring-in Mark Richardson to harangue Dayle Hadlee on the theme that better wickets would produce better cricketers. All in all, quite the build-up. Two days later we went into Lincoln township to get some food. There, in the middle of a roundabout, was Jesse's missing shoe. "Oh yeah," he said. "Now, I remember." No one dared ask, "Remember what?"

Neil Broom was, and still is, a very funny human. When the subject of pets came up, he revealed that he hated cats. Victoria and I were thinking, 'Where's this going?' We asked why. "Because every time I hear them meow," he said, "I think they're saying my name: 'Neeowl, Neeowl.'" From then on, whenever Broomy came out to bat, I'd give him a little "Neeowl". Then there was the time he tried to show off his gymnastic prowess by doing a backflip over a couch. The execution wouldn't have impressed the Russian judge and, in fact, necessitated another visit to A&E.

The Central Districts team were in town for a one-day game against Canterbury at Hagley Oval. They had injury issues and I was the next batter in line. We got skittled for 67 — my 11 was third-highest score — and Canterbury won by nine wickets with a mere 196 balls to spare.

Craig Spearman picked up an injury in that game so I was added to the squad. In Timaru, I roomed with Peter Ingram, a big-hitting opening batsman and future Black Cap from New Plymouth. There was a single bed and a double bed: seeing I was 18 and he was 24, the seniority system would've normally resolved the issue. But Peter, being a nice bloke, decided we should toss for it; I won. It didn't occur to me till later that, as the rookie, I should've insisted Peter took the double bed. He must have been devastated to lose the toss because he'd probably thought, 'I'll just make the gesture and Ross will say, "No, no, you take the double".' But instead, I said, "Yeah, fine, let's toss," called tails and to the victor the spoils.

Mark Greatbatch: Ross dominated in domestic cricket because he had good power. In 2003/04, CD played Canterbury in the final of the State Shield, the one-day competition, at Jade Stadium. Canterbury had nine or 10 current or former internationals. We also had a decent side — Craig Spearman, Jamie How, Mathew Sinclair, Jacob Oram, Ross — albeit a lot younger. In the 15th over we were 150 for none; Spearman took Paul Wiseman for 30 in an over. We got 354 for 5 — Ross top-scored with 95 off 86 balls — and bowled them out for 255. Watching those younger players up against the better, older New Zealand players of the time, I had the sense I was witnessing the emergence of a couple of guys who were going to be part of the next core group.

That remains one of my favourite games, but it was hardly a changing of the guard. We met again in the 2005/06 final at QE II Park in Christchurch. It was Chris Cairns' last game for Canterbury who, once again, were stacked — Brendon, Nathan Astle, Chris Harris, Shane Bond, Craig McMillan, et al. Only one of their team hadn't, or wouldn't, play for New Zealand. My focus going in was on being as relaxed as possible. I was so relaxed I forgot my cricket bag. The manager, who was also the physio, had to go back to the hotel for it. Our coach, the former England player Graeme Barlow, gave me a dressing-down.

But at least I was relaxed. I got 50, which was our top score, and had Peter Fulton caught at mid-wicket. Part-time bowlers never forget a wicket. But we got our arses kicked: Cairns signed off with four wickets and a brisk 40-odd not out and they won in a canter.

Speaking of which . . . CD's Palmerston North contingent — Mike Mason, Ewen Thompson, Jake Oram, Bevan Griggs, Jamie How, me and a few others — trained really hard. Our trainer Darryl Cochrane entered us in a 10-km race from Massey University into Palmerston North and back. I was the fastest sprinter, but ET and Mace were the distance guns: they'd do 10 km in 40 minutes, while Jake and a couple of others were 45 to 47-minute men. The heat was on me to break 50 minutes.

The start/finish line was in the Massey driveway. I was keeping up until I was hit by a strident call of nature on the Manawatu River bridge. I really, really needed to go. By the grace of God, the route went past my mate Marcus's flat in Graham Place, next to the hockey ground. I burst in and charged into the loo. Afterwards, the last thing I felt like doing was rejoining the race. I worked out the timing, waited a while, chucked some water on my face and got Marcus's flatmate to drive me to Massey.

He pulled over at the top of the Massey Hill and I slumped down in the passenger seat when the pack went past with Bev and Mace to the fore. I powered home, finishing just shy of breaking 50 minutes. Which was perfect — I didn't want to overdo it. The boys were high-fiving me: "Well done, Ross, great effort." I accepted their plaudits with due modesty. I rationalised that I was so fit from the training we'd done over winter that I would have done that sort of time if I hadn't been blindsided by my metabolism. Having said that, it has remained my little secret — until now. If Darryl Cochrane reads this he'll be going, "What a bloody fraud!"

For a while, Victoria was called "Sipper", because she'd sit on the same drink all night, and I was called "Tipper". Bevan Griggs had dubbed me "Tipper" after a CD end-of-season party at Mark Greatbatch's house, a sort of a mad Monday affair. Jesse was pouring what were known as "Jesse Goneburgers" — treble bourbons with a splash of Coke just to take the edge off. I wasn't a stranger to the beverage itself because my mates and I used to get trays of $2 bourbons at the Fitzherbert Pub in Palmerston North. I was hammered but had just enough sense to apply the brakes by giving it the old dribble down the neck. I was tipping half the glass out, hence "Tipper".

The boys got me back to the motel and tucked me in. I was fresh as a daisy for golf the following day while the rest of them were seriously hung over. Jesse played in scuffs. I don't know of anyone else who has played a round of golf with sponsors at a corporate golf day wearing scuffs.

Jamie How and I were good mates but, for whatever reason, our joint ventures were often borderline fiascos. There was the time we were meant to be flying to Whangarei. We boarded late, settled into the only unoccupied seats — which matched our tickets — and prepared for take-off. Even though the plane was full, a couple more passengers came on board. Their tickets also matched the seats we were in. Confusion reigned until Jamie asked, "Where's this plane going?" Taupo, as it turned out. Right seat numbers, wrong plane. We put our heads down and got off as quickly as we could.

During the Champion's Trophy in South Africa in 2009, we went to the Tom Cruise movie, *Lions for Lambs*. It had already started, so we made ourselves unpopular by squeezing past people to get to our seats. I wouldn't say it was the easiest plot to follow but after half an hour or so I was really getting into it when something odd happened: the words "The End" appeared on the screen. Right movie, wrong theatre. It was a multiplex cinema and we'd gone into the 1 pm showing instead of the

2 pm. Now and again, I think about tracking *Lions for Lambs* down and watching it from the start. Then I remember I know how it ends.

Chapter 4.
Foo (aka Black Cap 234)

In early 2006, Victoria and I and some Central Districts teammates were at a UB40 Concert at the Bowl of Brooklyn in New Plymouth. We were enveloped in a fog of marijuana fumes emanating from a nearby group — which we certainly weren't used to — and surrounded by happy people singing 'Red Red Wine'. My phone was on silent so I missed a call from chairman of selectors Sir Richard Hadlee. He'd left a voice message saying congratulations, I was in the New Zealand side for the last two ODIs against the West Indies. It wasn't a bombshell in that I'd been making runs so I had to be part of the selection conversation. And coach John Bracewell had told me early in the season that I wouldn't make the ODI team, but wasn't far way. For all that, though, it's a moment you never forget and a thrill that nothing else can quite match. I debuted a week before my twenty-second birthday. Since you ask, I was run out for 15. We won.

Fittingly, the call came before a game at Pukekura Park, one of my favourite grounds. (I doubt many bowlers feel that way about it.) To me, it's the most picturesque ground in the country. The crowd is fantastic. CD teams have long appreciated and admired their ruthlessness when it comes to having a laugh at our opponents' expense. After BJ Watling had got a duck, they tossed bread at him when he was in the field.

I'd attended next to no international cricket — a couple of ODIs in Napier, neither of which I watched from beginning to end. The first time I went to a test match, I took part in it. More to the point, though, I had accumulated a reasonable amount of playing experience before I was picked for New Zealand.

I had a poor season of domestic cricket in 2004/05. NZC's technical director, Ashley Ross, pointed me to a playing opportunity in the ACT for six or seven weeks in August/ September. When I arrived, they asked me where I wanted to bat. Unaware that they had quite a strong middle order, I gave the reply they were hoping for: "I'll bat wherever you want me to." Wrong answer: they wanted me to open the batting.

ACT played in the New South Wales regional competition against four Sydney teams — North, South, East and West — and NSW Country. I performed respectably rather than spectacularly, but it was a great preparation for the New Zealand season. Six months later I was playing international cricket. It was also a valuable insight into Aussie cricketers' take-no-prisoners approach on and off the field. The ACT coach was telling a joke in the showers which faced the changing room. Everyone was losing it. "Hang on, boys," he said. "Wait till you hear the punch line." We weren't cracking up at the joke: our skipper, who was standing next to him in the shower, was peeing down his leg.

I played for New Zealand A. Some players shine at that level, but I never really enjoyed it and wasn't very successful. I found New Zealand A to be a manufactured team and the contests to be a bit artificial. It didn't help that there's no real consensus about what an A team should be: some countries see them primarily as a development pathway, so their A teams are not genuine second XIs; some go the other way and load their A teams with guys who have already played international cricket. Plus, you're so close to your goal of playing for your country that you burden yourself with expectations and focus on outcomes, instead of just playing what's in front of you and going through your normal process.

Victoria Taylor: I got a job in Te Awamutu which meant another year of trying to catch up with each other. I remember the awkward feeling of being brand-new in the job and having to explain that I wanted to take a couple of days off to watch my partner make his Black Caps debut in Napier. You sort of don't know what to say, but they were really good about it. I did a year there, but it just got too much so I gave up my job and moved to Palmerston North. Ross was trying to cement his place in the team so every game counted. As a partner that's quite stressful.

I was the new boy so I was head down, bum up, taking everything in. My nickname in the team was "Foo". Growing up in Masterton, "foo" was the equivalent of cool: "That's a foo car." For some reason, I went back to using it; Daryl Tuffey and Shane Bond picked up on it and started calling me "Foo Boy". Ian Smith claims that, when he first heard someone call me Foo, he thought they were saying "food". That made perfect sense to him because, every time I went to his and Louise's place, they'd have to do a big shop the next day to replenish their food stocks.

John "Braces" Bracewell was a no-nonsense operator, which suited me because I like that sort of coach. But I was being mentored by Martin "Hogan" Crowe who wasn't a Braces fan. Apparently, they didn't get on as teammates and time hadn't softened their opinion of each other. Hogan was very big on getting me to play straight. At training a day out from my first test in New Zealand — against England at Seddon Park in 2008 — I was getting annoyed with myself whenever I didn't play straight. Braces came down and said, "Ross, what are doing?" When I explained, he said I was focusing too much on playing straight and getting away from my strengths and natural flair. That night, Hogan asked me how training had gone. When I told him Braces thought I was trying to play too straight, Hogan went nuts: "What would he know?"

I could see both points of view: I wanted to play straighter but didn't want to curb my instinct to do what came naturally and what had got me into the team. That sort of difference of opinion isn't unusual. You're unlikely to coach at the top level without having firm views on the game and how it should be played. But, because coaches are individuals and there are many different paths to success in cricket, those views are going to differ, sometimes subtly, sometimes dramatically, from coach to coach.

Over the course of a career, you get a lot of advice from many different sources, some of which is contradictory. This can be confusing and unhelpful for young players whose natural instinct is to pay attention to whatever coaches or advisors — rep team coach, club coach, first XI coach, father, best mate's father — tell them. With experience and achievement comes the confidence to filter out advice that isn't useful or comes from sources who aren't on your wavelength and don't understand your method. And, at the same time, that experience and achievement make people hesitant about offering advice on the basis that you know it all — which you don't — or have heard it all before, which is more likely to be the case.

Interestingly, Braces — an outstanding off-spinner in his playing days — rated my off-spin, whereas I never did. Eventually he worked out that I really just wanted to bat.

In 2007, I got a century in an ODI against Australia at Eden Park. Our victory put us 2–0 up in a three-match series, meaning we'd won the Chappell–Hadlee Trophy for the first time. Shane Watson particularly and Matthew Hayden sledged me and I went back hard at them. Between overs my batting partner Peter Fulton told me to treat it as a badge of honour: "If they're sledging you, they must rate you." That hadn't occurred to me. Wise words from Fults, who got 76 not out off 65 balls and he and Brendon brought us home.

Glenn McGrath didn't sledge me. Maybe he thought it would be overkill given the chatter from Hayden and Watson. I nicked a McGrath delivery to third man for a single. When I got up the other end, McGrath gave me a look and said, "Shit, you've got a lot to say for a young bloke." I said, "Mate, you can say whatever you want to me, but I'm not taking it from f---n Shane Watson." After the game, Stephen Fleming, our skipper, came over and told me he'd liked the way I'd stuck up for myself.

Before Flem's last test in Napier in 2008, we went to the Trinity Hill winery and met the founder, John Hancock, and head winemaker Warren Gibson. I bought my first Trinity Hill Homage Syrah, which is one of my favourite wines. A couple of years later I went back with Jeetan Patel, but they'd run out of the normal-sized bottles of Homage because Steven Spielberg had bought the last 11 dozen. I bought a couple of magnums and Jeets got a six-litre bottle. A bit later, I went to Jeets' house in Wellington and there was this $1500 bottle of wine just sitting in the hallway.

Despite my perception of him at the time, and the public perception pretty well throughout, Shane Watson's a good bloke. I played with him at the Rajasthan Royals in the Indian Premier League (IPL): a nice guy, a family man who loves wine and playing his guitar. The perception of who he was as a cricketer and a person was way off the mark, and that applied on both sides of the Tasman. He came out to bat in the 2015 World Cup final in Melbourne to a barrage of boos. There was no way the Kiwi contingent in the crowd could have generated that noise; they had plenty of help from the locals.

I made my test debut against South Africa at the new Wanderers stadium in Johannesburg in November 2007. It was a brutal and deflating introduction to cricket at the highest level in the most demanding form of the game.

South Africa won the toss and batted. We bowled them out for 226 with Bondy and Chris Martin leading the way. It was all downhill from there. We found their intimidating pace attack — Dale Steyn, Makhaya Ntini, Andre Nel and Jacques Kallis — too hot to handle, getting rolled for 118. Flem made a counterattacking 40; my 15 was the second-highest score. My enduring memories of that innings are the surge of relief when I got off the mark and being pointlessly sledged in Afrikaans by Nel, who was an ogre, quite possibly the angriest man in the game. After Hashim Amla and Kallis had filled their boots, we needed a mere 531 to win; we got 172. Steyn took 10 wickets in the match and did it again in the second test at Centurion, which South Africa won by an innings. I got 17 and 8 and was then dumped from the test team.

At my first review with New Zealand Cricket, manager Lindsay Crocker said, "Ross, I notice you spend a lot of time in your room: are you okay?" He probably suspected that this young guy wasn't at ease in the environment; if anything, it indicated the opposite. I'm pretty comfortable in my own skin and operate on my own clock: when I'm hungry, I eat; when I'm tired, I sleep. I don't need to be around people. When I was with the Black Caps, I'd spend a lot of the downtime sitting in cafés, drinking coffee and people-watching. If someone was around, I might say, "I'm off to a winery, do you want to come?" If not, I was more than happy to fly solo.

Not that it was a bed of roses. We had "Leading Teams", a team-building concept that NZC High Performance manager Ric Charlesworth, a legendary Australian hockey player and coach, brought in from AFL. Basically, it involved revealing yourself to your teammates by telling each other what you're feeling and thinking. I wasn't a big fan — it seemed like trying to manufacture a culture out of hot air — and I wasn't the only one. It hastened the departure of a few players, notably Nathan Astle.

And there was too much of a critical focus on small stuff. You were fined for being late, but some guys in the team wanted you to be late; they got a kick out of others copping a fine. People make mistakes. If they keep doing it, you've got to deal with it but, if it's a one-off, why make it into a bigger deal than it actually is? The culture now is much less judgemental. Back then, if you didn't want to train, you were lazy, so we trained for the sake of it. Cricket at the top level is largely in the mind so those extra training sessions weren't making us better players.

We used to have jobs: tickets, scorebook, flag, baggage — everyone had one. It wasn't a universally popular arrangement and eventually fell by the wayside. Now, the manager and assistant manager do everything.

But tickets were a good gig because you got to keep the leftovers. I was on tickets at the 2009 Twenty20 World Cup in England. I strained my hamstring against South Africa and was out for a week or so. Because I wasn't playing against Ireland, the first game of a double-header at Trent Bridge, I wasn't really tuned in and missed the bus to the ground. The hotel was on the outskirts of Nottingham. I jumped in a taxi, only to realise that I'd forgotten my wallet. I said to the driver, "Mate, I've got no money, but I do have four tickets to the cricket." New Zealand vs Ireland mightn't have been much of a carrot to dangle but the second game was England vs South Africa. The cabbie said, "Yeah great, I'll pick up my dad and we'll watch the afternoon game." It would've been a challenging negotiation if he hadn't been a cricket fan.

Being a young buck and therefore supposedly up to speed with the latest in music and technology, I was on music for the whole 2008 tour of England. The tour ended in Aberdeen, of all places, where we played an ODI tri-series against Ireland and Scotland. After a three-test series (lost) and a five ODI series (won) against England in the space of seven weeks, it would be fair to say the boys weren't laser-focused on the Aberdeen leg. We played an under-strength Ireland at Mannofield Park in front of 100 spectators. Brendon McCullum and James Marshall put on 274 for the first wicket, which is the highest Black Caps ODI partnership for any wicket. Scotty Styris wasn't playing so he sauntered over to the fast-food caravan and brought back 15 hot dogs. To say Braces was unimpressed doesn't begin to convey the negativity of his response. (I was next in, so I couldn't have one.)

I got 59 not out off 24 balls, my fastest ODI half-century, we got to 402/2 and knocked over Ireland for 112.

Afterwards, we were having a few in the changing room which, as you'd expect, wasn't quite up to the standard of Lord's or Old Trafford. It was small but not cosy, with hard wooden benches. I got up to change the music and sat back down on a banana which squelched all over the back of my shorts. Peter Fulton was directly across the room from me. I asked him, "Who did it?" Fults probably couldn't hear me over the music, but he could lipread. He pointed to my left. On my left, drinking beer, supposedly absorbed in another conversation and trying to pretend he didn't know what had happened, was TG Southee: 19 years old and already showing glimpses of his rare talent for winding people up and being a pain.

I grabbed Tim, wrestled him down onto the bench and for whatever reason — blind rage might've had something to do with it — sat on his head and bounced up and down. I didn't think it was that funny, but Fults was in hysterics. When I finally let Tim up, Fults said, "It wasn't Tim, it was Jeets" — Jeetan Patel who was sitting on my right. My apology wasn't overly sincere: I figured Tim had either done or would soon do something that warranted a roughing up. Jeets got off scot-free. Well, he's older than me and I was brought up to respect my elders.

Tim loves that sort of argy-bargy. He's a very good story-teller — as is Trent Boult — and that incident is part of his back-of-the-bus repertoire.

In 2010, I got a century off 81 balls against Australia at Seddon Park. At the time, it was the fastest test century by a Kiwi. Brendon subsequently surpassed it three times, and his century off 54 balls in his final test is the fastest of all time. I knew Mum and Dad were leaving just before midday so I started playing some shots, trying to get to 100 before they left the ground to go to the airport. I thought I'd missed the boat but Peter, my father-in-law, figured out what was going on and drove them back to the ground in time to see me reach three figures.

One of my two favourite ODI innings was the 131 not out against Pakistan at Pallekele in Sri Lanka at the 2011 World Cup. (It was my birthday. The other favourite was on the day before my birthday seven years later — 181 not out against England in Dunedin.) Indian fans still come up to me or message to thank me for pumping Shoaib Akhtar and beating Pakistan. Interestingly, I also get plenty of social media stuff from Pakistanis saying it was one of their favourite innings. And, every year on my birthday, Indian fans message me to say that Kamran Akmal, who was the Pakistani keeper that day and played a significant part in proceedings, sends his regards.

Kane Williamson always reckoned he could tell how I was going to go in a game by how I batted in the nets. It was counter-intuitive: a crap net meant a big innings was coming up. Boy, did I have a crap net in Pallekele — I got cleaned up three times in the space of five balls. I was woefully out of form and the happy birthday messages from home somehow made it worse.

Dan Vettori won the toss and we batted. Martin Guptill was going well but Brendon went six and out and Jamie How struggled. I went in at 55/2 in the 13th over. My second ball, bowled by Shoaib Akhtar, went for four between Akmal and Younis Khan at first slip. I put the next one through backward point, then nicked a goober to Akmal. He shelled it. I'd faced four balls, been dropped twice and hit two fours, one of which actually wasn't an edge.

I had to grind it out. It took me close to 100 balls to get to 60, but I was fighting just to get a score. The wicket was okay, but I was struggling for confidence. And, on top of the game situation, both the team and I needed a boost to get us into the tournament. The key moment was slog-sweeping Shahid Afridi for six. He was someone that I never looked to play that shot against because he bowled flat and quick and could get under the bat. My plan was to see him off, so I must've played the slog sweep on instinct. But it gave me momentum. I took 28 off a Shoaib over, 30 off one from Abdul Razzaq, and Jake and I pillaged 92 off the last four overs to get us to 302. Pakistan got 192. Coming in at number three, poor old Kamran Akmal had the opportunity to redeem himself but offered me a chance off Tim's bowling. I didn't spurn it.

We played South Africa at the Shere Bangla National Stadium in Mirpur, Bangladesh in the quarter-finals. Our coach, John Wright, wanted to have a training session, but Dan dug his toes in, telling Wrighty, "The boys are cooked." Billy Bowden had umpired the West Indies–Pakistan quarter-final at the stadium; he told Wrighty that, if we won the toss and batted, 220 to 230 would be enough because it was really hard to score once the lights came on. South Africa were the top-ranked team — they had Amla, Kallis, Steyn, Graeme Smith, AB de Villiers, Morné Morkel — while we were eighth. Not surprisingly, the media wrote us off. In fact, I doubt anyone outside the group gave us a chance.

Faf du Plessis lit the fuse by talking about the semi-finals, the implication being that the quarter-final was a foregone conclusion. He also made the strange claim that he knew his game better than any 26-year-old in world cricket. This was a guy in his first year of international cricket; he'd never played a test, just a handful of ODIs. The consensus among the boys was that this Faf du Plessis was a very confident character.

We won the toss, which was a great start. Brendon and Guppy went early: we were 16/2 after six overs. Jesse and I were just trying to get a partnership going. My job then, and for a long time afterwards, was to get to 35 overs. Wrighty drummed that into me: "Wickets in hand, Ross. Just get to 35 overs." That night I got to the 33rd. Jesse and I put on 114. It wasn't spectacular but we were very conscious of Billy's formula for success. Jesse batted fantastically well for 83, the highest individual score in the game by some distance. Kane smacked 38 not out and we scraped over Billy's bottom line: 221. We knew we'd have to bowl well, but we were competitive.

Jesse was cramping up big-time and didn't go out to field. I went off at the first drinks break to find him face down in the corner of the dressing room, not the most hygienic spot in Bangladesh I would have thought. The slightest movement was causing him to cramp up. I asked how he was going; he turned his head a millimetre or so to reply and went rigid. I said, "She's right, mate, just stay there."

Du Plessis was always going to cop it but, when he ran out AB in his first over at the crease, it went off. Dan and Scotty led the way. Styris loved that stuff; I'm sure he thinks the current team is far too gentlemanly. I didn't see our waterboy, Kyle Mills, run onto the field and give Faf a spray, but I did see Faf's retaliatory shove. Growing up in Masterton, the eleventh commandment was, "If something's going down, you stand by your mates." I told du Plessis, in pretty blunt language, to keep his hands to himself or he'd wear one. To my family's embarrassment a photograph of the incident, in which I can be seen snarling at Faf, was widely circulated.

Credit to Faf, though. The boys went at him hard — I'm pretty sure he wouldn't have had that much abuse in his entire international career to that point — but he stood up to it and batted really well. While he was there, they were in with a chance. But we got across the line, dismissing them for 172 in the 44th over.

We were elated at winning a big game when no one had given us a chance. That would have to be one of my favourite victories because of the way we stuck together. Kiwis play better when we're up against it and we battled hard that day. Millsy probably doesn't remember it quite as fondly: he got fined, even though he hadn't taken part in the game and then was packed off home with an injury.

Another fond memory of playing on the subcontinent was the first test against India in Ahmedabad in 2010. Hamish Bennett, playing in his first —and only — test, went down on the first morning, which left us with a pace attack of Chris Martin and Jesse Ryder. Virender Sehwag, a player I loved watching, got 173 off 199 balls, just hitting it wherever he wanted. Jesse and Kane — who, by the way, was on debut — got centuries to keep us in the game and we had India 15/5 in their second innings. Guppy ran out Sehwag and Chris knocked over Gautam Gambhir, Rahul Dravid, Sachin Tendulkar and Suresh Raina. That spell on a flat wicket at the end of day four put us in a position to win the game, but we just couldn't get Harbhajan Singh and VVS Laxman.

Well, at least our specialist bowlers couldn't. To be fair, by tea on the fifth afternoon they were knackered. The game was petering out, so Brendon and I were doing the bowling. Baz bowled spin in the nets but medium pace in games for some reason. My plan to Harbhajan, who was on 116, was to not go for too many so I had three or four guys out on the leg-side boundary. Harbhajan said, "Oh come on, Ross, at least bring up long on and I'll take him on." So, I brought long on up and went around the wicket, thinking he was going to run at me and try to tonk it back over my head. I unintentionally bowled a high full toss — hip height, definitely marginal but not called. Harbhajan had a wild mow, top-edged it into his helmet and it looped to BJ at 45 to give me my first test wicket.

Next over, I nicked off Sreesanth, a legit dismissal, to finish with 2 for 4 off 4.4 overs. When you tour England all the official ECB publications have full stats so, hilariously, there I'd be at the top of the test bowling averages. And the best was yet to come.

The other notable feature of that series was that Sachin was closing in on 100 international centuries. When he batted, the ground was full and the crowd was humming. When he got out, 80 per cent of the crowd had buggered off by the time he got back to the pavilion.

Victoria Taylor: I was doing relief teaching, which was great because it meant I could come and go. If Ross was overseas for a long time I could just pack up and shoot over to join him. Obviously, you pick and choose the best trips to go on.

We'd been in Palmy for two or three years and he was hardly ever home — literally a couple of weeks a year. When we got engaged, I said, "This is crazy: if you're never going to be around, I'm not staying in Palmy. We need to be where my family is, so let's move to Hamilton." I never got registered because not long after we bought a house in Hamilton, I was pregnant with Mackenzie and that was the end of my teaching career. My cricketing career went the same way. It got to the point where I was working and training and spending my summers away playing cricket. Something had to give.

There was a player revolt against Andy Moles who'd succeeded Braces. I wasn't involved. My mindset — at that stage — was a product of my upbringing: you respected the coach whoever he was and however he operated. The senior players just weren't happy with him. That came as a surprise to me because Andy didn't seem much different to the other coaches I'd had. He was very much cut from the same cloth as Mike Hesson and Gary Stead — a facilitator. In fact, Andy was probably more of a hands-on coach than Hess. But he had to go. Mark Greatbatch came in as the batting coach and over time sort of assumed the head coach role.

I was still the archetypal young player who keeps his head down and tries to steer clear of the manoeuvring and politicking, but I started to get the impression that the relationship between Dan and vice-captain Brendon was getting a bit rocky. I didn't really understand it because they were quite close. Maybe Dan felt Brendon was getting too big for his boots, picking and choosing where he batted, wanting to give up the gloves.

Mark Greatbatch: I did think during my tenure as batting coach/coach that there was a bit of immaturity from some, Brendon particularly. Daniel was trying to

get him to help lead the group, but he wasn't doing a
lot of leading. It was all about him. Three or four years
after that, though, he did mature. I recall Dan saying in
a selection meeting that he wanted Baz to be his vice-
captain, but he wasn't mature enough, he wasn't leading,
he was a negative influence on the group.

Quite possibly that decision planted the seeds of what
happened down the track in terms of Ross and Brendon.
They're very different guys with different personalities.

When we got home from India, Brendon was relieved of the vice-
captaincy and I was told that, if Vettori went down, I'd captain
the team. Except they didn't make it public. It was as if they were
scared of Brendon.

Eventually it started to trickle out, although I still hadn't heard
a peep from Dan. CD played Otago in Dunedin. When I went out
to bat, Brendon, his brother Nathan and Craig Cumming sledged
me. They called me "the Prince of New Zealand Cricket" and
"untouchable" and suggested "my dad" — Mark Greatbatch — had
got me the vice-captaincy. Starting when I was 14, I'd had plenty
of guys sledge me and tell me afterwards, "Nothing personal,
mate." This was definitely personal. In fairness, Nathan came up
afterwards and congratulated me on getting the vice-captaincy.

Our next game was against Northern Districts in Hamilton.
I still hadn't heard from Vettori. I was starting to fret about it
because he was all-powerful: selector, captain, de facto coach. I
saw him at the start of the game: nothing. By then, my read on it
was that they'd felt they had to name someone; it couldn't really be
another bowler, and I was next cab off the rank, but Dan obviously
wasn't that shook on me either.

We had to win to make the final of the HRV Cup, the T20
competition. I got lucky: I hit a full toss straight up in the air,
but they didn't lay a hand on it. Then I smacked Tim for six to
win the game and ran around the field like a headless chook. It

was an overflow of the emotions stirred up by the carry-on in Dunedin and the uncertainty created by Vettori's silence, which he maintained after the game.

We played Auckland in the final at good old Pukekura Park. They had an impressive bowling line-up — six guys who had or would play white-ball cricket for New Zealand, plus England all-rounder Ravi Bopara — but it was one of those days. I got 80 off 30 balls with eight sixes, Kieran Noema-Barnett got in on the act and we won by 78 runs.

The Black Caps assembled a few days later. Dan finally uttered what, apart from "sorry", seemed to be the hardest words to say: "Ross is the vice-captain."

Up until that point, I felt I'd had an interesting relationship with Brendon. Away from cricket, we didn't have a whole lot in common: I wasn't a beer drinker, wasn't into horse racing and didn't play golf, all of which meant I wasn't in his orbit that much. In hindsight, the vice-captaincy mini-drama may have been the tipping point.

There's no doubt that the IPL had already created a rivalry. In 2008, Brendon's US$700,000 deal with Kolkata understandably caused quite a stir. I went to Bangalore for US$100,000. After that first tournament I re-signed with Bangalore for US$700,000. Vettori and Oram were also on big money, but the narrative was that Brendon was the highest-paid Kiwi. No one mentioned me, but he knew we were on the same money. Flying under the radar didn't bother me. I was a boy from the Bush who'd lived on spaghetti and eggs. US$700,000? I'd never dreamed I'd make that sort of money.

PART TWO:
SCAR TISSUE

Chapter 5.
Be Careful What You Wish For

In mid-2010 we played a triangular ODI tournament in Sri Lanka. With Dan Vettori and Brendon McCullum on paternity leave, I was captain. Before the first game against India in Dambulla, Tony Greig, who was doing commentary, walked past our warm-up as Mark Greatbatch was nicking catches to the slips. Greig told him, "You should be good at that — it's all you ever did as a player." Batchy took it in his stride: "Nice to see you too, Tony."

It was Kane Williamson's first tour. Thinking I couldn't chuck the young debutant — he'd turned 20 two days earlier — in at the deep end, I batted at three with Kane at four. It didn't go according to plan: Kane got a nine-ball duck. (He bowled well though.) Scotty Styris and I put on 190; we got 288 and rolled India for 88; I took four catches. Captaincy didn't seem like that big a deal.

But by halfway through the tournament, I was ringing my manager Leanne McGoldrick to say, "I'm not ready to captain this team." (Vettori had signalled his intention to give up the captaincy after the 2011 World Cup.) I didn't think I could captain in all three formats. I was making big strides with my batting but felt two or three years away from being ready for the captaincy. Leanne told me to soldier on and we'd talk about it when I got home.

Batchy had been roped in as coach, a prime example of being

in the wrong place at the wrong time. After that big win in Dambulla, the wheels came off. We missed out on the final of the triangular tournament after India turned the tables on us in the rematch. That was the start of an 11-game losing streak in ODIs. Dan returned as captain for the tour of Bangladesh: we lost the ODI series 4–0 which, at that time, was seen as pretty much rock-bottom. Then we went to India and lost the ODIs 5–0. Three of the losses in Bangladesh were really close, but in India we simply weren't competitive.

Mark Greatbatch: I didn't have a great experience with the group in Bangladesh. The second IPL auction was coming up. We were getting scores of 180 to 200 and playing like we were trying to get 280 to 310. I said to them, "I don't know what's going on here: we've talked these being 220 to 240 wickets. Score those runs and we've got a great chance of winning the game with our bowlers and our fielders. Getting 20 or 30 off 10 or 15 balls might look great, but it doesn't do a lot for your team." I had no doubt that some players were auditioning for IPL contracts.

There was a real immaturity in the group at that time. They'd probably say they were just playing their game, but they weren't playing with many brains. It really disappointed me that they were using playing for their country to audition for big-money contracts. There were probably four or five of them in that mould. I don't know what level it was later on, but there was definitely that negativity and immaturity when I was there. It was subtle at times, but other times it was pretty blatant.

Dan ran the team on and off the field so being his vice-captain didn't require me to do a great deal. Even if he wasn't playing, he'd do the talking. That was fine by me because I wasn't comfortable with that aspect of the role. I hated talking, hated the sound of my own voice.

I don't know whether Dan set out to accumulate power — he doesn't come across as that sort of person — or it just happened that way. The instability in the coaching set-up created a vacuum that he filled. Dan's an intelligent guy. He probably took the view that it was his head on the chopping block so he should be in control. The problem was that some players didn't feel comfortable talking to him. You're probably not going to share your fears and insecurities with the captain under a conventional structure; when the captain is also the coach and selector, you're even less likely to do so.

I had a pretty good relationship with Dan. He was a hard individual to get to know — he didn't let his guard down very often — but he was always respectful. After he retired, he would always text to congratulate me when I did well. The other dimension to our relationship was that my father-in-law had coached Dan and my parents-in-law are friends of Dan's parents.

When I got back from Sri Lanka, I met with New Zealand Cricket's general manager of cricket, Geoff Allott, and high-performance director Roger Mortimer to review my performance as captain and, I suppose, look ahead to life after Vettori. My self-analysis was that I was quite good tactically but not good at doing the talking in group situations — team meetings and huddles. I said my approach would be to lead from the front, try to get the best out of players through one-on-one discussions and endeavour to get better in group situations over time.

They seemed happy with that and undertook to ensure that structures were put in place to help me in the areas where I wasn't strong, like dealing with the media. I wasn't media savvy and didn't have a comfortable relationship with journalists. They thought I was guarded and unforthcoming, but it was more that I simply wasn't confident. It was a reassuring discussion: there was clarity around my strengths and weaknesses and the areas in which I needed help. I set great store on the assurances that NZC would put things in place to enable me to cope and grow into the role. Silly me. I was innocent in the ways of the world and NZC.

I guess you could say the underlying assumption was "when rather than if" I became Black Caps captain. That sense grew stronger after a conversation with new coach John Wright in Chennai before the World Cup got under way. We were having a drink in the team room at the hotel: the subject of the captaincy — and the whispers that there would be a competitive process to determine who succeeded Vettori — came up. "Don't worry about it," said Wrighty. "You're my man."

It was a strange — and very public — process. In his autobiography, Brendon wrote that, on our return from the World Cup, he'd had a coffee with CEO Justin Vaughan who told him NZC wanted him to put his name forward for the captaincy and that both of us would be required to present to an interview panel. I was given only a week's notice: I'd actually heard that Brendon was preparing a PowerPoint presentation before I was officially informed that I'd have to present. I didn't hear from Justin Vaughan until I was driving to Lincoln for the presentation/interview.

I had an ambition to be captain, but it was too soon. The problem is that you don't determine when these opportunities arise and, in that sense, perfect timing is a rare commodity in professional sport. At one point I said to Leanne and Victoria, "You two want the captaincy more than I do." They — rightly — came back with, "You don't know if you're going to get another shot at it."

Because I had issues around dealing with the media, I'd been working with Amanda Millar, a TV journalist and media trainer. Once the process was confirmed, she gave me job interview coaching and helped me prepare my presentation. A PowerPoint presentation wasn't an option for me. We wrote a presentation, Amanda critiqued my delivery and we tweaked a few things in consultation with Leanne and Victoria, although Victoria's input was limited because she was pregnant and we were about to get married.

(We got married at the Hilton in Taupo. At some point during the evening, I was at the bar with Martin Crowe, aka Hogan, Ian Smith and Mark Greatbatch. Hogan proposed a toast to New Zealand cricket captains which we all were. Hogan captained New Zealand from 1990 to 1993; Smithy was in charge for a test against Sri Lanka at Eden Park in 1991 when Hogan was injured; and both Batchy and I had captained in ODIs. We drank the toast. Hogan then said, "Now we're drinking to New Zealand test captains, so Ross and Batchy: see you later.")

A few hours before I delivered my presentation, I had a review with John Buchanan, the former massively successful coach of Australia who'd joined NZC as director of cricket. (He was on the interview panel, along with John Wright and Batchy.) At the end of the review, he asked, "Are you looking forward to tonight?" I told him I was pretty nervous, which was a considerable understatement. At school I hadn't been any good at making speeches, but the worst that could happen then was that I embarrassed myself, as opposed to blowing a once-in-a-career opportunity to captain my country. John said, "Just be yourself; it's a formality — the coach will get who he wants." 'Well, if that's the case,' I thought, 'I'm in good shape given what Wrighty told me in Chennai.'

I met Leanne to go over my presentation. Her main concern was that I wasn't late so I got to Lincoln half an hour early. Sitting in the rental car I watched through the pavilion window as an animated Brendon rolled out his high-tech presentation. I rang Leanne. "Maybe we underestimated this," I said. "Maybe I should have done a PowerPoint presentation."

"It's a bit late now," she said. "Just be authentic." It was a strange feeling being back at Lincoln, where I'd been at the Academy and met Victoria, to apply for the Black Caps captaincy. To this day

I wonder if Brendon hung around and watched me through the pavilion window.

John Wright: They both interviewed well and it wasn't an easy decision. I suppose the thing that swayed me in the end was Ross had played very well during the World Cup. There was a game against Pakistan that we needed to win to get to the quarter-finals. Dan got injured and Ross made 131 not out then did a very good job of captaining the side in the field. I thought he had leadership potential.

Mark Greatbatch: The two presentations were very, very different. One was a top presentation, thorough to a degree, but felt like it was put together by multiple people, whereas Ross's was more natural and his passion and willingness to help others showed out. All of us thought Ross was the right guy to lead the ship at that time.

John Buchanan: I had Brendon at the Kolkata Knight Riders. The first year he was just a player and it was the first season of IPL so everything sort of rolled. The second season, I made him joint captain. Brendon was a gambler, a risk taker, and that certainly didn't fit John Wright's approach to cricket.

More importantly, John wanted to try to attack this culture whereby the Players' Association, through its various tentacles, controlled what happened with the Black Caps. Ross stood apart from the Players' Association. He wasn't as directly influenced or directly involved as a McCullum or a Vettori or an Oram, that sort of senior playing group. So, Ross, in John's mind, was the logical choice. And, certainly, in mine as well. Here was a way that, if we got things right, we could set about changing some of that culture. That was probably naive on both of our parts, simply because we just didn't realise the power and strength of the Players' Association, the control it had right throughout New Zealand cricket.

Obviously, Ross was thrilled to be appointed captain, believed he could really do the job, believed he was going to bring something different to the culture of the team, and that's what he set out to do.

That night Batchy rang to give me the heads-up that I'd got the job. (The official confirmation came later from John Buchanan.) Batchy mentioned that Brendon had lost credibility by revealing that he wanted Tim Southee as his vice-captain. Over time, Tim has become one of the leaders, so you could say Brendon spotted something in him that wasn't evident to many others. At that stage, though, Tim lacked the maturity to take on a leadership role.

Brendon must have suspected that I was Wrighty's preference; furthermore, another panel member was my "dad", Mark Greatbatch. I suspect his supporters, some of whom were on the NZC board, had assured him that he'd blow the panel away with his presentation, I wouldn't have the skillset to compete and the panel would realise the error of their preconceived ideas. Those weren't unreasonable assumptions.

Mark Greatbatch: People have said we got it wrong, that we should have stuck to the natural order of succession, that Ross should never have been captain. You've got to think about where they were at the time: the maturity of one and the maturity of the other were chalk and cheese. Yes, you've got to have some innovation and instinct for the game but there are other qualities that you need — maturity and the ability to lead people and be responsible.

I'd been working with sport psychologist Gary Hermansson

since 2003–04, both one on one and through his role with Central Districts. Gary was also the Black Caps' in-house sports psychologist from 2005 to 2008.

> **Gary Hermansson:** I could see that there were elements in the team that made division and discord likely. They weren't going too well, nothing like they are now. I was with the team when the IPL thing activated and you then had separation between those who got contracts, those who didn't and those who were never likely to.
>
> There wasn't the kind of unity that would have been valuable. The IPL created a bit of a rift within the team — not an outward one, an inward one. There were people with lots of money and those without, and there were things that happened around who got fined and who didn't get fined, who needed to pay up and who could pay up easily. It was almost like there was a class division in the team that wasn't fully evident externally. There was muttering and eyeball rolling and whatever in the team space so it wasn't a great surprise to me to see it evolve in that direction. And there was a little piece of privilege in the team, an old boys' senior player type thing.
>
> I think the aspiration to the captaincy was evident earlier for Brendon than it was Ross. Ross didn't have that driving ambition; I think it was almost like he had his own objectives for his performance. It's almost like the captaincy became his by default. He deserved it in terms of his performance, but you've got to question whether he was necessarily captain material for where the team was at the time.

The first tour following the appointment was to Zimbabwe in October and November 2011. We had a 6 am flight from Harare to Bulawayo on the day of the Rugby World Cup final — All Blacks vs

France at Eden Park — and a lot of thought had gone into working out where we'd watch it. As we boarded, I noticed that, assuming her name badge could be believed, one of the air hostesses was called "Farewell". We'd got up at four so half the team were asleep before we taxied onto the runway. I was wide awake thinking that having an air hostess called Farewell was tempting fate. As we were going down the runway, the brakes were slammed on. BJ Watling and Kane woke up with a start: "Jesus, are we there already?" There was something amiss with the plane so we taxied back to the terminal and disembarked. It was going to be a few hours before the plane was good to go so our carefully laid plans for watching the rugby were up in smoke.

We'd already checked out of the hotel so we went to the Harare Sports Club, the cricket ground, to watch the start of the final. Then we had to go back to the airport for our flight. We ended up watching that nail-biter at the airport on Nathan McCullum's laptop. His partner back in New Zealand skyped it off her TV screen. All's well that ends well: the All Blacks won and, when we reboarded the plane, Farewell was nowhere to be seen.

In the selection discussion before the test, my first as captain, Wrighty and I spent some time on the balance of the bowling attack, specifically who would be third seamer behind Chris Martin and Doug Bracewell who was making his debut, as was Dean Brownlie. Wrighty said he'd seen Dean bowl and he was good enough to do the job, so we went with him as the third seamer and with Dan and Jeetan Patel to bowl spin.

I won the toss and we batted. Just before lunch on day three, by which time we'd bowled 60 overs, I chucked Dean the ball and said, "Good luck, mate. It's a flat wicket so we'll set a straight field — just pitch it up and get hit straight." His first two balls were long hops that got cut to point. I went down to check that Dean was okay — he assured me he was — and repeat the message about pitching up and getting hit down the ground. The next ball was an action replay: another half-tracker, another cut shot. I moved from slip to gully, thinking, 'What the hell have you done here, Wrighty?'

Last ball of the over Vusi Sibanda, on 93, cut it straight to me: Dean had a wicket in his first over in test cricket and my mood had improved out of sight. When I congratulated Dean, I asked him if he'd been a bit nervous. He said, "Yeah, I haven't bowled for a couple of years."

We won the test — not by much — and Dean had dismissed a well-set batter, so Wrighty could claim it as a masterstroke. It would be fair to say, though, that my confidence in Dean's bowling was never fully restored. He bowled three more overs in the first innings and just one in the second as the sixth bowler after Martin Guptill, who also took a wicket. After Zimbabwe we went to Australia for a two-test series. I gave Dean three overs in Brisbane and actually reviewed an lbw shout against Ricky Ponting. Ball tracker showed it going over the stumps, a possibility that hadn't occurred to me.

Dean grew up in Perth and apparently had potential as a bowler until he injured his knee playing AFL. After that, he hardly ever bowled because it caused his knee to flare up. He bowled 51 overs in test and first-class cricket and has Wrighty to thank for his solitary wicket. How things have changed: in 2011 a crocked, very occasional bowler was our third seamer; in 2022 Kyle Jamieson is our fourth seamer.

The first test at the Gabba was one to forget. It was my first experience of being a father on tour and I didn't get as much sleep as I would've liked. Victoria and Mackenzie flew home on day three. At the airport, Victoria watched me get my first golden duck in 58 test innings — a New Zealand record — thinking, 'I'm going to get the blame for this.' It was all over shortly after lunch on day four: we lost by nine wickets. The only bright spot was Shane Warne putting out a tweet along the lines of, "When you go to kiss Liz Hurley and she says, 'Not now, I'm watching Ross.'" (I'd played with Warnie — and met Liz — in the Indian Premier League.)

Neil Taylor: While that test match was on, we went over to see our eldest daughter, Rebecca, who lives on the Gold Coast. I went up to Brisbane on the train, which was late. I got off the train, walked into the Gabba and looked at the scoreboard: Taylor out for a duck. I enjoyed the train trip but not the cricket. I saw Tim Southee's parents who asked if I was going to Hobart. I said, "You wouldn't want to go after this, would you?"

I obviously wasn't brimming with confidence going into the second test at Bellerive Oval. Our bowling coach, Damien Wright, had played a lot of cricket for Tasmania; before the game, he got local boy Tim Paine, who had played for Australia but wasn't involved in that series, to come and give us some inside information on the wicket and the conditions. Tim's advice was that it was a bowl-first wicket, but losing the toss wasn't the end of the world because getting 240–250 in the fourth innings would be far from easy. You'd have to say he was spot on. The prospect of us pulling off an upset didn't seem to bother him, but then he probably went along with the consensus that it was highly unlikely, if not unthinkable.

The wicket was emerald-green. Clarke won the toss and naturally chose to field. I apologised to the boys for losing the toss — the openers, Guppy and Brendon, were probably thinking, 'You useless prick.' I was on my way out to the middle in the third over. I got to six before Peter Siddle seamed one back and I was given lbw; I reviewed but it was just clipping the bails. I walked off shaking my head.

We were bowled out for 150. Only Dean, who got 56, passed 20. The next morning the *Dominion Post* ran a front-page photo of Jesse Ryder on his way back to the pavilion. "Day of shame" thundered the accompanying headline. In case the readers didn't get the message, the subheading labelled us "a laughing stock".

When I came out to bat in the second innings, Clarke chirped me: "Come on, boys, let's get Captain Unlucky out." You had to fight for every run on that wicket but that made me fight harder. I took 142 balls to get to what I'm sure was my slowest half-century. The captaincy didn't affect my batting, as happens with some players. Both Wrighty and Batchy were strongly of the view that, if I made runs, the rest would fall into place. Wrighty would say, "This team needs your runs more than they need a good captain." That became my mindset to the point that the captaincy brought out the best in my batting.

Clarke brought their part-time trundlers into the attack. I got lucky — dropped by the late Phil Hughes off Michael Hussey. Jesse was stumped by Brad Haddin off Huss, a horrible dismissal on a couple of counts. Ricky Ponting bowled the last over of the day. He was about to turn 37 and very much a part-time bowler so I was thinking, 'You can't get out to this guy.' He trotted in off a short run and bowled a really heavy ball that also swung. I was happy to get off the field. At stumps on day two we were 153 ahead with seven wickets in hand, clearly in front in what was going to be a very tight game.

But when Clarke came out to bat in Australia's second innings, things had shifted in their favour: they were 159/3, needing 241, and David Warner seemed to be batting on a different surface to everybody else. I didn't sledge very often but I thought, 'Nah, bugger it, I'm going to have a word here.' Referencing Clarke's famous falling-out with Simon Katich, I said something along the lines of, "Wouldn't it be great to have a gutsy, veteran left-handed opener out here helping you win the test match? You know the guy I mean: you personally got him kicked out of the team." Clarke pulled out of his stance and gave me an icy stare. If looks could kill, my earthly existence would've ended then and there.

A couple of balls later Clarke nicked off to Doug Bracewell. Captain Unlucky didn't get it first go but caught it on the rebound. I was so pleased with myself I hoofed the ball into the air. Afterwards people were asking me if I had a sore foot; I probably did, but I was too pumped to notice. I didn't give Clarke a send-off. I've always thought send-offs were a bit weak — once you get them out, you've won the battle.

Hussey came in to face the last ball of the over. He was hit on the pads, given not out. The boys were in two minds about referring, but I went for it and the decision was overturned. If there was anyone in their side we wanted to see the back of in that situation, it was Huss. In the space of nine balls, Doug had got Ponting, Clarke and Hussey, they'd gone from 158/2 to 159/5 and the game had turned on its head.

Haddin and Warner put on 30-odd and the pendulum swung again. Then there was another collapse — in 10 balls four wickets went down for the addition of seven runs, leaving them on 199/9. Nathan Lyon was the last man. He was given out lbw to Tim, but ball tracker showed it pitching outside leg, which was a bit odd given Tim was bowling over the wicket. DRS seemed out of kilter throughout the entire match. Warner, who was on 100-odd, started playing a few shots and suddenly they needed fewer than 20. The media had been on my case since Brisbane: I was thinking, 'What the hell am I going to tell them if we lose this?'

Tim and Dougie had both bowled nearly 10 overs on the trot and the target was down below 10. We started the over to Lyon with three slips and two gullies, but Dougie wasn't swinging it as much as he had been. Lyon got an inside edge that went onto his pad and trickled back down the wicket. I thought, 'I don't know if it's a three/two field with Doug tiring a bit and not swinging it. I need to put in a mid-wicket and push mid-on straighter.' Bowlers can be reluctant to get too straight in case they get put away on the leg-side and Dougie was bowling too wide of off stump. I moved the second gully to mid-wicket; Lyon hit the next ball there. That field placing saved a run and kept Lyon on strike. If they'd got a single, Warner would have been on strike and one shot away from tying the match, two from winning it. Next ball Dougie clean bowled Lyon.

We won by seven runs. It was our first test win over Australia since 1993 and the first in Australia since 1985. The common factor in the three wins was Wrighty, who played in the two other games.

We caught phenomenally well that day. I took what was probably the best catch I've ever taken. Trent Boult, on debut, got Usman Khawaja to edge one that went between me and Guppy. Gup dived and got a fingertip to it, but I still managed to catch it. *His* take was that he deflected it into my hands, otherwise I would have dropped it. Which would have made two of us. He jumped in front of me again when I caught Clarke. It would be fair to say I've never let him forget it.

Warner was man of the match. I guess you can make the argument: he made 123 not out; the next highest score in the game was 56; the next highest score in their second innings was 23. But you would have thought Dougie, with match figures of 9/60 in a winning cause, had a pretty compelling case. It didn't worry us because we'd won the test, but I thought it was typically Aussie. If nothing else, it gave the boys a good laugh.

At the post-match presentation, Clarke didn't acknowledge our existence, let alone our performance or victory. A couple of them put their heads around the changing room door to say "Well done" and Michael Hussey joined us at the bar when we got back to the hotel. He had me on about being dropped off his bowling, pulling out his pocket and saying, "Oooh, Rosco, you were nearly in my pocket." As for the rest of them, I suppose they just wanted to get out of Hobart as quickly as possible.

During the first test there'd been a lot of talk that the speed gun was all over the place. Tim and Chris Martin were clocked in the high 120s while Siddle was supposedly bowling at 150 kph. Dean Brownlie batted really well in that game, taking on Siddle's short stuff. "If that's 150," he said, "I'll face 170." (He now denies ever saying that.) When we got on top in Hobart, the speed gun had Tim bowling 142 kph for six overs in a row. At the hotel bar session, we got talking to a Kiwi who worked for the broadcaster, Channel 9. He told us that six speeds would come up: they'd normally use the median but, when Australia were on top, they'd use the highest number.

The next day's *Dominion Post* had a front-page photo of new bowling star Doug Bracewell celebrating a wicket. "Wizard of Oz" crowed the headline. "One for the history books." Meanwhile, Melbourne's *Herald-Sun* was telling its readers that the previous day's events in Hobart amounted to a "day of shame" for Australian cricket.

It wasn't until we got home that we realised what the win meant to the New Zealand public. For weeks afterwards people would come up at airports, supermarkets and petrol stations to pat you on the back. That was a first for me. In that heady aftermath it felt like almost anything was possible. And, indeed, it was.

Chapter 6.
Captain Cooked?

In mid-2012 I was playing for Delhi in the Indian Premier League when John Wright rang to say he was resigning as Black Caps coach. He couldn't see eye to eye with director of cricket John Buchanan and didn't feel he could do the job to his full capabilities. It was a shame because I got on well with both of them, but they just couldn't work together. "Sorry Ross," he said, "but you're on your own now. Be very careful because they're after you next." I said, "You've got to do what you've got to do, Wrighty," but I was thinking, 'There's one of my biggest allies gone.' I asked him what he thought the team needed in a coach; he replied, "This team needs a coach that can get on with you."

> **John Wright:** I resigned well before the 2012 West Indies tour, but they asked me if I'd do it anyway. In hindsight I shouldn't have. It was a difficult tour. The first thing that happened was that I was informed there was no money available for any camps. The only preparation was that the fast bowlers had three or four days in Australia with bowling coach Damien Wright. The rest of the team came out of the New Zealand winter and practising indoors and went straight to Miami where we played the West Indies in T20 games in very hot conditions. We hadn't played

on grass. I was very disappointed that there weren't any resources to prepare the national team and I sometimes wonder whether that was designed or just occurred.

John Buchanan wanted Kim Littlejohn, an Australian with a background in coaching and high-performance sports administration in cricket and lawn bowls, to be the manager. Players' Association CEO Heath Mills put a stop to that so Kim became a national selector. Having to deal with an Aussie he didn't know probably added to Wrighty's issues with Buchanan. I found Kim to be a very nice guy but thought the three of them were played off against each other and fed different information to make their relationship even more problematic.

Kim Littlejohn: I arrived in September 2011 just as they were about to name the team to head off to Zimbabwe. It appeared to me that John Wright was fighting a battle to bring about changes and allow Ross time to grow and develop as a captain. John was a hard guy to get to know — he didn't trust too many people and he did it his way. There were two camps: Ross and his supporters and Brendon and his crew. I was never allowed to get close enough to the group to find out what was really going on; I was kept at arm's length by the manager who we subsequently discovered was in the McCullum camp.

We were at an airport hotel in Los Angeles, en route to the Caribbean. I'd noticed that Martin Guptill and my manager Leanne McGoldrick's daughter Laura had started hanging out, going to movies and whatnot. Just before we flew out to Miami, Guppy pulled me aside: he was rather sheepish, almost apprehensive. He said, "I just wanted to tell you that Laura and I are sort of dating." I said, "You don't say? You've been going to the movies as 'friends' — I mean, who goes to the movies as friends?"

It was as if I was Laura's dad and he was seeking my permission to court her. To be fair, I'd known the McGoldrick family for longer than I'd known Gup.

In the first T20 game in Fort Lauderdale, I chased back trying to get under a Kieron Pollard skier, dropped the catch and suffered a level two tear to my shoulder labrum. I tried to bat but it was too sore. After the game, I was taken to hospital in an ambulance. They treated me with kid gloves, taking every precaution, presumably to ensure that I had no possible grounds on which to sue them.

The hospital was like a scene from *ER*. There was a guy with a gunshot wound to my left, a drug overdose to my right and a drunk spewing in the corner. Welcome to America. Despite the carnage in A&E, it was a nice enough hospital, certainly flasher than the Zimbabwean facility where I would have a testicle operation a few years later. I felt bad because our manager Mike Sandle had to spend his fiftieth birthday keeping me company at the hospital.

> **John Buchanan:** I was heavily involved in the interview process for the team manager role. We appointed Mike Sandle, a former policeman who interviewed well. I thought he really had the makings of a very good team manager, a very good support person for John Wright and Ross Taylor. But when Mike came back from his first tour, he was a changed person. He no longer seemed to me to be objective but was well and truly in the — inverted commas — Players' Association camp.

Mike was always in the background. He never put his head above the parapet and didn't do much, but he knew full well what was going on, first in the West Indies and then in Sri Lanka. He did provide a memorable moment on that trip, though. After Kruger van Wyk had made his debut against South Africa a few months earlier, he got the fern and his New Zealand test player number tattooed on his chest. Mike told Kruger he'd just been informed by New Zealand Cricket that the player numbers were all wrong because they hadn't counted someone back in 1955. Everyone was in on the joke except Kruger who was crestfallen. He was slumped in his seat moaning, "I've got the wrong number tattooed on my chest."

My injury paved the way for Brendon McCullum's return. He was supposedly rested for that tour, although it was unclear whose initiative that was. My understanding was that Wrighty was all for resting Brendon because he felt the tour would be my last chance to get the team I wanted and mould it. However, when I got injured, Wrighty flipped and wanted Brendon on a plane asap.

On a personal level, Wrighty and Brendon got on well. They had things in common — they both liked a beer, cigarettes and horses. On the cricket side of things, though, Wrighty knew where he stood with Brendon. When I did my calf during the previous home summer, Brendon captained the side against Zimbabwe and, by all accounts, made his presence felt. I had calls from Wrighty and batting and fielding coach Trent Woodhill telling me to hurry up and get fit because Brendon wasn't acting like a man who was just keeping my seat warm.

I'd addressed the issue of the team's drinking culture in my captaincy interview. I believed we drank more than an elite sports team should, especially an elite sports team that wasn't winning. The mindset was: "Lose, drink booze." We had great jobs — travelling the world playing cricket and representing our country — but some players treated it as a holiday rather than a job. Cricket sometimes seemed secondary to playing golf and getting on the piss. John Buchanan challenged me, asking if I'd impose curfews and how I would discipline players who breached them. They were good questions. Basically, I just didn't buy the notion that what happens at the bar is team culture.

Brendon took a different view and he had some enthusiastic followers. He was probably following the example set by the senior players when he first got into the team. To me, it seemed strange to be drinking till 11 o'clock or midnight the night before a game. On that tour, for instance, there were guys still at the bar after 11 pm when we were leaving the hotel at seven the next morning to play an ODI that started at 9 am. Don't get me wrong, there was many a night when I had a glass of wine or two with dinner, but staying up late drinking, which some guys did all the time, fell into a different category.

In terms of being undermined, that West Indies trip was actually worse than the Sri Lankan tour when it all came to a head. Some of the senior players would be down the back of the bus talking really loudly to people back home in New Zealand — the likes of Heath Mills — about me and the support staff. It was the opposite of being furtive — the whole point of the exercise was that the targets could hear every comment. When Daniel Vettori came over for the tests he said, "It's actually not that bad over here," which shows what sort of messages the folks back home were hearing.

It was hard to accept from Jake Oram, a Central Districts teammate for a number of years and someone I respected. At the end of the day, though, we're all human and he was getting towards the end of his career and looking after what he perceived to be his interests. And while Jake and I had been CD teammates in many games, we didn't spend a lot of time together off the field, whereas he and Kyle Mills were really close.

I understand it to an extent. Were they going to back me, knowing I didn't want them in the team, or back the other guy, knowing that, if he took charge, their places would be secure and their input welcomed? That doesn't make their behaviour okay: you've still got to respect the person in that position. Brendon would have faced it front on but that wasn't me; I just let it slide. I'm sure Wrighty took issue with them — he wouldn't have held back — but I'd grown up with that mindset of respecting your elders.

The senior players didn't like the fact that Wrighty exercised a lot of authority and they blamed me for not standing up to him. Where they were wrong was that Wrighty and I were on the same page: we discussed things and agreed on most of them, including our respective roles. The malcontents thought I was rolling over on selection calls, but I didn't want them in the team either. What they saw as weakness on my part was actually alignment. I probably should have involved them a bit more, and my communication skills could have been better, but I didn't trust them. It's hard to involve and communicate with people you don't trust.

John Wright: I don't think any of us had many happy memories of that tour. When you're losing, tours are never fun. I felt very sorry for players like Daniel Flynn and Dean Brownlie — I don't think they played much after that tour. It was hard on Ross because it was early in his captaincy career and there was a chain of events that made his role even more difficult. There were tensions. Brendon would have been disappointed at missing out on the captaincy and it's natural that leadership contenders have their supporters within the team.

Dropping Kyle Mills for the fourth ODI in Saint Kitts was probably the last straw. We named the team and had a warm-up. I went back to the dressing room to put on my gear for the toss and go to the toilet. While I was in there, Oram and Mills came in. Jake said, "I told you; I told you those f--kers were going to drop you." I waited till they left; they never knew I was in there. Once again, if that had happened to Brendon, he would have faced it front on.

I got 110 in that game. I'd missed three ODIs, I wasn't sure the labrum was going to stand up to it, there was all sorts of shit going on, most of it directed at me, and the wicket was a dust bowl so I was pretty proud of that knock. There's a highlights package on YouTube. It's easy to spot Millsy in the dugout when I reached 100

— he's the only one not standing up. A picture worth a thousand words, perhaps.

There was a debate over whether we should pick Brendon in the test team. I argued for his inclusion, not because I thought he deserved to be there — he was struggling with his batting — but because the clique was getting out of control. I figured they'd go even more rogue if he was left out.

It was almost as if New Zealand and the West Indies were playing off to decide who got the wooden spoon. The major teams in world cricket were a lot better than both of us at that stage. We were very disjointed: Wrighty tried his hardest, knowing it was his last go-round, but the players knew he was on the way out so it was easy to do what they did. The Windies had some big players — Shiv Chanderpaul, Chris Gayle, who was at his peak, and Sunil Narine, who had a major influence on proceedings — but there were enough holes for us to have exploited. In terms of our development, though, we were a couple of years away from being a winning team.

While we were in the West Indies, NZC chief executive David White led me to believe I'd be involved in the process of choosing Wrighty's successor. In fact, the extent of my involvement was hearing that the next coach would be a Kiwi. Seeing Mike Hesson was the only Kiwi on the short list, it was pretty clear he'd get the gig. (Interestingly, in 2018 NZC did seek my opinion on who should succeed Hess, even though I had no official leadership role in the team.) I wasn't even consulted as to who should have been coach. There's no way that would have happened to previous captains. They would have had a massive say in who was appointed. Things like that made me think I wasn't valued at all.

John Buchanan: There were plenty of applicants for the national coach job. We got down to a short list of four, but the outstanding applicant was David Parsons, the England Cricket Board performance director who ran the National

Performance Centre at Loughborough University and oversaw the Lions, the England A team. He was a really good operator. Second in line was Matthew Mott who'd done a fair bit of coaching with Australian state sides — I knew he'd be a good coach and a good team culture person.

But out of the blue, quite late in the piece, David White said there was another bloke we should interview. Mike Hesson didn't make the top four in our opinion, but David made sure that he was on the list, so we ended up interviewing five. Then David said he'd chair the interview process to make sure it was all done properly.

It became more and more obvious through the interview process that David was manoeuvring Mike Hesson into the role. When we'd look at the other applicants, he'd always find a reason why they shouldn't be compared to Mike. So, in the end, Mike was awarded the role. I remember saying to him that there were some good people around him and the best way forward was to keep communicating. I don't know that he really leaned on any of my experiences or kept the communication up. The exception to that was he did make some statement to me very early that one of the first things he wanted to do was change the captain. He just didn't believe the captain was the right person, which really took me by surprise.

Hess came on board for the tour of India. The wicket for the first test In Hyderabad looked flat, as Indian wickets do. But, when I went out to have a look on game day, it was a different wicket. As we were going out to toss, I asked the Indian skipper, MS Dhoni, why they'd changed the wicket. He said, "Because whoever won the toss would still be batting on day four." That wouldn't happen anywhere else. I just thought, 'I'm a rookie captain in the powerhouse of India, I'm not kicking up a fuss.'

It was the same old story: India won the toss and batted big. We got rolled, followed on and got rolled again. Off-spinner Ravichandran Ashwin took 12 wickets; left-arm orthodox spinner Pragyan Ojha took six. Thanks for coming.

Before the first test, Hess gave us the big spiel, a less than riveting presentation about his philosophies. He was clearly nervous. In both innings he came and sat beside me and talked to me when I was next into bat. I thought, 'Cricket 101: has this guy never been around a team before?' I didn't have the heart to tell him to bugger off. He did it again during the next test in Bangalore which we also lost, although we were more competitive. After Hyderabad, I was pretty happy to get 113 in the first innings.

There was no DRS in India at that time and a number of calls went against us. Hess did a lot of complaining to the match referee, something Wrighty very rarely did. I felt duty-bound to back Hess up, so I'd accompany him. In hindsight, I should have just let him do it himself — it didn't make the slightest difference.

Wrighty's assistants, Trent Woodhill and Damien Wright, were both Aussies. I think there was a view at the top of NZC that there were way too many Australians in and around the Black Caps set-up. Neither Trent nor Damien lasted long once Wrighty had moved on. The Canterbury coach, Bob Carter, came in as batting coach. When he got back from the Indian tour, he was highly critical of me to a group of NZC people.

John Buchanan: We were watching an A game at Lincoln when Bob Carter suddenly started tearing Ross apart, saying he couldn't captain, he'd lost the dressing room, his behaviour was terrible. Kim and I were scratching our heads thinking, 'Are we talking about the same person?' Bob was adamant. Again, hindsight: Bob was a carrier pigeon. He'd been a hard-working coach for a long time and been given an opportunity to be around the elite team, so he became a mouthpiece for others further up the food chain. I liked Bob but always felt he was carrying some things about Ross and what was going on that were just not accurate. Interestingly, before I left New Zealand, Bob came back and apologised, saying what he'd said wasn't right.

Kim Littlejohn: With Ross's protector in John Wright no longer there, it was a whole different scenario. Mike Hesson was very much a Brendon McCullum supporter and it was all about Brendon. I don't think Ross was ever given the chance to be able to grow in to the role.

There are so many different elements to the captaincy, so many things you need to learn and become good at. Man-management is an obvious example because an international test team is going to contain a variety of individuals. By the end of my international career, I was a 38-year-old with three children who'd played well over 400 games for New Zealand; that's a very different beast to a 22-year-old single guy on debut. You have to treat different people differently. The notion that you treat everyone the same way is a nonsense.

I don't think any captain has all the attributes: every captain needs help. Dealing with conflict probably isn't Kane's favourite part of the job, although he has got better at it. Stephen Fleming was a great captain and had a lot of the attributes but didn't do justice to his batting talent. To some extent, that was also true of Brendon. What approach do you take: focus on being captain and hope the batting takes care of itself or vice versa?

We used to have captain's meetings the night before a test match. Flem and Dan, who were both very articulate, were good at them. Brendon was also very articulate, but I sometimes felt he was more thinking out loud about what he was going to do than addressing and engaging with the rest of us. Some days Kane talks a lot, some days he doesn't. Under Fleming we had meetings before one-day games as well, but those petered out under Vettori.

I inherited the practice but would have been a better captain without captain's meetings. Sometimes I was okay, but other times I just talked for the sake of it and I'm sure it didn't sound authentic. It just didn't come naturally. I used to stew over what I was going to say, which isn't a worthwhile use of time and mental energy going into a test match.

At school, I was one of those kids who keep their eyes down in class, hoping the teacher won't ask them a question or choose them to read something out. Victoria, who was a schoolteacher, told me those are the kids teachers look out for with the aim of drawing them out of themselves and bolstering their confidence. I said, "Now you're telling me." If I'd known that when I was 13 or 14, I would have been staring at the teacher and trying to bluff them.

Now, we don't have captain's meetings at all. We nearly always have a guest speaker and, over time, we decided that it amounted to stealing their thunder: the guest speaker would have their say, then the captain or the coach would get up and start talking. Now, the guest speaker speaks, the guys collect their caps, shake hands and go off to get ready for the next day.

I also had a cultural issue. When I captained for a couple of games at the 2011 World Cup after Dan injured his knee, I got him to do the team talks: because of my upbringing and background I was uncomfortable, as a younger player, addressing the senior players. That deeply ingrained principle of respecting your elders worked to my detriment as a captain. By the time I became the senior player in the team, I was much more confident in group settings and had no problem offering my opinion whenever it was sought.

John Buchanan: We went around all the players to get their self-assessment and the amazing thing to us was the absolute high ranking that a lot of them gave themselves. Ross, in fact, was one of our surprising results in that he didn't rank himself as high as some other players who were far less skilled.

Towards the end, Trent Woodhill said, "If you've got something to say, Ross, say it; if not, just let Wrighty talk." Wrighty and I were on the same page so, from then on, I let him do most of the talking. Under Hess, there were a lot of awkward silences because we weren't on the same page. I raised the subject with John Buchanan who said, "Ross, you're fine — Steve Waugh hardly ever talked." He didn't say "You're just like Steve Waugh," but he made the point that Waugh, a highly successful captain, actually said very little.

When Brendon became captain, I overheard a couple of conversations between him and Hess in which they were working out what each of them was going to say: "You cover that, Brendon, and I'll do this bit." I never had that conversation with Hess when I was captain. Fast forward a few years: Kane was sick so I took over for a game in Kolkata. Hess said to me, "I'll say this, Ross, and then you say that." I said "Yeah, cool." Then we got into the meeting and Hess said all the stuff I was meant to say. I was wondering if I'd heard right so I said to him afterwards, "Wasn't I supposed to say that?" Hess said, "Oh yeah, sorry."

Captaincy is hard on an individual — you have to grow up quickly — but it's also hard to step down: to give up having the power, the perks and the profile that come with it, and go from being the leader to just another player and perhaps a lieutenant whose advice the new captain may or may not want. I was able to do that because I wasn't captain for long and went back to the ranks quite early in my career. Apart from Hess and Brendon having to work out whether I was going to try to undermine them, there was never a problem.

If the captaincy appointments had proceeded according to natural succession — Fleming to Vettori to McCullum to Taylor — I obviously would have been better prepared when my time came. There are a few beguiling assumptions embedded in the natural succession theory: that there wouldn't have been the acrimony; that there would have been a seamless transition from Brendon to me; that I would have ended up having an extended run as captain of a much better team. Life doesn't necessarily work that way: in some respects, Brendon was more ready for the captaincy in 2012 than I was, but in other ways he was less. You can't assume that, if that one thing had been done differently, everything would have fallen into place.

Besides, it was Brendon who stuffed up the natural succession. If he'd been a dutiful vice-captain and remained in the role until Dan stepped down, he almost certainly would have been appointed ahead of me.

Chapter 7.
Blindsided

My first encounter with Mike Hesson provided a foretaste of things to come. It was July 2012: we were in Antigua to play a test against the West Indies when word came through that Hess was the new Black Caps coach, replacing John Wright. New Zealand Cricket boss David White and Mike Sandle arranged for us to have a "getting acquainted" phone conversation.

At that time, I was working with Gilbert Enoka, the long-time All Blacks mental skills coach. I checked in with him beforehand: his advice was that I had to have an open mind and be upfront and honest so that was the attitude I went in with. Hess's assurance that our chat would be confidential — "This won't go anywhere" — reinforced my inclination to address the elephant in the room.

It was common knowledge that Hess and Brendon, fellow Dunedinites, were close. I asked Hess, "How's your relationship with Baz going to affect the team?" Judging by his tone of voice, he was taken aback: it was as if the issue had never occurred to him, which I found strange. He said, "Oh, me and Baz don't agree on everything. We can question each other."

Twenty-four hours later, following the announcement of his appointment, Hess did a TV interview in which he revealed that I'd asked him about his relationship with Brendon. My manager, Leanne, immediately started getting messages on the theme of,

"What a way to start." She rang David White who told her that, as far as he was concerned, nothing untoward had occurred.

About a week after we got home from the West Indies, I met Hess in Pokeno. I was still mindful of Gilbert's advice so I went in with a positive attitude. For the most part, the meeting went okay but we still managed to take each other by surprise. I asked him about his relationship with John Buchanan, his boss. Hess said he and Mike Sandle were working on sidelining John. I thought, 'Wow, you've only just got the job and you're already throwing your weight around.'

In the spirit of transparency, I told Hess that I didn't see Nathan McCullum, Kyle Mills and Jacob Oram making the 2015 World Cup squad. His face fell. All three were Team McCullum, but that wasn't the reason I didn't see them going through to the World Cup. Wrighty and I had simply believed there were better options — younger players with more upside.

Fast forward a couple of months: we were in Sri Lanka, about to play the second ODI at Pallekele in the city of Kandy. Mum had just called to tell me my Grandma Sylvia, whom I adored, had died. I was absolutely devastated but we were actually on our way to the ground so I had to pull myself together in a hurry. I'd also picked up a bug and was vomiting before I went out to bat. Brendon wasn't playing because he had a sore back. Hess said to me, "If you can't field, I think Nathan should be captain." I said, "Are you joking?" Both Kane Williamson, who'd captained the side in the West Indies when I injured my shoulder, and Kyle Mills were playing; Nathan was a long way down the list. After that, I was going to field regardless of how crook I felt.

When we got home from Sri Lanka, I recounted that discussion about Nathan in a media interview. I wasn't in a great space and shouldn't have done it — Leanne told me off afterwards — but I wanted to flag that the captaincy drama wasn't just about cricketing issues: personal relationships and the Otago connection were factors.

Postscript to that meeting with Hess in Pokeno: as I was heading home, Dad rang to ask how it had gone. Being inclined to look on the bright side, as I then was, I told him I wouldn't be captain in a year's time.

I did contemplate resigning. Leanne would tell me that I'd find a way of making it a positive experience. But positivity was in short supply, given what we were hearing from people inside NZC: with the exception of John Buchanan, the people that counted — chairman Chris Moller, CEO David White and Hess — seemed resistant to any suggestion that they should publicly endorse me as captain. In hindsight, that in itself indicates that things were happening behind the scenes in the months leading up to the move against me. Along with the deafening silence, there were leaks and off-the-record briefings that just encouraged the media to question my position and speculate on my future.

After the tour of India, I went to South Africa to play for Delhi Daredevils in the Champions League. Back home, the speculation intensified every time Hess spurned an opportunity to say that I had his support. That reticence culminated in him announcing that the NZC board had decided Ross Taylor would be captain for the Sri Lanka tour. It was an obvious red flag, since it practically demanded the interpretation that Hess wanted to distance himself from the decision and, once the tour was out of the way, all bets were off.

I discussed it with Gilbert and Leanne. We decided I needed to talk to Hess and ask for feedback and guidance, seeing he obviously had significant concerns about my captaincy. I rang him; he responded with an email that didn't really get us anywhere. Leanne, meanwhile, was ringing David White, trying to get him to engage constructively — trying her best to get me, Hess and the management team around the table over in Sri Lanka. On their third call, David said, "We are not changing the captaincy." The fourth call took place just as the Sri Lanka tour was getting under way. It wasn't a pleasant exchange: White told Leanne to stay out of it, it was nothing to do with her — or him; Mike and Ross, he said, would sort it out between them.

It felt like they were pushing me into a corner in the hope that I'd see my position was hopeless and resign. The problem with that was I would have been seen as tossing it in and leaving the team in the lurch on the eve of the tour. We didn't have an NZC media person with us for the test portion of the Sri Lanka tour: apparently the view at NZC was that there was very little public interest in what was happening with the test team. An interesting call given what was about to unfold.

Hess and I had a meeting two days after we arrived, but once we got into the ODI series — which didn't go well — the communication dried up. The weather was a big factor in that series: we lost a couple of Duckworth Lewis games, then were rained off when we were in a winning position. I was getting frustrated with the lack of support. Four days before the first test in Galle I said to Hess, "Aren't we supposed to meet once a week?" He said we'd meet that afternoon.

About 15 minutes before the meeting was due to take place, batting coach Bob Carter came to see me. He wanted the meeting canned. I said, "No, we're just going to talk about making me a better captain." Bob said, "I don't think it's the right time." He knew what was coming; he dropped a few hints that I was walking into an ambush, but I didn't pick up on them.

Hess, Bob and Mike Sandle came to my room. "It would be remiss of me," said Hess, "not to say what's really going on. There are leaders and there are followers, and I think you're a *follower*. There are senior players in the team who don't want you as captain. It's my job to make sure this team has a strong captain and you're not a strong captain."

Then Mike Sandle took over, saying I'd let myself down with some of my behaviour. I'd kicked a rubbish bin outside a dressing room, sending rubbish everywhere, so fair enough to pull me up on that. (It wasn't in public view and I did pick up the rubbish and put it back in the bin.) He also suggested I'd abused spectators and smashed up dressing rooms. It was all bullshit, self-serving exaggerations of very minor incidents.

(Some of the stuff that found its way into the media over this period bordered on the surreal. A huge deal was made of the fact that I'd sworn in the changing room. A changing room is a place where cricketers go to get changed, talk shit and swear. Did my departure as captain put an end to profanity in the changing room? That could be a Tui billboard. I had to threaten a New Zealand news outlet with defamation proceedings if they ran a story claiming that I'd very nearly been arrested by the Sri Lankan police for assaulting a rubbish bin. As it happened, I was on very good terms with the senior police officer who was in charge of the police and military units that provided security at the grounds. He was a really nice guy. I sometimes sat next to him at breakfast and, at the end of that and subsequent tours of Sri Lanka, he gave me tea as a going-away present.)

Hess asked if I had any questions. I didn't; I'd been blindsided and was in a state of shock. I knew I wasn't going to last in the role but hadn't see it coming before the first test. Hess left; Mike Sandle stayed just long enough to put in a strong entry for understatement of the year: "That must be a lot to take in."

I rang Victoria, Leanne and Martin Guptill, my closest friend in the team, to tell them what had happened. I texted Shane Bond, our bowling coach, to ask if he could drop by. He said he'd be there in 10 minutes. On the way, Bondy ran into Bob Carter who told him what had happened, so he wouldn't have been surprised to find me in a pretty emotional state. Bondy was the most trustworthy, professional and hardest-working player I ever played with: I didn't want his sympathy; I just wanted his honest opinion on whether I should continue as captain. He said, "Yeah, you've got your faults, but you should carry on." I also spoke to Gilbert who was adamant that a good leader wouldn't quit — "Make them push you."

(I later read that Bondy had been at an earlier management meeting at which the idea of changing the captain was aired. Asked for his opinion, he said that, while the coach was entitled to have the captain he wanted, dumping the incumbent in mid-tour just before a test match wasn't appropriate.)

At 9 o'clock the next morning, there was a knock on my door. It was Hess. He sat where Bondy had sat and said, "Ross, you can think I'm a c--t, but it's what I believe in. John Buchanan's coming over and I'm going to recommend to him that we have a new captain for South Africa. Have you got anything you want to ask me?" I just said I'd carry on as captain. I suspect the idea behind the ambush was that I'd accept my fate and volunteer to quit: what normal individual would carry on under those circumstances? At no point, though, did Hess come out and say that maybe it would be better if I stood down.

We lost the first test by 10 wickets in two-and-a-half days. We batted poorly — I made nine and 18 — but the bowlers performed pretty well in trying conditions. I had a meeting with John Buchanan who said he'd heard that I'd forbidden Tim Southee from talking to Brendon on the field. What had happened was that Brendon had ants in his pants which isn't ideal for fielding in the slips. After he'd put one down at third slip, he went to mid-off. He was talking to Tim after every ball and they kept moving the field.

Brendon used to give me his five cents' worth and, at times, I could see from his body language that he was frustrated by some of my decisions. That never worried me. It's natural: I didn't agree with everything Kane Williamson and Tom Latham did. I didn't mind if Brendon wanted to move the field now and again, but they were doing it all the time. So, I went over to them and suggested that they might like to include me in some of those discussions.

When I raised it with Tim, he was adamant that all he'd said to anyone about the incident was that I'd objected to not being consulted. That was where it had got to: people in the camp telling exaggerated tales on the captain while Brendon acted as if I wasn't on the field. It was disrespectful and pretty hard to take after being told the senior players didn't want me as captain.

We trained in Galle on what would have been the fifth day of the test. Afterwards Brendon pulled me aside. "Are you alright, mate?" he said. "You don't seem the same — you're very standoffish towards me. I don't know what's going on with you and Hesson but I back you 100 per cent. I don't want the captaincy. If the best player wants the captaincy, then I don't want it."

The next day we travelled to Colombo where I had another meeting with John Buchanan. He said he was going to recommend that I stayed on as captain — "I think you're doing a good job; I disagree with all this stuff." Deep down I knew that wasn't going to happen, but it was nice to hear and gave me a sense that I couldn't have been all that bad.

I told John about my conversation with Brendon, saying he didn't seem to know what was going on. John was bemused because he'd discussed the captaincy ructions with Brendon's advisor, Stephen Fleming, just before coming to Sri Lanka and with Brendon himself on arrival. Fleming's response was that he thought Brendon should be the captain but didn't think the timing was right or that it would be a good look, given Brendon's relationship with Hess. Brendon would later tell the media that he had no idea about what was happening around the captaincy until we got back to New Zealand.

John Buchanan: This all happened after the one-day series at the start of the tour and it seemed I needed to get over there for the test series. I met with the team management: Mike Sandle talked about Ross hitting rubbish bins and getting wild and just very poor behaviour around his team and the officials. (I later asked the umpires about Ross and his behaviour: they said he and Mahela Jayawardene were two of the easiest captains in international cricket to work with.) Mike Hesson and

Bob Carter were still of the belief that Ross was a very poor captain who didn't have the support of the playing group and so on. He just wasn't the right person to lead the team and the outcome of this was that they had to replace him. Mike had said to me very early in his tenure that one of the first things he wanted to do was change the captain. Here he was, following through on that, and they were just building their own case for his removal.

I'd also gone to Stephen Fleming about it and I'd gone to Brendon McCullum about it. Brendon denied any knowledge of what was going on, and that might be accurate. I had Brendon with me at the Kolkata Knight Riders and we got along really well there — I made him and Brad Hodge sort of joint captains.

Then I met with Ross and walked through all those issues with him. He admitted he'd probably lost his cool, but he was hardly the first captain or cricketer to lose his cool. Having been around the Australian team a bit, I would have thought that, while not necessarily desirable behaviour, it wasn't something that you would recount as being unique to Ross Taylor. In terms of the tactical side, there was an acknowledgement from other players around the world that he knew what he was doing.

After we'd trained in Colombo, Brendon ran back to the hotel. I knew something was up because I hadn't seen him do that since our New Zealand Under-19 days. On the contrary, he often complained about how sore his knee and/or back were. It wasn't that Brendon hadn't helped others before that, because he had, but now he was throwing for half the training, talking to all the batters and generally behaving like a bloke who'd made a New Year's resolution to be more responsible.

I'd put off telling Mum and Dad because it was obviously going to upset them. I rang them from Colombo. They were great. Dad basically said, "To hell with them — forget about going to South Africa." I was leaning towards not going to South Africa but had fretted about telling them that so for him to be that clear-cut was a relief. Knowing I had their blessing not to go to South Africa gave me a lot of clarity going into the second test.

At stumps on day one we were 223/2; I was on 109, Kane was on 95. My job as a cricketer was to score runs but there was definitely an element of wondering, 'How did I do that?' Having had two hours' sleep every night for a fortnight, I could hardly believe my body and mind were capable of it. The first 20 runs were horrendous, but Martin Crowe's words just kept running through my head: "Don't get out; just bat. Be there at the end of the day."

The captaincy tended to bring out the best in my batting. When I won the batting cup a couple of years later, I told an interviewer that I went out to bat with the mindset that I was still captain. I liked the extra responsibility. And sometimes issues and dramas can actually help by blocking out other potential distractions. Injuries can work that way. Would I have batted that well if I hadn't had the captaincy drama to motivate me?

After the tour Kevin Pietersen rang me to commiserate. I really appreciated him taking the time and trouble to do that. He'd been through something similar when he was England captain. And, earlier that year, there'd been a huge blow-up over his contact with South African players during their series in England: KP, who was born and brought up in South Africa, supposedly told the Proteas how they should bowl to his successor, Andrew Strauss. With all hell breaking loose, KP went out and played one of his greatest innings: a dominating 149 against a bowling line-up of Dale Steyn, Morné Morkel, Vernon Philander and Jacques Kallis.

After that innings, KP said, "It's not easy being me in this team." International cricketers spend more time with their teammates than their families. It's not like rugby: play for 90 minutes, have a shower, have a beer and head home. You have a bad day on and off the field, see the same guys at breakfast, then do it all again.

I adopted a mindset of, 'The longer I bat, the less time I have to spend in the changing room.' As I walked off after getting 142 in the first innings, I was thinking, 'Enjoy it, but don't get too carried away — you're going to have to do it again in the second innings.'

> **Victoria Taylor:** I don't think he knew he had it in him until he had to go through those times. He was ringing me in the middle of the night, he wasn't sleeping, he lost so much weight. It was just mind-consuming and he had to overcome that. He had to find a way to put that aside and score runs.
>
> Had we had a crystal ball, of course, he would have said no to the captaincy. But, on a positive note, had it not happened I don't think he would have been the player he became. As much hurt and anguish as it caused, it made him a better, mentally tougher player.

In the second innings I got 74. Tim Southee ran me out which, in itself, didn't bother me. It was more the fact that I'd told him I was about to declare, but he was in his own little world. There were claims that I was pissed off because I wanted another hundred. That was nonsense because we would have had to have batted another four or five overs and I wanted to have a decent crack at them that evening. We had 15 overs at them: Doug Bracewell got Kumar Sangakkara in the 12th and Mahela in the 14th, the two key wickets that we wouldn't have got that evening if we'd batted another four or five overs. I couldn't have cared less about a hundred, but I'd earned a not out and I wanted to achieve the goal that Hogan had set for me — be there at the end. The 74 was as good as the 142. I had to work my arse off on a tough wicket to get us into a winning position.

At tea on day four Hess spoke to me the first time since our pre-game selection discussion. He'd just let me do it, stayed out of my way and hadn't said a thing. We were 322 ahead with five second-innings wickets in hand so I guess he was having to contemplate the prospect of us winning the game and squaring the series. He was friendly to the point of overdoing it; Gilbert had some psychological term for it. We set Sri Lanka 363 and won by 167 runs. Between them, Tim and Trent Boult had match figures of 15/195.

How celebrated cartoonist Tom Scott saw the captaincy issue in the *Dominion Post*.

I still don't know how I captained that team knowing half the players didn't want me, and the coach was actively engaged in making their wishes come true. It's a tough thing to say, but I honestly felt — rightly or wrongly — some of them wanted us to lose to make it easier to head off John Buchanan and implement their plan. Us winning, and me getting player of the match, was their worst nightmare. If we'd lost, the New Zealand public would have been thanking Hess for getting rid of me. Bob Carter later told me that, on the flight home, he warned Hess that he'd be crucified if he dumped me.

John Buchanan: I wrote a detailed report back to David White to explain everything that was going on; how I disagreed with what they were doing and the way they were going about it. Maybe Ross wasn't as good a captain as we thought, in terms of a leader on the field, but there needed to be a different process to go through rather than what they were doing, which was just an ambush, incredibly clandestine. I recommended that Ross be retained as captain, that I became the person to work with Ross and Mike to make sure that you got that relationship going and help build the team culture. I got a negative response from David White — I was wrong and Mike Hesson, Sandle and Bob Carter had it nailed.

We flew into Auckland at about 10.30 on Friday night so I got to Hamilton about 1.30 am. I weighed 86 kg; I hadn't been 86 kg since I was 14. Mackenzie was 14 months old and I'd been there for two of those months. Victoria was hugely stressed. Even though I hadn't slept on the flight, I couldn't sleep. I flicked on TV. There was a replay of a Super Rugby game in Hamilton earlier that night with Smithy commentating. I texted him at 2.30 am asking if he was still in Hamilton and, if so, could we meet. I fully expected that he was actually tucked up in bed back home in Havelock North and I wouldn't hear from him till the next morning, but an hour later he texted back from the Hamilton casino.

We met early the next morning. Smithy was blown away when he heard what had happened. He knew me well and I respected his opinion, so I wanted to get his take on what I should do on various fronts. I'd pretty much given up on the captaincy, but I wanted to hear what he thought about me not going to South Africa.

Ian Smith: Ross was at my motel just after 6 am. He wasn't in a good place — clearly agitated and upset, a different Ross Taylor to the happy-go-lucky one I'd known.

He wasn't a conflict guy; he'd never been in any trouble.

He didn't want to go to South Africa. He said, "I'm not sure I could play with these guys." My advice was that he shouldn't go. It was too soon; I didn't think there'd be a winner at the end of it. I imagine he sought other people's opinions and, in the end, he made himself unavailable. In hindsight, that was one of his best decisions because it could quite easily have gone pear-shaped, given his state of mind. We left it at a point where I said, "You can't finish with cricket, you're too young. Sit back at home and see if the hunger to play cricket comes back."

Leanne McGoldrick: I tried very hard to talk Ross into going to South Africa because I was so worried about the repercussions and how he would be perceived. When he got back from Sri Lanka, I flew up to Hamilton. Within seconds of seeing him, I knew he couldn't go. I'd never seen him like that. He was a shadow of his former self. It was awful.

The thing about Ross was that he was basically a very happy person who just went about his business. He trusted everybody and took things at face value. If somebody looked him in the eye and said something, he trusted their word and that they were being sincere and honest because that's the type of person he was. Because of that, it was astonishing to him that people could behave in completely the opposite manner. That whole episode seemed to instil in him a general sense of mistrust in people, something which had never been a part of his nature before.

On the Monday, Leanne and I had a meeting with Players' Association CEO Heath Mills in Mercer. On the way there, I got a call from Hess to say that he was going to recommend to the board that I stayed on as test captain with Brendon taking over as the ODI and T20 captain. Leanne and I looked at each other, dumbfounded. It was the first time I'd heard any mention of a split captaincy — it hadn't come up at either of the meetings in Sri Lanka. I thanked him and asked for a couple of days to think about it.

> **Ian Smith:** There were suggestions that they never meant to say Ross wouldn't be the captain in one form of the game. When I had that first chat to him, Ross was absolutely certain in his mind that he was not going to be the New Zealand cricket captain in any form of the game. I'll never forget that.

The Players' Association had started to get involved, perhaps because there'd been some comment about the fact that they'd been very quiet. Heath's view was that I should accept the test captaincy and go to South Africa.

> **Kim Littlejohn:** I guess it speaks for itself that the all-powerful Players' Association suddenly went extremely quiet. If the boot had been on the other foot, if New Zealand Cricket had been removing Brendon, I guarantee they would have been all over the media; they would have been in my ear going on about why Brendon is being treated so shabbily. I never had a phone call from them.

On the Tuesday, I got a call from David White to say the board had ratified the split-captaincy proposal and an announcement would be made on Friday. He was flying back from Dubai and wanted to meet face to face on the Thursday.

Leanne and I were just about to go into that meeting when Brendon called to say I should take the test captaincy. It was hard to know where he was coming from: maybe there was an element of him not wanting the test captaincy and/or being able to say to the media that he'd tried to convince me to do it — by that stage they knew they had a potential PR problem.

If I'd accepted the test captaincy offer, the arrangement wouldn't have lasted. It would have been just a matter of months before I got binned again. Then the spin would have been, "Well, we tried but Ross just wasn't prepared, or wasn't good enough, to make it work."

Brendon needed to be the boss: it wasn't in his nature to be satisfied with a split-leadership arrangement. And because of what had happened, my relationship with Hess and his supporters was non-existent; I simply didn't — couldn't — trust them. It hadn't been great before they blindsided me but, once the media and public knew the background, it would've been impossible.

I told David White that I wasn't going to accept the test captaincy and wouldn't be going to South Africa. He went to great lengths to try to get me to change my mind on South Africa, offering to pay for me and the family to have a holiday in Fiji and to fly Victoria, Mackenzie and Leanne to South Africa business class. I just said, "Thanks, but no thanks." I asked him if he'd known in advance about the ambush; he said he hadn't. I asked him whether, in that case, Hess had gone outside his jurisdiction to try to sack me without informing, let alone getting sign-off from, the board and CEO. David said he didn't know. He gave that response to a number of other questions.

It's hard, but not impossible, to believe that Hess had acted on his own initiative. Talking to NZC insiders and people who'd been involved in cricket administration at senior levels, the consistent feedback was that the board would not have tolerated a coach unilaterally deciding to sack the captain in mid-tour. As was pointed out, the captaincy is a board decision, not a coach decision. The coach recommends, the board approves. That, in turn, suggests that the board had made an in-principle decision to replace me.

As was also pointed out, at that time the NZC board, and Chris

Moller in particular, were very hands-on, much more so than previously when it had sat above the organisation at a governance level. I was told there was a group on the board who were pushing for change on a broad front. Justin Vaughan had been replaced as CEO by David White, who seemed to have been brought in as an agent of change. The board faction wanted to see big changes because they felt the team wasn't performing as well as it should have been and nor was the organisation.

Whether those board members were comfortable with the way Hess went about it and the fallout from that is another matter. I guess they rationalised it by looking at the big picture — mission accomplished — and telling themselves there was little to be gained from public hand-wringing over how they got there. The end justifies the means.

Bryan Waddle: It seemed to me at the time the change was made that the dressing room was more McCullum's than it was Taylor's. And that basically solved the issue, which is why I had no problem with whatever the new coach wanted to do in those situations. They had the right to do what they wanted with the captaincy, but you don't treat people like that. I just couldn't accept the way Taylor was treated by the hierarchy of New Zealand Cricket, the stories that went around, the things that you weren't allowed to say in terms of injunctions.

Gary Hermansson: There may be some legitimate reasons as to why the captaincy might have changed and, in hindsight, you could argue that it was a good decision, although there are some dynamics about that to do with Mike and Brendon that are interesting in themselves. But Ross felt really hurt and abandoned. The organisation had put him in the position of having that responsibility and then they'd abandoned him, even though it became clear that the captaincy issue wasn't handled well. There was no reprimand or any kind of resolution. Everybody just joined the abandonment really.

I wouldn't say that Ross had post-traumatic stress disorder as a clinical diagnosis, but he certainly had all the elements of it — that whole kind of empty despair, the sense of rejection. He's not easy with animosity or with conflict and negativity, so it put him in that space.

The captaincy definitely came too early for me. I was still learning my game and coming to terms with international cricket. Kane, Brendon, Dan and Flem were all very good captains in their different ways but, as a general rule, if you don't have a good team, you're not going to win. Good captains add value, usually in small ways, but if you don't have a good team, you're not going to win games of cricket consistently, no matter how good your captain is at the one-percenters.

That might suggest it gnaws away at me that I never got the chance to prove what I could do with a good side. Not so: while it would've been nice to have had the confidence and the support from within the team and NZC to have captained the way I wanted to, the flip side is that I wouldn't have played for as long as I did. If I'd captained for five or six years, there's no way I would have still been a Black Cap in 2022. Things happen for a reason.

Chapter 8.
Forgive but don't Forget

We spent a lot of that summer at Victoria's parents' bach at Waihi Beach. I didn't do much apart from taking Mackenzie to the beach and watching darts on television. I rang Martin Crowe to fill him in on the captaincy saga and broke down when he told me his cancer had returned. By and large I felt okay, although I clearly wasn't: my father-in-law Peter became concerned because I was so quiet, almost blank. He wondered if I'd ever play cricket again.

> **Leanne McGoldrick:** I got criticised because people thought I'd encouraged him not to go to South Africa, but it was the complete opposite. I was worried that, if he didn't go, he'd never play cricket in New Zealand again. One of the things that really concerned me was how some people viewed Ross not going. His explanation was just dismissed. I don't think any of them realised or cared that Ross wasn't in a healthy psychological state. Ross had medical advice that he shouldn't go.

> **Brendon McCullum** (in his 2016 autobiography *Declared*): If you looked at it objectively, [Ross Taylor's] decision not to come on the South African tour was quite bizarre and really only explicable in terms of people fuelling his

emotions behind the scenes. If anything, that probably made him feel worse, more hard done by. But the brutal truth is that no one is New Zealand captain as of right: you either do your job or you get dropped.

Not for one moment did I believe that I was New Zealand captain as of right. Indeed, as I indicated to Dad after my first face-to-face meeting with Hess, I took it for granted that I was on borrowed time in the role. It was never about losing the captaincy: I understood that NZC and the coach could appoint whoever they liked, whenever they liked and that they weren't bound by decisions made by their predecessors. It was about the way it was done: the intrigue, the undermining, the hidden agendas. And, after it was done, it was about the utter indifference to the impact it had on me and those close to me.

* * *

It was raining so Victoria and I decided to go to the mall in Mount Maunganui. I put the car radio on, not onto Radio Sport because that was the last thing I wanted to listen to. Almost immediately the announcer said, "We're crossing live to a New Zealand Cricket press conference about the captaincy issue." NZC chairman Chris Moller came on: "First of all," he said, "we'd like to apologise to Ross Taylor and his family for the way things have been handled."

It was a strange way of going about it, to say the least. There was no apology in person. (There hasn't been to this day.) Instead, it was delivered via the media without any prior notification. The fact that I wouldn't have heard it unless I'd happened to turn on the radio made it less meaningful in my mind — it seemed more like a PR ploy than a genuine apology. It would have meant a lot more if Chris Moller had picked up the phone and spoken directly to me. There was also an apology in writing — a two-sentence letter that was sent to Leanne even though NZC knew my address — and some follow-up communication from David White.

Over in South Africa with the Black Caps, Martin Guptill was sick to the point that there were discussions about him coming home. Furthermore, being a close friend of mine wasn't necessarily a plus point under the new regime. After not playing the first T20 he texted me before the second saying, "There are times when you go to the ground and you know it's just not your day — you're not going to get any runs. Mate, that's me today." I messaged back, basically doing for Guppy what Hogan did for me: "You know you're a good player; be that player." He went out and made 101 not out off 69 balls, hitting a boundary off the last delivery to win the game. The next highest score was 25.

Afterwards, he told the media that talking to me had helped him. I was watching it, thinking, 'That's not going to go down well.' The official narrative was that I was a poor leader who couldn't motivate players, but Gup was crediting me with helping him get out of his sick bed to make a match-winning hundred. Gup didn't have an agenda. He made an innocent comment but, as I later heard from others, it wasn't seen that way.

John Buchanan: Martin Guptill was a person that we really believed would be great a support for Ross because he just didn't seem to buy into everything else that was going on. Whether that was because it didn't matter to him who was captain, he was always just going to be his own person but, even if that was the case, he would have been more of an ally than someone that wouldn't support Ross.

Shane Bond's situation became awkward when a letter he'd written to NZC was leaked to the media. Bondy's a straight arrow and was very uneasy with some of the accounts of what had happened in Sri Lanka — particularly in regard to the split captaincy — that were finding their way into the public domain.

He told NZC CEO David White that some of what was being said wasn't right. David told him to put it in writing. Bondy wrote a letter and sent it to Leanne, who was also his manager. She asked if he was quite sure he wanted to follow through with it, pointing out that it could jeopardise his position with NZC then and in the future. (Later on, it was conveyed to me that the letter also contained some criticism of my captaincy.) Leanne told him to sleep on it. The letter was emailed to David the following day.

I had a huge amount of respect for what Bondy did. Brendon and Hess thought he was trying to sabotage them and pretty much ostracised him. Over time, though, I think they realised he was an asset and someone who just tells it the way he sees it.

To some extent, the question of who leaked Bondy's letter to broadcaster Tony Veitch overshadowed its contents. A lot of people were convinced that Leanne was the leaker. That was nuts: why on earth would Leanne put her client Bondy in such a difficult position with Brendon and Hess, and potentially damage his coaching prospects?

Besides, the leak didn't do me any good either. I'd got to the point of picking up a bat and starting to think about playing cricket again, but the leak triggered a whole new round of media coverage that set me back. Something else that didn't help was hearing how a senior Black Cap who'd been in Sri Lanka reacted to the revived controversy: "We knew Bondy would be the one who'd stuff it up."

When the Black Caps got back from South Africa, Leanne and I met Hess at the Novotel in Auckland. (By then I'd indicated to David White that I'd be available for the upcoming games against England.) As it turned out, neither Bob Carter nor Mike Sandle could make the meeting and Brendon decided it would be better if he didn't attend, so it was just Hess and his mentor from SPARC (now Sport New Zealand.)

Hess was visibly ill at ease. He denied that he'd said I was a follower, not a leader, and that the senior players didn't want me as

First media appearance: this photo of me, aged seven, at the Wairarapa Bush vs Romania rugby match in 1991 appeared in the *Wairarapa Times-Age*.
Inset: That's a big hat for a wee boy: me as a toddler.

With my sisters Elianna (left) and Rebecca at home in Masterton. Note the oversized sports shoe.

The boys from the Bush: me — with my first batting award — and Jesse Ryder. Our shared cricketing odyssey took us from the York Street kindergarten to Bangalore, via numerous rep teams, New Zealand Under 19s, Central Districts and the Black Caps. *WAIRARAPA TIMES-AGE*

Wielding my first proper cricket bat, a Waugh Zone V-100 bought for me by Grandad Jack, as a 13-year-old, playing for the Wairarapa College first XI.

WAIRARAPA TIMES-AGE

On my way to 95 in Central Districts' 2003/04 State Shield final victory over a star-studded Canterbury side. Still one of my favourite games. *PHOTOSPORT*

Old boys' reunion: Palmerston North Boys' High School old boys, left to right, Mathew "Skippy" Sinclair, me and keeper Bevan Griggs in full voice for the Central Stags against the Auckland Aces at Eden Park in 2005.

I wondered where that CD kit got to. My best mate, Marcus Emery, decked out in my CD training kit, can't wait to congratulate me on scoring a century for the Stags against the Wellington Firebirds at Fitzherbert Park, Palmerston North in 2006.

Taking a measured approach on my ODI debut against the West Indies at McLean Park, Napier in 2006.

Proof that I have bowled in an ODI — against Australia at the WACA in Perth in 2007. Non-striker Ricky Ponting watches with trepidation. (My two overs went for 16 runs, without reward.)

This cover drive was probably the highlight of my brutal and deflating introduction to test cricket — against South Africa at The Wanderers ground in Johannesburg in 2007.

GETTY

The original tongue poke — on reaching 100 in an ODI against Australia at Eden Park in 2007. It was intended as a cheeky acknowledgement of the fun and games that had taken place — I'd had some luck and sparred verbally with some of the Aussies. My daughter Mackenzie saw it on the TV highlights and wanted me to do it again. It became our little ritual.

PHOTOSPORT

Get a haircut and get a real job: me and Jesse at Black Caps training in 2008.

Celebrating my maiden test century — against England at Seddon Park, Hamilton in 2008.

"You're a good player, Ross, but remember: soft forearms." With future Black Caps coach John Wright in 2008.

The Taylor Squad — made up of sisters and cousins — making their presence felt at Westpac Stadium in Wellington in 2009.

At the 2009 Abu Dhabi grand prix with the boss — Royal Challengers Bangalore owner Vijay Mallya — and Bollywood star Deepika Padukone.

RCB warm-ups: Rahul Dravid is pointing out that he's 11 years older than me but having no trouble keeping up.

I wasn't in the same league as my great mentor, Martin Crowe, when it came to stylish batting, but perhaps there's a hint of Hogan in this cover drive against Pakistan at the Basin Reserve, Wellington, in 2009.

PHOTOSPORT

With Black Caps coach Mark Greatbatch at the Dambulla International Stadium in Sri Lanka in 2009. I've known Batchy since I was 13; he had a big influence on my career.

GETTY

One of the eight sixes I hit on my way to 80 off 30 balls in the 2010 Twenty20 final against the Aces at my favourite New Zealand ground: Pukekura Park, New Plymouth. PHOTOSPORT

Black Caps team photo taken during the Seddon Park test against Pakistan in January 2011 which coincided with the IPL auction. From left to right: Tim McIntosh, Jesse, me (vice-captain), Daniel Vettori (captain), Chris Martin and Brendon McCullum. It was Dan's second to last test as captain; within a few months Brendon and I would be auditioning to replace him.

GETTY

All fired up at reaching 100 in a must win game against Pakistan at the 2011 World Cup. One of my two favourite ODI innings.

GETTY

The international contingent lead out the Rajasthan Royals during the 2011 IPL. From left to right, Johan Botha, skipper Shane Warne, Shane Watson and me. 2011 was Warnie's last season as an IPL player.

Smacking it for the Royals against the Chennai Super Kings.

You wouldn't think from Aussie captain Michael Clarke's expression that he has just won the toss and sent us in to bat on one of the greenest wickets of all time: Bellerive Oval, Hobart, 2011. PHOTOSPORT

Catching David Warner off Chris Martin at Bellerive, to Martin Guptill's delight. We bowled Australia out for 136 in their first innings and went on to win by seven runs. We haven't beaten them in a test since. PHOTOSPORT

Being interviewed by Bryan Waddle, the voice of New Zealand cricket, before the third test against South Africa at the Basin in 2012. PHOTOSPORT

Feeling the pain of what proved to be a broken arm inflicted by South African paceman Morné Morkel. Morné was very apologetic. PHOTOSPORT

With Leanne McGoldrick, my long-time manager and, according to the *Times of India*, my wife, at the Taj Mahal in 2012. *TIMES OF INDIA*

I go two from two — two safaris, two tiger sightings — at the Ranthambore National Park in 2012. Rahul Dravid is behind the driver; I'm in the back seat in the white t-shirt. Inset: teammate Nayan Doshi takes photos while Rahul and I can only watch in wonder. M.D. PARASHAR captain, although he conceded he might have implied something of the sort. I was taken aback: it wasn't a statement that was open to misinterpretation or likely to be forgotten. He complained that much of what I'd said to the media amounted to a personal attack on him, which had really upset his family. I said it wasn't a personal attack, I'd simply given my side of the story. What I was thinking, though, was that, at no stage in the whole business, did he or Brendon show the slightest concern about how it had affected me and my family.

We'd agreed at the outset that, whatever transpired in the meeting, we'd restrict our comments afterwards to the message that it was a work in progress and things were going well. However, Hess departed from the party line when he spoke to the media.

It was a story that wouldn't die. On the contrary, it just seemed to mushroom and mutate. There was the campaign, headed by former New Zealand batsman John Parker and involving a number of former captains and cricketing luminaries, that zeroed in on the captaincy issue as part of a wider critique of NZC. Brendon stopped that in its tracks by initiating defamation action. Brendon also sought and obtained an injunction to prevent publication of his email exchange over the captaincy with his former mental skills coach Kerry Schwalger. I understand anyone who read the emails would have had no trouble realising why he went to such lengths to prevent them seeing the light of day.

Gary Hermansson: It became messy with the ex-players starting their campaign and Brendon suing people and taking out injunctions. Ross was the one in the washing machine being thrown all around the place. It could have destroyed him as a person and as a cricket player and, from the mental health point of view, pushed him into a space that would have been really difficult to cope with. But he had some people who cared a lot for him and people on his side who had integrity and could see what was happening, so they provided that bit of help, keeping him pointing to a true north. Martin Crowe was a key anchor point for him. It could have been an absolute disaster, and it did have its disastrous elements. But as difficult as it's been — two steps forward, one step back at times — it's been a journey which has been one of challenges but also of real strength coming through as a person.

Even though a couple of years had passed, it took me back to square one.

With me and John Wright out of the way, John Buchanan and Kim Littlejohn were in the crosshairs. I'm sure they knew that. The honesty and integrity of John Buchanan and Wrighty shone like beacons in the murky New Zealand cricket landscape. Sadly, their relationship was probably never going to work: they'd gone up against each other as head coaches of India and Australia in some high-stakes series and games, including the 2003 World Cup final. Wrighty wanted to do things his way, without having to report to John, but part of John's remit was overseeing Wrighty. The division between them presented an opportunity that was exploited to the hilt.

When I began my comeback with Central Districts, Gary Hermansson, who worked with the CD team, used to say to me, "Remember Ross: forgive, but don't forget." That became a mantra I recited to myself many times in the months and years that followed.

Shortly after I returned to the Black Caps fold, Bob Carter sought me out. We met for a coffee in Wellington. He offered a sort of general apology and reminded me that he'd tried to get me to put off the fateful meeting. He knew what was coming because he'd tried to talk Hess out of doing anything while we were on tour, but Hess had made up his mind to act. Bob confirmed my recollection of Hess's case for a change of captain. He remembered my response to Hess's claim that the senior players didn't want me: "I can guess who they are." Bob also said he hadn't heard any mention of a split captaincy until we were back in New Zealand.

I'd heard that a lot of the stuff I'd asked for as captain was now being implemented. When I went back into the environment, I saw for myself that was very definitely the case.

> **Leanne McGoldrick:** While Ross was honoured to be considered for the captaincy, he had some misgivings. He has never overestimated his own ability: he recognised his shortcomings and that he had much to learn if he was going to captain New Zealand. He was forthright about the support, training and guidance he would need to become an effective leader and was assured it would be forthcoming. It never eventuated.

The management talked about having to "reintegrate" me into the Black Caps which, I felt, characterised my non-participation in the tour of South Africa as a transgression. If they'd understood me a bit better, they would have known I wasn't coming back in with the intention of causing trouble. I can honestly say I never undermined a captain in my entire career. Besides, to what end? Once the captaincy was taken off me, I had zero ambition to do it again.

For me it was straightforward: there was only one New Zealand men's cricket team, I had goals I wanted to achieve, mostly that Hogan had set for me, and the only way I could achieve them was by playing for the Black Caps. Therefore, I had to go back into the team, try to put the Schwalger emails out of my mind and just get on with it. In a way it was harder for my family, who were feeling the same hurt but didn't have my focus and opportunity.

I'd confided in very few of my teammates so not many of them knew my side of the story. Those who were in Brendon's camp from the outset obviously accepted the NZC/Hess/Brendon line that I and my shortcomings were the problem. Even those who could acknowledge that I'd been shafted — and the neutrals may have fallen into this category — may have viewed me as not a true team player, because a true team player would've just sucked it up, kept his mouth shut and moved on.

There were some jarring moments. I ran into Brendon in the lift and asked him where he was going: he was on his way to an NZC board meeting. I was never asked to attend a board meeting. When I was captain, Hess wanted a senior players group. He'd have a chat to Brendon and Dan to get their opinion, then tell me, "I've spoken to Dan and Brendon and this is what we're going do." Under Brendon, there was no senior players group.

Hess, particularly, Brendon and a number of players were standoffish. It felt weird, as if I was a newcomer to the environment. It didn't help that I wasn't there mentally and didn't perform very well at all. In the first game at Eden Park, I dropped a couple of catches, one of them a goober. The crowd were great, but I was so zonked that I didn't realise they'd given me a standing ovation until Victoria mentioned it when I got back to the hotel.

Gary Hermansson: I'd give Ross his due that he could step up and try to make it work but, psychologically, it's a bit like in a tribal sense: if you're in the tribe and you've had a clear indication that there are people in the tribe who haven't wished you well, who've made things difficult and have actually hurt you to the core, then it becomes hard to go out and do what you need to do. There's a feeling of alienation and wondering, 'Who do I look to?' I think with Ross there was also a resistance to creating a clique of his own: there were people who were very supportive of him, but the dilemma was how do you embrace that friendship and support without risking it escalating into creating further division?

In his book, Brendon said something to the effect that, when I came back, I was detached from the team. I certainly spent a fair bit of time in my room, but I'd always had done that. I didn't tag along when they got on the beer: again, nothing new there. I preferred to go and have dinner with my relations or catch up with friends. If we won a test match or ODI I'd certainly have a beer or a wine with the boys, but I was never at the bar the night before a game. If you reckon that makes me a bad teammate, you're saying that what suits a select few socially is the team culture and you have to buy into it whether you like it or not. What suits some team members socially isn't — and cannot be — a genuine, inclusive team culture.

I didn't want to be seen as trying to keep the captaincy drama alive or to form a clique so I kept everything that had happened to myself and was particularly careful around the younger players. No doubt, some of them saw me as insular. There are guys I've played a lot of international cricket with who still don't know what went on and what I was dealing with. That was sometimes quite hard to accept, given that they would have understood me a lot better if they'd known the full story.

I focused on doing my job, scoring runs, ticking off the goals Hogan had set for me. It made me very stats driven, but I'd like to think it benefitted the team. Just for the record, when I captained in test cricket, I averaged 47.2; under Brendon's captaincy, I averaged 49.1. In short, I actually performed slightly better under Brendon than when I was captain. Brendon averaged 45.2 in test matches when he captained, 29.5 when I was captain.

Ian Smith: Ross found new reasons to play and they were personal milestones. I probably hadn't met a bloke since Richard Hadlee who was so stats focused. Richard was absolutely driven by personal milestones and, because he achieved them, the team did well.

At the 2014 Indian Premier League, the Delhi Daredevils bowling coach, Eric Simons, introduced me to Paddy Upton, a South African-born cricket and mental skills coach. I talked to Paddy about being an outsider in a team environment. (He has no fewer than four university degrees and, when not coaching cricket teams, is a university professor in Melbourne. He has also written fascinatingly on the subject of corporate psychopaths and how they present and behave in team sport.) He said you either have to leave, because the leadership will make your life a misery if you oppose them, or you have to find a way to keep your head down, bite your tongue and get on with it. I wasn't going to walk away and the other option was what I was doing anyway.

> **John Wright:** When you're a coach you sometimes align with the bloc you think can get the job done. That's the way it is. As it turned out, McCullum worked well with Hesson, but it was very tough on Ross and I had a huge amount of respect for the way he swallowed it and got on with it. For him, playing under that regime must have been like playing with a cloud over your head.

Sean Fitzpatrick presented the caps before a test at Lord's. He talked about Laurie Mains coming in as All Blacks coach in 1992 and wanting his Otago boy Mike Brewer as captain, and how tricky that was. I couldn't stop looking at Hess and Brendon. It was comical in a sense: here was the legendary All Blacks captain commanding the room and certainly not trying to get a laugh, but I was struggling to keep a straight face. I just kept thinking about the Otago link and how much Laurie Mains and Mike Brewer sounded like Hess and Brendon. I doubt anyone else made the connection, but it certainly resonated with me.

We had all sorts of people come and talk to the team and present the caps. Some were really good, some were average. I have to say none of the others engaged me as much as Fitzy did that day.

Together, Hess and Brendon were a powerful force. After Brendon retired from international cricket, my relationship with Hess improved and, by the end of his stint, we got along okay. And, over time, things got better between me and Brendon. Before the falling out over the captaincy, I used to buy him a bottle of wine when he made a century and vice versa. That had stopped with the ledger in Brendon's favour. I took a few bottles down to Dunedin for the first test of the 2013/14 summer — against the Windies — to give to Brendon. I suppose you'd call it a peace offering. We had a 195-run partnership with both of us getting centuries, but the weather deprived us of what would have been the first test win of Brendon's captaincy. But we went on to win in Wellington and Hamilton, giving us our first series win over a top-eight nation since 2006. I got hundreds in both games and, at the end of the series, Brendon gave me seven or eight bottles of wine.

When we were in Adelaide in late 2015 for the first pink-ball test, we were invited, via a contact of mine in the wine trade, to visit the Penfolds Magill Estate. About 18 of us, including some partners, went along: we paid for lunch and Penfolds supplied the wine. I could sense the boys losing interest during the tour of the estate — they just wanted to get stuck into some fine wine. It was sort of my show so I took the attitude that as long as they got to taste some Grange Hermitage, an iconic wine by world standards, my job was done: they could say they'd tried a wine worth $800 a bottle.

We had a tasting of Penfolds' top of the range wines, including the 2011 Grange. The boys were happy; job done. Then our host said he had some nice stuff to have with lunch and brought out five bottles of 1984 Grange, which was amazing. I used to buy a special bottle to commemorate a century and there was no better time or place to push the boat out, having just got 290 in Perth. I bought a magnum of 2010 Grange, which came in a nice box. When we got back to the hotel after lunch, it slipped out of my hand and hit the deck. Knowing what it had cost, the boys thought it was hilarious.

The box had a polystyrene casing, but I was still mightily relieved to open it up and find the bottle intact. Brendon bought me a fantastic bottle of wine that day: a Bin 620 Cabernet Shiraz, the first one that Penfolds had released for 50 years.

One area that improved out of sight under Brendon was media relations. I'd struggled with the media. I got off to a bad start, not only losing my train of thought in a press conference but owning up to it. That made the news. I was always worried about saying the wrong thing and seemed to get slammed for every little misstep or borderline decision. There were journalists who wanted to cosy up to me and have a direct line, but it wasn't in my nature to develop those relationships. I think I learnt to give them something, but I just couldn't play the game and ultimately paid a price for it. I would have been better served to have allied myself with two or three of them.

Brendon was the polar opposite: he put a lot of time into cultivating the media and getting them on side and, in terms of the general atmosphere and tenor of the media coverage, it paid dividends. Brendon was good at the game. I've no doubt that his media savvy and the way he presented himself were considerations for those who promoted him, especially looking ahead to the 2015 World Cup.

The media loves black-and-white narratives and therefore has very little interest in explaining that, while winning takes care of everything, it's really hard to win if you haven't got the players and you're up against teams that have. This is where the media and public criticism sometimes gets silly: you look at two teams and think, 'They could play 10 games, and team A is going to win nine of them because they're just a better team and the conditions suit them.' The record books show that it doesn't matter who you are: if you're in India and it's turning square, it's incredibly hard to win. But, if you lose, you'll still get hammered and people will be ringing talkback to say you're hopeless, you've got no fighting spirit, no pride in the black cap et cetera.

When Tiger Woods got the first tournament win of his post-disgrace comeback, Nike rushed out an ad with the slogan, "Winning takes care of everything." Nike copped a lot of stick for it, but they were absolutely on the money: as soon as Tiger started winning again, everybody forgot about the scandal that many had predicted would ruin his reputation and career. When the Black Caps started doing well, all the questions that had swirled around the change of captaincy, the way it was done and the manner in which some of the protagonists had behaved became irrelevant. The results spoke for themselves. Winning takes care of everything.

I won the Sir Richard Hadlee Medal for player of the year in 2012/13, when there wasn't an awards ceremony, and again in 2013/14. I'd made five centuries but, given that Brendon had become the first New Zealander to make a test triple century and had also made a double hundred, I knew it had to be a close call. I didn't realise just how close. The player of the year was chosen by a panel of former New Zealand selector and cricket identity Don Neely, the then convenor, Ian Smith, and Bryan Waddle. They deliberated and communicated their decision — that Ross Taylor was player of the year — to New Zealand Cricket. NZC came straight back asking them to reconsider.

Ian Smith: Don said we'd been asked to review. I don't think he said we must make another choice, but someone from NZC told Don we had to look at it again. We did get pressure, there's no doubt about that. In the end, we basically said, "No, we're not looking at it again. We made that decision in the first place and that decision stands." It wasn't out of sympathy or anything like that. We didn't pick Ross because we felt sorry for him — he just had a damn good year.

It was an interesting awards night. Stuart Heal, the recently installed NZC chairman, and a former chairman of Otago cricket, presented Brendon with a special award to mark his triple century. During the evening I walked past Heal three times: he didn't say a word to me. A couple of board members did congratulate me on winning back-to-back Sir Richard Hadlee medals, but they were certainly in the minority. I assumed the others categorised me as a troublemaker because I hadn't gone quietly.

A few years later history almost repeated itself.

Bryan Waddle: The one with Brendon I'm not sure about the background because I wasn't the convenor at that stage, but I was aware there was a push against Ross. The one that I know about is 2017/18 when Trent Boult got the award. We had the same panel — Don Neely, Ian Smith and myself. I'd been doing it for a good 10 years and we had a system by which we decided when all the figures were made available. Test cricket had the highest rating, then ODIs, then T20s. Our judgements were based on the figures and I don't think we ever got one wrong.

New Zealand Cricket had their awards the night after the final test and the decision was pretty tight: there were three players in the running and we ended up pretty much deadlocked. It was one-all and I had to make the final call. NZC were after me for the name because they had to get their stuff ready to present on television.

Someone from NZC got in touch with me a couple of times to find out where we were at. I explained the situation to him and said that it looked as though it was going to be Ross Taylor. That led to an exchange of views: he expressed a preference for Trent Boult. I discussed it with the others — they held firm and I stuck by my opinion. I went back and said, "This is our recommendation, this is what you've asked us to do. They're your awards and you don't have to accept our recommendation if that's the way you feel about it." I thought that was the only reasonable way to get out of it. They could do whatever they wanted — and they did: Trent Boult was the winner.

Hess and Brendon were at the peak of their powers, both as individuals and as a combination, at the 2015 World Cup. I was fully "reintegrated" but had no leadership role. Kane was vice-captain. On the field I would give Brendon my opinion if asked, which didn't happen that often. Off the field, I was out of the loop. Guppy and Jesse Ryder had been opening the batting in ODIs with Brendon at five, but Jesse had gone, Grant Elliott had come in and Brendon was going to open.

It was a very settled team. The only real changes came when Adam Milne got injured. Mitch played against Bangladesh but didn't have a great outing so Matt Henry came in for the semi-final. When we walked out for the national anthem, we spotted 2011 Rugby World Cup hero Stephen Donald in the stand. We were saying to Matt, "Come on mate, you're going to be our Beaver." In fact, Grant Elliott was the hero that day.

The games against Australia and South Africa at Eden Park were fantastic, the best atmospheres I'd experienced in New Zealand by a long shot. My form was pretty average. I got stumped against Sri Lanka in the first game, scratched around for a few not out against England after Brendon had absolutely blitzed them, and got cleaned up against Australia.

Competition details were not one of my strengths. In an ODI, you normally bowl 50 overs, or pretty close to it, then have a 40-minute break in which to gather your thoughts and get ready to bat. But when we fielded first in 2015, we often bowled teams out so quickly that there was only a 10-minute break between innings. I'd tell myself the competition details had changed and I had to change accordingly, but I didn't really manage to do that.

The game against Australia at Eden Park was a case in point.

(Hogan was getting inducted into the International Cricket Council Hall of Fame, which created a bit of an emotional challenge for me.) We bowled them out in 32 overs and were straight back out there. I got in at the seventh over after Brendon had gone berserk and ran one down to third man off Pat Cummins to get off the mark. They brought Mitchell Starc back to bowl the last over before the proper break. His first ball sent my off pole flying and provided an emphatic, if belated, answer to the question I'd just put to Kane: "Any swing?" My father-in-law and brother-in-law, who are Pakeha, were shocked at the racial abuse directed at me after I was skittled by Starc. They felt embarrassed and sorry for my sisters and cousins, having to hear it from the people I was supposedly representing.

Very few Black Caps had played at the MCG, so in late 2014 a group of us went to Melbourne on a familiarisation exercise. Hess's thinking was that, if we did make the World Cup final, we wouldn't want to be in the position of most of the team never having set foot in what is a unique and intimidating arena.

It was sound in theory, although I'm not sure how valuable it turned out to be in practice: they were resewing the MCG outfield so we couldn't walk on it and, by the time we returned for the final, Kane had forgotten how to get from the changing room to the viewing area. And the reality is that no amount of familiarisation can prepare you for the experience of walking out to bat in front of 93,000 spectators, the vast majority of whom are vociferously supporting your opponents.

On the morning of the final against Australia in Melbourne I'd been in the lift with David Warner and his wife who were fine. But then Victoria and I found ourselves in the lift with Brad Haddin. I said, "Hi," but he didn't really want to engage with us or even make eye contact. I guess it was in keeping with his pre-game comments about the Black Caps being too nice and the Aussies deciding they were going to play hardball.

It was nothing new. As a player, Ricky Ponting would never

acknowledge you around the hotel. Now that he's a coach, he's more affable. Andrew Symonds might raise an eyebrow; Matthew Hayden would say, "Good morning, Tails." (He and one of my hockey coaches were the only people who ever called me that.) So, you could pass the three of them on your way to breakfast and get three different reactions. The IPL broke down those barriers. On the field, of course, all the Aussies went hard, but that was okay.

Staying in the same hotel as the opposition is unusual, if not unknown, in most sports, but it's part and parcel of international cricket. I have to admit I didn't like it; it made it harder to switch off. And there's nothing worse than seeing a bowler at breakfast after he'd nicked you off in the first innings. You say, "Good morning, Broady," but you're thinking, 'This guy's going to nick me off again.'

We'd played all our games at home so we were still on New Zealand time when we got to Australia for the final. When we went down for a late breakfast on the morning of the game, I was struck by the nervous air around the team. It was an unsettling atmosphere, so I said to Victoria, "Let's get out of here." We went for a walk and met up with my brother-in-law and his wife at a café. The boys had played some fantastic cricket to get to the final, but on game day it felt like the nerves got to people and we froze. The only guys who said anything on the bus going to the MCG were Grant Elliott, Dan Vettori and me.

Before the final, Hogan had written a nice piece on the theme of Ross and Martin: the two sons I never had. We didn't catch up beforehand, but he was the first person I saw when we came off the field. It was a pretty emotional moment and a few tears were shed. Gup and I took him down to the changing room. As a rule, Hogan, like a lot of ex-players, wasn't particularly comfortable in that setting and being around the current team, but that night in Melbourne was the exception: he was visibly delighted to be there. It was a bittersweet occasion.

Hogan was telling us that, while he was doing studio work in

Sydney for the semi-finals, he'd stayed at his movie star cousin Russell Crowe's apartment. Hogan had come over without a suit jacket which he was going to need for his on-camera work for *CricInfo* during the final. He rang Russell, who was in Los Angeles, to ask if could borrow a jacket. Russell said, "Yeah, sure, look in the wardrobe in my son's room." There were 50 brand-new Armani suits, mostly black with a few greys. Being a bit eccentric in his attire choices, Hogan picked a brown tartan jacket with a waistcoat.

At some point during the game, Hogan got a text from Russell saying, "Great choice, looks good on you." As we were having a laugh about it, Hogan added, "I just got another text from Russell asking when I am returning the jacket."

The next morning a big group of us went down for breakfast at the Langham Hotel where both teams were staying. Some of the Aussie players were in the bar, still in their playing kit. There was a bit of good-natured banter. Their captain, Michael Clarke, who'd batted authoritatively the night before, came over to pay his respects to Hogan.

After we'd had breakfast, and to everyone's amazement, Gup ordered and consumed a huge plate of ice cream. His explanation was that he was shouting himself for being the highest run-scorer in the tournament. He'd certainly earned it.

PART THREE:
WELCOME TO MY WORLD

Chapter 9.
Eyeballs

Injuries are the professional athlete's occupational hazard. I've had my share but, luckily, none of them kept me out of the game for too long.

My calves and hamstrings have been troublesome since my first hamstring tear at an under-18 hockey tournament. They say calf muscles are an old man's injury, but mine started pinging during the home series against Zimbabwe in early 2012. A couple of months later, I met All Blacks coach Steve Hansen at the Halberg Awards — the Black Caps were nominated for beating the Aussies in Hobart. He asked how the calf was and gave me this advice: when you think it's right, give it another week. I've followed that formula ever since.

I got hit on the arm by Morné Morkel in a test against South Africa at the Basin Reserve in 2012. Our physio Paul Close got me to squeeze his fingers: there was no pain, so he said I was okay. I popped a couple of Panadols, played the next ball out to backward point and instantly regretted it. Pain is the body's way of telling you something's wrong, and this message couldn't be ignored. I walked straight off. This was just after lunch on day four of a weather-affected game: when I left the field, we were 160/3 in our first innings; South Africa had made 474.

I went for an x-ray at a nearby clinic. It showed the arm was broken. My first thought, as I sat there with Mum, was, 'That big contract I just signed with Delhi is out the window.' (Morné, who's a nice, kind-hearted guy, sent me an apologetic message that night. Later, when we played together in the IPL, he was forever saying sorry for breaking my arm.)

The surgeon could fit me in the next morning, but what if I needed to bat in the second innings to save the game? I said it wouldn't come to that. He assured me the Indian Premier League was still a goer; in fact, he reckoned I'd be able to do a handstand after the operation, although he wouldn't recommend it because it would have been very painful. If I hadn't had the operation, I probably would have missed the entire IPL. As it was, I ended up missing three IPL games.

At the end of day four, South Africa were 274 ahead with all their second-innings wickets intact. I figured they'd have a dip in the morning and give themselves two and a half sessions to bowl us out on what was a pretty good wicket.

I had the operation: the surgeon inserted a 12-cm plate with six screws. Back at the hotel, and still very drowsy, I settled down in front of the TV to watch what I hoped would be a tame draw. South Africa set us 389 to win or, realistically, 80-odd overs to survive. After five overs we were 1/2, with Daniel Flynn and Brendon both out for nought. Kane and Martin Guptill made it through to lunch at 26/2.

At tea we were 103/5, with Kane on 58 playing a heroic hand against the formidable South African pace quartet: Marchant de Lange, Morkel, Vernon Philander and Dale Steyn. He and Kruger van Wyk batted for almost 20 overs after the break before Morkel, who ended with 6/23 off 16.4 overs, made the breakthrough. Dougie Bracewell went out to join Kane. That left Mark Gillespie, Chris Martin — and yours truly. Coach John Wright's concerns for my well-being were now balanced by alarm that we might lose the test match. He got on the phone to Mike Sandle, telling him, "Get Ross down here."

We were driving to the Basin with the radio on. It was rush hour; the traffic was at a near-standstill. Mike was starting to fret. "If we lose another wicket," he said, "you might have to leg it."

We got stuck at the lights on Cambridge Terrace so I got out and walked the rest of the way. I was still pretty drowsy, so it was the closest I've come to sleep-walking — as far as I know. Chris Martin perked up big-time when I walked into the changing room, but Kane and Doug held firm so neither of us had to bat. It was an interesting dilemma: you obviously don't want to bat with a broken arm a few hours after you've been under anaesthetic, but I was the New Zealand captain.

In August 2015 we were in Zimbabwe for a three-match ODI series in Harare. I got 112 not out in the first game, but their leg-spinner, Graeme Cremer, bowled with a fielder at 45 and square leg up, a deep mid-wicket which made the slog-sweep a risky option, and a long on. With that field, the single was to mid-wicket, whereas you can often nudge a good delivery to square leg for one. We got 303/4; Zimbabwe got 304/3. I didn't get a bat in game two: we chased down 235 without losing a wicket, with Gup and Tom Latham making tons.

We had an extra day before the third game. I wanted to come up with a way to make Cremer push square leg back and bring mid-wicket up, thereby opening up cow corner. I decided the sweep shot was the way to go. At training, I'd faced George Worker, bowling left-arm finger spin, and Ish Sodhi bowling leggies, and swept everything. Ish bowled a full one: I went down to sweep, missed it and it bounced up into the bottom of my box, forcing it up. I went down like a sack of spuds and everybody laughed their heads off. As I would have done if it had happened to someone else: cricketers are hard-wired to laugh when someone gets hit in the "lower abdomen". I felt a sharp pain just below my well-defined abs but got up and carried on. Not for long.

I hobbled to the changing room, inconveniently located on the other side of the ground. The affected area was three or four

times its normal size so the medical team decided I should have
an ultrasound. Getting to the right place involved a magical
mystery tour that took us back to where we'd started. The
ultrasound revealed two haematomas. Our doctor immediately
ruled me out of game three and sought a specialist's opinion.
After another ultrasound, the specialist confirmed that I did
indeed have two haematomas, they'd got bigger since the first
ultrasound and there was a laceration that required an operation.
That prospect hadn't crossed my mind. I rang Victoria who
wanted to know what the hospital was like; I said it was okay,
although the Ebola signs everywhere were a bit disconcerting.
Only one of us found that amusing.

The operation cost around US$1600, payment in advance. The
late Ross Dykes, who was filling in for our usual manager, Mike
Sandle, handed over his credit card, but the hospital didn't accept
them. Ross and an elderly liaison officer had to traipse around
Harare's money machines accumulating cash. I was in a fair bit
of pain and wondering why the hell it was taking so long: the
operation was scheduled for 5 pm but Ross didn't get back with the
cash until about 8.30 pm.

I was apprehensive enough as it was. Then I got a text from
Grant Elliott asking if I was sure I should have the operation in
Zimbabwe, and wouldn't it be better to organise an air ambulance
to South Africa? It was a little late in the day for that: they were just
about to wheel me into the operating theatre.

I woke up at 4.30 am, probably because the other person in the
room was vomiting noisily. There was no one from New Zealand
Cricket and no liaison officer: I was on my own They'd taken my
cell phone — to ensure it wasn't stolen apparently — so I couldn't
let Victoria know I was still alive. After hearing nothing all day,
Victoria texted Gup, but he didn't know what was going on. She
finally rang Mike Sandle, who wasn't even over there, to ask if he
could find out how the operation had gone.

The surgeon, who was Congolese and had studied in Belgium,

explained in a thick French accent that they'd drained the haematomas and stitched up the laceration. He'd also sent photos taken during the operation to our doctor.

A couple of days later, trussed up in a medical version of a jockstrap that the surgeon had made for me, I flew out with Players' Association personal development manager Sanjeewa Silva, who helped me with my bags. Back in Hamilton, I went to a urologist to get the stitches removed. He'd worked in Kenya and said the stitches were sheep intestines, which was quite common in Africa. He also said I was lucky not to have lost a testicle. The Congolese surgeon had done a good job and it had healed well, but it was an uncomfortable couple of weeks.

I first began to wonder if my eyesight was 100 per cent when we were playing day/night games in England in 2013. I dropped a couple of catches; in fact, I didn't even lay a hand on them. I didn't like fielding under lights — and the English lights are quite low — or on windy or cloudy days. I wore sunglasses to counteract the wind, rather than the glare.

Catching had never been a problem for me. As a kid, I took on board Dad's mantra that it wasn't enough to be a good batter or bowler — you had to be a good fielder as well. I couldn't guarantee runs or wickets, but I rarely dropped a catch, so it was a real cause for concern when I started putting them down. The nature of this game is that, when you dwell on your failures, your mind starts playing tricks on you. And while all that was going on, I was getting out early or starting even more scratchily than normal.

I went into the first test against Australia at the Gabba in November 2015 without having had much time in the middle. I got a duck in the first warm-up game, 16 in the second and the third was abandoned when the Cricket Australia XI's opening partnership ended at 503; Aaron Finch was 288 not out. It shows how dire things were that Kane, Brendon, Gup, Tom and I bowled 39 overs between us. Tom actually took the wicket. It was far from ideal preparation and did little to allay my apprehension at the thought of Mitchell Johnson's and Mitchell Starc's 150-kph inswingers honing in on my groin.

I got 0 and 26 in the first test. During Australia's first innings, I came off at a drinks break and told our video analyst, Paul Warren, that I just wasn't picking up the ball. Not long afterwards I took a one-handed screamer off David Warner: at the end of the day's play, Paul said, "You must have seen that one okay." Nevertheless, I went to an optometrist who said I'd have to have an operation at some stage, but it wasn't urgent.

I walked out with mixed feelings: there was an issue with my eyes so it wasn't all in the mind; on the other hand, eye problems are just about the last thing a professional cricketer needs. Then I focused on the fact that, while something was amiss, it was fixable. And perhaps the eye drops I'd got from the optometrist helped. Martin Crowe had sent me his foreword for this book, which I found inspirational so, all in all, I went into the second test at the WACA in Perth in a better frame of mind.

My 290 in that game is obviously one of my proudest achievements. Not being a scoreboard watcher, I wasn't aware I was on 197 and brought up the double century with an extravagant cover drive. If I'd known, there's no way I would have played that shot: I was in a nice rhythm and it would have annoyed me no end if I'd got out on 197 playing a million-dollar cover drive.

I got hit quite a few times by Johnson, Starc, Josh Hazlewood and Mitchell Marsh. My hands took such a battering that I went for an x-ray, but it was only bone bruising. I'd never batted through a full day of test cricket before and took a lot of pride in doing that in 40-degree heat, going for an x-ray, having a restless night and making some more runs the next day. (I was on 235 overnight.)

There were a couple of interesting examples of how batters' perceptions play a part in determining their mindsets. On day three, Starc supposedly bowled the fastest ball ever in test cricket — around 160 kph. I say "supposedly" because there have long

been rumours that the Aussies pump up the ball-speed ratings
for propaganda purposes. When the number went up, Warner
started woo-hooing. I was batting well and feeling comfortable
and that particular ball didn't seem any quicker than the others,
but the fact that it was clocked at 160 kph made me think, 'Shit,
he's bowling really quick.' I didn't move my feet to the next ball and
was dropped by Marsh in the gully. It was the only chance I gave
and it wasn't a dolly — Marsh had to dive and got one hand on it.
Even though Starc was the faster bowler, Tim Southee and Trent
Boult were freaked out by Johnson, perhaps because of the way
he'd intimidated England in the 2013/14 Ashes series: they wanted
me to take Johnson, even when that meant facing Starc. It was all
about perception.

It was a high-class bowling attack and, while it was a flat wicket,
there was a big crack outside off stump at one end. As long as you
got in behind the ball, you would have been outside the line if you
got hit on the pads. Even so, it was impossible not to think of Tony
Greig — or was it Billy Birmingham? — losing his car keys down a
crack at the WACA.

Boulty and I put on 37 for the 10th wicket, with him getting
the lion's share. He was going along nicely but eventually he said,
"Ross, can you hurry up and get 300 because I'm shitting myself."
In hindsight, I should have told him not to worry about it and
stayed in my game plan; instead, I tried to take Nathan Lyon over
cow corner and was caught by the substitute fielder who was on
for Usman Khawaja. If it had been Khawaja out there, he mightn't
have got to it, but the young sub had fresh legs.

In radio commentary, the former Aussie quick, Dirk Nannes,
was critical of the Australian players for not congratulating me
as I walked off. I played it down, saying I went off pretty quickly,
which I did. But I walked past a few of them, not one of whom said
a word. It was the highest score by a visiting player in Australia,
surpassing England's R.E. "Tip" Foster who made 287 — on debut
— in Sydney in 1903. Incidentally, Foster, one of seven brothers

who played first-class cricket, is the only man to captain England in both cricket and football.

Funnily enough, if I'd got out for 200, normally a cause for celebration, we might have lost. We got 624 in reply to Australia's 559/9. If they'd started their second innings 100 or so ahead, we could've been hard-pressed to get away with a draw. As it was, we actually had a sniff when they were 46/2, but Adam Voges and Steve Smith got hundreds.

I caught Joe Burns off Tim in the third over. After batting for so long, I could have pleaded fatigue and put my feet up, which was probably why Ian Chappell in the Channel 9 commentary box praised what was a regulation catch. Slip fielders in Perth and Brisbane stand a long way back, which is a mixed blessing: you get a good look at it, but you also have time to think about it.

My Uncle Max was there with his partner Lynn, visiting her daughter. It was nice to get a little tap on the back from him after each session, especially as there weren't many Kiwis in that section of the stand.

I got agonisingly close to a test triple century but, if I'd been offered 290 beforehand, I'd have taken it in a heartbeat. It's the same with getting a 70 or 80: I would have loved a century, but I'll take it. To be honest, 300 wasn't even in my mind when I got to the ground. Hogan was proud of me but only semi-joking when he complained that I'd snaffled the only record he took pride in: the highest score by a Kiwi against Australia — 188 in that famous win at the Gabba in 1985.

How does it rank? Certainly, in my top five. I'd put the 142 against Sri Lanka in 2012 at the top of the list, given the circumstances. I don't think I've batted any better than when I made my first overseas test hundred — 154 not out — in Manchester in 2008. One of the hardest innings, and therefore a big favourite, was 104 off 133 balls against Pakistan in Dubai in 2014. To give it context, the next highest score in both second innings was 45. We were in the mire and the wicket was turning square; in one session I took us out of danger and gave us a chance of winning. The match was drawn but it was a momentum shift: we'd been well beaten in the first test and went on to square the series in the third. And I'd probably go for the 80 at Edgbaston in 2021, again because of the circumstances.

KFC was a sponsor of Australian cricket. After that innings, Ian Smith, who was commentating for Channel 9 and has always been concerned that I don't get enough to eat, said something along the lines of, "Ross must be salivating at the thought of tucking into some KFC." He texted to say he was working on getting me some KFC vouchers.

We went on to Adelaide for the first pink-ball test. In an interview with Ian Healy before the start of play on day three, I said that Aussie wicketkeeper Phil Neville had batted really well. Smithy and Mark "Tubby" Taylor, who were down on the ground doing their preview segment, were going, "Who? Phil Neville played fullback for Manchester United. It's Peter Nevill, you idiot." I was blissfully unaware of this gaffe, not that it would have concerned me one little bit after "Heals" handed me a $290 KFC voucher. But then someone from Cricket Australia told me it was only redeemable in Australia and had to be used in one go. We lost the test that day and flew home the next morning, me with a useless voucher in my kit.

My sister Rebecca, who lives on the Gold Coast, came home for Christmas. Seeing I wasn't going to be in Australia anytime soon, I gave her the voucher with a warning it had to be used in one go, so she'd need to round up all her friends. In fact, Rebecca lives just around the corner from the KFC in Southport and the manager let her use it however she liked.

A fun fact about the Perth innings: although I batted for 567 minutes — facing 374 balls — in serious heat, I never changed gloves. It was quite a dry heat so I just left my gloves out in the sun during the breaks. I don't really sweat much, so even in India and Sri Lanka I rarely changed gloves. The fact that I'm superstitious also had something to do with it.

If I was more tolerant of damp gloves than most, it was because nothing did my head in more than a batter changing his gloves every few overs. It kills the flow of the game. The only respect in which I'm high maintenance is applying ChapStick to my lips because they dry out quickly.

I just don't sweat from my scalp so my hair never gets damp. It's like Steelo. In India, it would be stinking hot and humid; the boys would be saying, "Ross, come on, please tell me you're sweating." I'd take my cap or floppy off so they could check for themselves. My hair would be bone dry.

Colombo can be challenging, but the test in Kolkata in 2016, when I captained because Kane was sick, was horrible, definitely the hottest conditions I ever played in. You knew it was off-the-charts hot when the Indians were wilting. Cheteshwar Pujara looked almost relieved to get out, even though he was on 87. If the India batters were cooked, imagine what it was like for the poor fielding team from temperate Aotearoa.

We lost the toss in all three tests on that tour — one of those was on me — and got hammered in all three. Once again, I wasn't picking the ball up that well and struggled in both the tests and the ODI series which we lost 2–3. Back home, I went to an optometrist in Christchurch before the first test against Pakistan. He compared what they found with the results of the tests I'd had done in Brisbane a year earlier: the pterygium, a growth on the white of the eye, had grown quicker than expected and I needed an operation within six months. The optometrist said he'd actually noticed it when he saw me interviewed on TV and wondered when I was going to get it seen to.

They call pterygium "surfer's eye". It's quite common in the Pacific Islands. The growth actually starts on your nose and moves across to the eye. In layperson's terms, it pulls your eye out of shape, from round to oval. If it gets to the pupil, you're stuffed and mine was getting close. (My eyes had been getting really red and bloodshot, to the point where I'd go down to breakfast and someone would say, "Jeepers, Ross, what time did you get to bed?" They assumed from the state of my eyes that I'd had a big night when, in fact, I'd been in bed by 10 o'clock.)

That test at Hagley Oval was a low-scoring affair. I got 11 in my only bat and once again had problems picking up the ball. Hardly surprising, I suppose, given an optometrist had just told me I needed to get my eyes fixed. I wanted to get the operation over and done with, so NZC arranged it for straight after the second test in Hamilton.

Before that game I let it be known that I was having the operation and would miss the subsequent ODI series in Australia. Mike Hesson suggested I should sit out the second test: he had a "duty of care," he said, not to put me in that situation. However, I felt up to the challenge. I got a quick-fire 37 in the first innings and 102 not out in the second; 92 of my 139 runs came in boundaries. We took nine wickets in the last session of the game to take the series 2–0.

Afterwards, Hess took me aside and said the eye obviously wasn't too bad, why not postpone the operation until after the series in Australia? He hadn't wanted me to play in Hamilton but changed his tune when I got a century. I was set on having it done asap for my own peace of mind, so we had a bit of a to and fro, him pushing me to go to Australia, me pushing back on that idea. We'd had a frosty relationship since the captaincy ambush and this was another episode in that long-running series.

I stayed at home and had the operation. They scraped the pterygium away, cut a bit from underneath my eyelid and glued it over the scraped area to prevent regrowth. It wasn't that painful but direct sunlight was hard to handle and the stitches scratching the eyelid was like having a grain of sand in your eye.

Just before Christmas I got blindsided again: as Mackenzie and I were about to go into the movie *Moana*, selector Gavin Larsen rang to tell me I'd been dropped from the Twenty20 team. It came as a bit of a shock considering we hadn't played any T20 games since the World Cup in India early in the year. When I'd had my player review with Hess, he'd said I was an important member of the team in all three formats. I couldn't help but wonder if my refusal to go to Australia had irked him.

One of the odd things about being dropped is that you start hearing from other players wanting to share their negative experiences with that coach. It happened then and it happened in relation to Steady in 2020. You feel a bit better, knowing you're not the only one and some of the others have been treated worse than you. Overall, though, it just made me more frustrated.

Gav's justification was that I hadn't had a great World Cup. Which was true, but I certainly wasn't the only one. The wickets were poor, so you really wanted to bat in the top three. We got 126/7 against India and won comfortably. Their all-star batting line-up — Rohit Sharma, Shikhar Dhawan, Virat Kohli, Suresh Raina, Yuvraj Singh, MS Dhoni, Hardik Pandya and Ravi Jadeja — could only muster 79. Mitchell Santner took 4/11 and between them our spinners — Mitch, Nathan McCullum and Ish — took 9/44. The first time I played a white-ball game under lights in India post the operation, I got 95 and played spin better than I'd ever played it.

Bangladesh toured, playing three ODIs, three T20s and two tests, in that order. I'd been hitting balls and was ready to play the ODIs, but Hess basically said, no, take your time, it's just Bangladesh. They picked Neil Broom, who'd actually opted out of an NZC contract to take up a multi-year deal to play county cricket — his father was born in England — before reversing his decision.

When I started hitting balls two-and-a-half weeks after the operation it was the first time I'd seen the ball swing from the thrower's hand. Not wanted by the Black Caps, I made my comeback with Central Districts in the Super Smash at Pukekura Park, the old happy hunting ground. I made a couple of 80s, hitting 14 sixes in the process. I don't know if I was seeing the ball better, but I was certainly wanting to prove a point.

A lot was made of my post-operation form, but I'm not sure it was simply a case of having better eyesight. I think I derived confidence from, firstly, realising that I'd had a problem, secondly, being able to re-evaluate past performances in the context of that problem and, thirdly, knowing the problem was now fixed.

The surgeon said there was very little data on elite sportspeople having a pterygium fixed. I'd had to have it done on health grounds, but he couldn't say what effect it would have on performance. It seems only common sense that it would help, since picking up the ball and the length is a crucial part of batting: the earlier you do so, the better. What batters who've been around for a while fear most is their eyesight deteriorating. Once that starts, it's hard to remedy.

The 181 not out against England in Dunedin in 2018 was one of my best ODI innings. We were 2–1 down in the series. I made a hundred in the first game in Hamilton, which we won, but got run out in the second game at the Mount, which we lost. I took off for a run, David Willey pulled off a smart bit of fielding, Gup sent me back and I did my quad trying to regain my ground.

I missed the third game in Wellington. My quad was still a bit tight, but game four was a must-win. I walked out at 2/2, chasing 335. It should have been a lot more. Jonny Bairstow and Joe Root put on 190 for the second wicket; they were on 267 when Bairstow got out in the 37th over. None of the next five batters got more than five. Ish did the damage, dismissing Jos Buttler, Ben Stokes and Moeen Ali. They probably should have got 380, but they hit the accelerator too soon, both as individuals and a batting group.

Kane and I worked hard to get us back into the game and reduce the run rate to a manageable number. Tom and I put on 187, which set the platform, and Colin de Grandhomme produced a typically swashbuckling cameo. Just after I got to 100, I reinjured my quad. Same thing: stretching to avoid being run out. At least this time I got home.

With runners having gone by the board, I hobbled a few singles but otherwise I was swinging for the fences. I was effectively batting on one leg, so I had to improvise: I could still play my natural slog, but almost had to play it off the back foot, which had the effect of making me hold my shape and clear the hip better. It was a prime example of "Beware the injured batsman" syndrome because I'm not sure I would have done it if I'd been fully fit.

Chapter 10.
Mind Game

Talent is what you see from the outside: what this guy can do with the ball, what that guy can do with the bat. But there aren't many sports in which the mental component looms as large as it does in cricket, and it's hard to tell from the outside where a player is at mentally. This batter mightn't be as talented as that batter, but he could be mentally stronger; he might have unshakeable self-belief and a ravenous appetite for runs.

As a kid, I was a big fan of Mark Waugh. Mark was a sublime talent, but his twin brother Steve had a significantly better test record, averaging 51 with 32 centuries compared to his brother's 41.8 with 20 centuries. (Mark had the better ODI record.) I don't believe for one minute that Mark was mentally weak; it just seemed to me that he didn't have Steve's hunger. Steve made 150 or more against all the other test-playing nations; Mark reached 150 just once in 128 tests. Steve seemed to operate on the old principle that, when you get to 100, you should take fresh guard and start again. What's more, he really liked being not out, which was something I strived to do. When Mark got to 100, it was almost as if he'd had enough.

Not that long ago, using a sport psychologist/mental skills coach was seen by the public and many players as a sign of weakness rather than a sensible response to the reality that cricket is very much a mental game. Perceptions are changing: it's becoming standard in elite sport — the All Blacks have been using Gilbert Enoka for years — and more widely accepted as a legitimate and effective part of self-improvement. Sports psychologists have been a massive help to me and a big influence on my career. I started with Gary Hermansson, but also worked with Gilbert and Pete Sanford, the New Zealand Cricket (NZC) mental skills coach. Eventually, I came full circle back to Gary.

You're on the road, growing up in the public eye, dealing with failure, form fluctuations and media criticism. However hard you try to avoid seeing or hearing what the media are saying, it gets back to you one way or another. And, when that happens, you have to understand that your family and friends have good intentions. Furthermore, while they revel in your success, the media and public criticism hits them hard. As a professional sportsperson, you have the tools to deal with criticism and the opportunity to go out there and set the narrative. Family and friends don't have those tools or that opportunity.

Athletes face an array of challenges over the course of their careers — including teammates and coaches doing their heads in — and can become prone to jumping at shadows. A sports psychologist can help you get on top of an issue before it becomes a significant or even overwhelming distraction.

A lot of it is just an offload; as Mike Sandle often says, "A problem shared is a problem halved." A good psychologist knows you well enough to recognise what you need from them at a given time. That could be just hearing you out or reassuring you that it's not just you, everybody goes through this in some shape or form. It could be pumping your tyres or telling you to pull your head in. I think most of the Black Caps now use sports psychologists, but in different ways: some use them a lot, some use them sporadically. Some only use them when they're in trouble and it's too late. I quickly came to the view that it was essential to have regular contact, in good times and bad.

Gary and I go back a long way. I'm not sure why Central Districts coach Graeme Barlow put me onto Gary Hermansson, but I did suffer from second-season syndrome in 2003/04 and wasn't living up to my own high expectations. Gary was ideal: he'd worked with Commonwealth and Olympic Games athletes and lived in Palmerston North.

Gary Hermansson: Ross came around to my place and started to unpackage what was going on for him. It was largely about attending to the task and being divided between trying to control what he needed to do for the team and also for his own aspirations.

He was very open to being reflective about what was happening, open to thinking about what I was putting forward to him — essentially that he was focusing on things that were uncontrollable. We tried to identify some things that could trigger his brain in the direction of being in the moment. He really connected with the concept of trust: trust your skills, you've done a lot of work. Whether that was the cause or not — I think it probably was, given that it's been an ongoing process for him — he began to enjoy things a bit more and get some runs on the board.

We related well and things sort of fell into place. Graeme Barlow got Gary involved with the CD team — he's been with them ever since — which meant we connected regularly throughout that season and over the winter months as well. In 2005, Gary gave up his position at Massey University to set up in private practice and then took over from Gilbert as the Black Caps' in-house psychologist. Gary likes to say he got the Black Caps job after working wonders on me. Having him in the camp certainly made it a lot easier for me to adjust to being a Black Cap and feel settled in the environment.

What could possibly go wrong? From left to right, Mike Hesson, New Zealand Cricket CEO David White and Director of Cricket John Buchanan at the press conference at which Hess was unveiled as the new Black Caps coach.

PHOTOSPORT

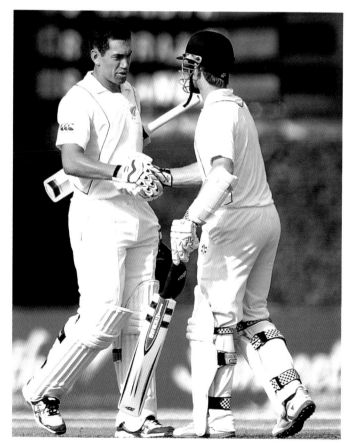

Kane Williamson congratulates me on reaching a century in my last test as Black Caps captain — against Sri Lanka in Colombo in 2012. I always enjoyed batting with Kane, who also got a century in that innings.

GETTY

I was very close to Grandpa Jack and Grandma Sylvia. They had a huge influence on me when I was growing up and I was shattered when Grandma Sylvia passed away during the 2012 Sri Lanka tour.

"Remember Ross: forgive but don't forget." It was always good to reconnect with sport psychologist Gary "Blue" Hermansson, but especially so when I returned to cricket with Central Districts in early 2013 after the captaincy drama and missing the Black Caps tour of South Africa.

Hogan with "the two sons he never had" — Guppy and me — in the MCG changing room after the 2015 World Cup final.

"That's for you, Grandma Sylvia": reaching 200 against Australia in Perth in 2015.

Acknowledging the ovation after being dismissed for 290, the highest-ever score in Australia by a visiting player.

Former Aussie wicketkeeper turned commentator Ian Healy has just presented me with a $290 KFC voucher, but we're laughing because it has just been pointed out that, in my interview, I mixed up Manchester United defender Phil Neville and Aussie wicketkeeper Peter Nevill.

At the 2015/16 Cricket Awards: left to right Guppy, his wife Laura McGoldrick, Leanne, me, my wife Victoria and Black Cap Corey Anderson.

Chin music: avoiding a bouncer from the Windies' Shannon Gabriel at the Basin in 2017.   GETTY

Beware the wounded batsman. My other favourite ODI innings: 181 not out on one leg against England at the University Oval, Dunedin in 2018.

"It's all in the way you tell them, Steady." With Black Caps coach Gary Stead during the second test against Bangladesh at the Basin in 2019.

Victoria and me at the 2018/19 Cricket Awards at Sky City Casino.

Gup and me with former Black Cap turned commentary box doyen Ian Smith during the 2019 World Cup. I've known Smithy since my school days and he has always been a good sounding board and a source of encouragement.

I wouldn't have had the career I've had without Leanne's nurturing, guidance and unwavering support.

Consoling the West Indies' Carlos Braithwaite whose brilliant innings all but took our 2019 World Cup pool game away from us.

PHOTOSPORT

The moment I knew we were in the final of the 2019 World Cup: the third umpire confirms that India's master finisher, MS Dhoni, was run out by Guppy's direct hit.

PHOTOSPORT

With Jonty and Mackenzie during my 100th test — against India at the Basin in 2020. I thereby became the first player to play 100 games for their country in all three formats. Our other daughter, Adelaide, decided to stay with Mum.

PHOTOSPORT

Professional sport can be a lonely occupation. Down on confidence and beset by self-doubt, I wait to bat against England at Edgbaston, Birmingham in 2021. I had to dig very deep that day, hence I regard the 80 I got as one of my best innings.

PHOTOSPORT

"We're bloody world champions and no-one can take that away." Relief and redemption at the Rose Bowl after Kane and I have got us over the line in the World Test Championship final against India at The Rose Bowl, Southampton, 2021.

GETTY

Winners are grinners, especially when there's plenty of sponsor's product at hand. With the ICC World Test Championship mace.
KANE WILLIAMSON

My final test match — against Bangladesh at Hagley Oval in Christchurch in January 2022. The guard of honour was a lovely gesture from the Bangladesh boys.
PHOTOSPORT

Fairy tale finish: I bow out of test cricket with a bowling average of 16 and everyone seems pretty pleased about it.

With Mum and Dad and Victoria and the kids — Adelaide, Jonty and Mackenzie — after my final test.

Gup helps me keep a lid on my emotions before my last-ever game for New Zealand: an ODI against the Netherlands at Seddon Park.   GETTY

Another lovely gesture: the Netherlands team form a guard of honour.   GETTY

My very last act in international cricket: taking an absolute screamer to end the Netherlands innings.   GETTY

I'll miss international cricket and being in the Black Caps environment but all good things must come to an end. I look forward to more of this: with Victoria and the kids at Mount Maunganui, Christmas Day 2020.

TAYLOR COLLECTION

Gary Hermansson: On my first tour, which was to South Africa, we watched the movie Old School on a bus trip. Some of the boys decided to name me after the character of Blue, the oldest member of the fraternity, who dies of a heart attack in compromising circumstances. Since then, I've been called "Blue" — in the cricket environment only — which I tolerate but don't feel altogether comfortable with.

The CD contingent — Ross, Jacob Oram, Jamie How, Michael Mason — were referred to as "Blue's boys". They were very comfortable with my presence and involvement. The others were a little bit wary. This was their way of both accepting me into the space, but also being a little bit divisive.

When I left in 2008, Ross and I continued our contact. He was less and less in the CD environment but would check in occasionally for a little warrant of fitness. It was all the elements around performance, particularly how to manage your head under the pressure to perform. As the expectations got greater for him, that tension became more consistent, so we just tweaked it as we went along.

I pushed to have a psychologist on tour. Mike Hesson was always against it: I think because he felt he could perform that role if the need arose. My view was that sometimes things needed to be talked about straightaway. If it takes two or three days to connect because of time zones and the New Zealand-based psychologist's other commitments, the problem will get worse and the test match might be over. There were times I was just lucky that Gary happened to be still awake.

The sport psychology worked in tandem with Martin Crowe's mentorship. Hogan was the cricket mentor while the psychologists were about equipping myself mentally for both cricket and life in general.

I knew I was good at white-ball cricket, but I wanted to get better at test cricket. Who better to talk to than New Zealand's best test batter? I didn't really know much about Hogan, apart from his exploits at the 1992 World Cup, but I knew how highly rated he was. My manager, Leanne McGoldrick, who'd known Hogan for a long time, initiated the contact. He used to tell people that I cold-called him, but Leanne told me to ring after she'd broached the subject with him. (She didn't have the heart to tell me his instant reaction was that he'd seen me play and I was "nothing but a dirty slogger".)

I took a bottle of Martinborough pinot noir to our first meeting; he supplied one from Central Otago. We talked a lot about wine before we got on to cricket. He thought Nathan Astle and Stephen Fleming were very good players but felt they would have been more productive if they'd been more goal-oriented. He'd jotted down some goals for me: make 17 test hundreds and the most ODI hundreds; be the highest run-scorer in test and ODI cricket; be a permanent fixture in the top 10 of the world rankings. I'd never contemplated any of it.

We didn't know how things would pan out, but it wasn't in my nature to dismiss his various theories, which some Black Caps did. That probably had more to do with the ideas man than the ideas. When I became a Black Cap, I realised a lot of the senior players rather resented that great team of the 1980s, particularly the individuals who were still involved in the game in some capacity. In Hogan's case, some of them may have taken exception to his typically forthright TV commentaries. I had no baggage in that regard.

The next day we went to the gym. Hogan wore fluorescent tights and a bandana. I thought he was having a laugh. He got me jumping off a weights bench with my eyes closed. As I landed, he'd tell me which way to go: push off your back foot to go forward, off your front foot to go back. Of all the coaches and advisors I've had, only Hogan and Mark O'Neill, a former Sheffield Shield player and the Black Caps batting coach when I first made the team, talked about batting on your toes.

Anyone watching us that day must have thought, 'What are these guys on?' It didn't worry me. The only time I was embarrassed by Hogan was when he took me to training in a convertible Jaguar. Driving through Hamilton with the top down, I was thinking, 'Jeepers, Hogan, I have to live here.'

Hogan was different. He could be hard on me, but I knew he was coming from a good place and I loved his honesty. NZC high-performance director Roger Mortimer once heard Hogan blast me in brutally direct language and said afterwards, "Ross, I've got to commend you because I don't know many athletes who could have taken what you just copped."

We did have fun — it was Hogan who really got me started collecting wine — but early on I needed that harsh appraisal. And maybe it was his way of reinforcing that he was the teacher and I was the student. He also knew when I needed to be picked up and set back on my feet. The hard talk stopped once I'd worked out my game and he could see where I was going; after that he found different ways of pushing my buttons. He'd had an up and down relationship with NZC and I think it was his way of giving something back to the game in this country without having to deal with them.

Once you have a technique, batting at the top level becomes largely mental, and Hogan was massive on the mental side: dealing with the other pressures such as the media, getting through dips in form, scoring runs and then having to go out and do it again, not getting carried away because you made a hundred. In cricket, no two days are exactly the same. How do you get yourself into that space where you can perform regardless of how you slept, how the game's going, how the team's going, how your family and friends are getting on and the distractions around that? Everyone has stuff, good and bad, going on in their lives. At the end of the day, though, you've got a job to do: make runs. No matter what's going on in the changing room or what's happening in your life, you've got to go out there and find a way to get the job done.

> **Mark Greatbatch:** Knowing Martin, he was certainly blunt enough to call Ross "a dirty slogger". But a good dirty slogger who actually worked hard on the technical side of things. He was predominantly a leg-side player and changing that took a lot of work. The mental side was probably an area that he wasn't as strong in. He had to learn to respect bowlers who could bowl in good areas for longer periods of time and how to survive through technique and patience. Martin definitely helped him to improve that mental side and compete at the highest level.
>
> Ross worked the test game out. He learnt to leave well. You've got to be patient; you've got to let them come to you. If you leave well, after a while they bowl a bit straighter and he always had that strength of hitting the ball leg-side. Through the second half of his career, he scored a lot of his runs straight and leg-side, but it was based on good thinking, good strategy.

When I scored my first overseas test century in Manchester in 2008, the top six in our batting order were Jamie How, Aaron Redmond, James Marshall, mc, Brendon McCullum and Daniel Flynn — not the most experienced batting line-up. Being a young guy in a young team, you can get fast-tracked, but you can also sink without trace. I had to learn for myself in those early years, so being able to draw on Hogan's extensive experience of English conditions — he played county cricket for Somerset for several years — helped enormously.

He was my sounding board outside the group, someone I trusted and knew always had my best interests at heart. The likes of Hess and Gary Stead are managers rather than coaches. There's a batting coach but he has to look after 14 other players; if there are overlapping squads for the different formats, with players rotating in and out, he might have to look after more than 20. A mentor knows you well enough to know how to push your buttons and what to say and not say in a particular situation. Unless the batting coach knows you, or is prepared to make the effort to get to know you — not easy when they're dealing with a large squad — they're just another member of the support staff.

Martin was a stable, constant mentor who could look at me in isolation and give me an honest opinion, one that wasn't influenced or compromised by what was going on with the team, good or bad. And while he was big on goals, he was equally insistent that records are made to be broken — you set the bar high for the next guy to come and knock you off: "The more people break your records, Ross, the better cricket here in New Zealand is going to get."

I always struggled with being not out overnight. You spend that night thinking about it to the point of mental overload, so you go out to bat the next morning feeling like you've already batted for three or four hours. Hogan tried two approaches. There were little reminders to watch the ball and play straight — basic stuff that you sometimes forget in the heat of battle — and a big-picture solution: "Drink more red wine." Whatever, I'd be out within half an hour. Maybe it was something in my morning routine.

Ian Smith: Ross's relationship with Martin was a lot stronger than I realised — they worked together very closely. Martin's nickname for him was "Tuisi" — as in too easy; he reckoned batting came too easy for Ross because of his natural ability to hit the ball. One of the last things Martin said to me was along the lines of "Make sure Ross gives that T20 stuff away — it's not doing his game any good. If he wants to be the best test and ODI player he can be, he should give that shit away." He used to tell Ross, "You'll always be in the all-time New Zealand team, but I'm sorry, son, you're going to have to bat at five." Martin Crowe was always going to bat at four.

I visited Hogan in Kohimarama when he was really battling with his illness. One of Victoria's uncles had died of bowel cancer several years earlier and, for some reason, I still had his beanie in the car. Hogan came out to meet me, complaining about the cold. I gave him Victoria's uncle's beanie: "This is a cool beanie, Ross," he said. "I'm not giving it back." I was pleased he liked it, but it was a sad thought that the beanie was passing from one cancer sufferer with no hair because of chemotherapy to another.

He was pretty fragile, but his wife Lorraine said it was fine to go for a walk. I'd been tossing up whether I should ask if he'd write the foreword for this book; in the end I did. He said he was going to write something whether I asked for it or not.

He sent me a message a couple of months before he passed away, the gist of which was that there was nothing more he could teach me. I'd learnt everything I needed to know: now it was a matter of going out there and executing. I hope I did him proud.

When I was 18 or 19, a guy in Palmerston North got me a gig with a club in England. He was getting into sports management and wanted to sign me up. About that time, the Indian equipment company BDM offered me what seemed like a lot of money to come on board — my arrangement with Gunn & Moore was gear-only at that stage. Ian Smith was always a good person to talk to about anything cricket-related, so I sought his advice. He suggested I talk to this woman who specialised in managing cricketers: Leanne McGoldrick.

Leanne was a huge influence on my career. She welcomed me almost as a son and often says, "You're like family, Ross." Apart from Victoria, she probably knows me better than anyone. She introduced me to Hogan and fostered that relationship, and she was a big factor in me doing well financially out of the game. But we always thought about career rather than money. If we'd been all about money, I would have quit test cricket after the captaincy drama and just played on the Twenty20 circuit.

Leanne knows cricket and has a lot of experience of managing other players. I was able to draw on that reservoir of knowledge and experience. She saw something in me that I probably didn't see myself. She had a vision for me and helped me make the vision a reality by pushing me to be the best player that I could be.

I wouldn't have had the career I had without Leanne's nurturing, guidance and unwavering support. I should have made more of an effort to let her know how grateful I was and am. It's like your parents: you thank them, but you don't thank them enough.

"Coach" is a problematic term because it can refer to a variety of roles — from hands-off manager to hands-on specialist — and different approaches. The purest coaches are those at age-group level who are all things to all kids — captain, technical coach, mentor, manager and sometimes surrogate parent.

Hess and Steady operated like football managers: they organised and oversaw trainings and devised a game plan in conjunction with the bowling and batting coaches and the captain. John Wright was actually a coach. I first came across Wrighty before he became Black Caps coach: he was working for NZC in a sort of talent ID and development role. He reckoned my bottom hand was too dominant, so he tied three fingers on my right hand together to force me to adopt a pinch grip, using just the thumb and forefinger. His mantra was "soft forearms". He'd say, "You're a good player, Ross, but remember: soft forearms." Wrighty was also probably the closest thing to a motivator coach that I played under; he worked for me in that capacity.

Under Hess, there was no structure to training. The top-order guys could bat for three hours if they wanted, not that I ever did because I would've been cooked. But some guys would bat for ages and the all-rounders and lower order would get hacked off because they weren't getting much time. Under Steady, training still went on for hours, but it was more structured. If you wanted to hit hundreds of balls, you had to wait till the end.

Mark O'Neill, son of Aussie great Norm, was probably the best batting coach I've come across, although you're a sponge when you're young; you're learning your game so you're very open to advice and direction. As a youngster, you're receptive to new ideas and prepared to try things; older players need a lot of convincing before they'll tinker with aspects of their game that have stood the test of time. Luke Ronchi, the current Black Caps batting coach, would give me ideas and try to push me. In the IPL, you tended to learn off your teammates rather than the batting coach: the Indian guys would pick the overseas players' brains about playing fast bowling while we wanted to learn how to play spin better.

I had Gary Kirsten at Delhi. Having won the 2011 World Cup with India, his standing over there was sky-high, which probably made things easier for him, but he just looked at things a bit differently. He was here with South Africa in 2012. JP Duminy didn't play in the first two tests. During the second test in Hamilton, Gary told JP to take some time out, get away from it all, so he went to Queenstown. When Jacques Kallis got injured, JP came into the team and made a hundred in the third test. Was that because Gary gave him some time out? You can't state that with any certainty, but what you can say is that the coach's handling of the individual had a good outcome. The Aussie, Stuart Law, was another coach I enjoyed, a positive influence in the Kirsten mould.

Ray Jennings, at Bangalore, was also South African but very different to Gary — more hard-nosed. I probably struck him at the right stage of my career; the older me mightn't have responded to that approach. He was pretty brusque at first but came around to the extent that, for quite a number of years, he never forgot my birthday.

At Nottingham, I had Peter Moores, a well-rounded coach and very popular with the players. It was a surprise to me that he wasn't more successful in his two stints with England. Peter had a famous falling-out with Kevin Pietersen: when the dust cleared, Peter was no longer coach and KP was no longer captain. The cricket world is a small one. When I was dumped as captain, KP rang to sympathise: he'd been through something similar. Seven years later I was playing for Nottingham, having a beer at Peter Moores' house and guys were asking him what happened with KP. Peter didn't bag KP once: he just said they'd had a few disagreements but Kevin was one of the hardest trainers he'd ever coached.

My message to young cricketers is that self-doubt, fear of failure and performance anxiety are natural, if not inevitable. When you bat for a living, a run of bad scores is obviously a cause for concern, but what's critical is how you bounce back. The key is acquiring the resilience and strength of mind to trust your game, to believe that you're still good enough, to have the confidence to know you can go out there and perform. Being in good form is great, but the most rewarding innings are the fighting 50s or 60s when you're coming off two hours' sleep and there's a lot going on in your life and in your head.

When I first came on the scene, guys who'd been around for a while commented on my confidence when I came out to bat. I was walking out the same way I always had. Playing against men at a young age is a bit make or break: it can set you back, but I saw it as a positive. I felt they'd sense if you were scared, so my mindset was around giving the opposite impression: don't go out there with a timid demeanour and downcast eyes; don't flinch, no matter how big and ugly the opposition fast bowlers are. When you're 14, someone bowling 130 kph is really quick, but I wasn't going to show fear.

I feel I was a resilient cricketer, but how much of that was ingrained and how much was learned I'm not sure. What I do know is that you need to be resilient to play this game.

Chapter 11.
Yellow Brick Road

The Indian Premier League (IPL) kicked off in 2008. Three Kiwis — Brendon McCullum, Jake Oram and Dan Vettori — went for big money in the first auction. Their teammates were proud of them and thrilled for them. Martin Crowe, who was head coach of Royal Challengers Bangalore (RCB), suggested I should put my name forward in the second auction. I got picked up for US$100,000 by, coincidentally, Bangalore. I'd love to say I got there off my own bat, so to speak, but Hogan wanted a Kiwi in the squad and I was probably the best of the bunch in the second auction.

I was excited to put it mildly. When Scotty Styris was injured during the 2007 Champions Trophy in India, I'd been flown up as a replacement but, by the time I got there, his hamstring had come good. Because of the rules around squad numbers, I couldn't be part of the team so they made me assistant manager. I was 22. I actually fielded in the game against Pakistan in Mohali and ran out Umar Gul with a direct hit which probably makes me the only assistant manager to have run someone out in an ODI. It was good to go to the IPL having had that exposure to India and with some idea of what to expect in terms of the conditions, the noise and the sheer volume of people, most of whom seemed to be cricket fanatics.

My modest price-tag and low profile relative to Rahul Dravid,

Anil Kumble, Jacques Kallis, Shivnarine Chanderpaul, Dale Steyn and Mark Boucher meant that I was hardly the focus of great expectations. Adding to the novelty, I had a close personal relationship with the coach. It was interesting to observe Hogan through the filter of the player–coach dynamic.

RCB was owned by Vijay Mallya whose father had founded United Breweries and built it into an international conglomerate that included the ill-fated Kingfisher Airlines. Mallya Jnr was also a co-owner of the Force India Formula One team, a Member of Parliament, and known as "the King of Good Times" for his extravagant lifestyle. He later became embroiled in financial controversies and, in 2016, relocated to the United Kingdom. He's one of the subjects of the Netflix documentary series *Bad Boy Billionaires: India*.

I got on well with Mallya. He was very good to me, inviting me to be his guest at the Formula One Grand Prix in Abu Dhabi. (His other guest was the famous Bollywood actress, Deepika Padukone.) I used to call him "Boss". Funnily enough, the Indians used to call me "Ross the Boss". Or "Rose". If there's one thing worse than being called Rose, it's being mixed up with Scott Styris. When we were warming up before a game in Galle, a spectator kept calling out to me, "Styris, Styris, give me your autograph." Scotty wasn't even on that tour.

Rahul Dravid was one of my favourite captains, the others being Anil Kumble and Shane Warne. What I really admired about Anil and Rahul was that, despite being superstars of the game and massive figures in India, they were very humble, down-to-earth guys who treated everyone equally. That mightn't sound like a huge deal but, believe me, it is, especially when you see how Indians elevate their top cricketers. It wouldn't be hard to lose your way.

The RCB roster included a teenage Virat Kohli who'd led India to the Under-19 World Cup earlier that year. When Virat was batting at an early training session, the Australian all-rounder Cameron White said to me, "Mate, watch this kid, he's going to be a gun." I thought, 'Well, he looks pretty good.' Cameron knew what he was talking about. Virat and I were sponges, peppering the international players with questions.

The very first IPL game was RCB against the Kolkata Knight Riders (KKR) — Brendon's team — in Bangalore. A troupe of Washington Redskins (now Washington Commanders) cheerleaders were flown in and there were parties and lots of razzamatazz: all in all, a very long way from Masterton. I didn't make the cut, which wasn't a bad thing as it turned out.

Just before the game got under way, Hogan came over to me. "Bloody hell, Brendon's fizzing," he said. "He's on the Red Bull. He'll either get a duck or 80." You wish. Brendon went nuts, making 158 not out off 73 balls with 13 sixes and 10 fours. RCB managed to get just over half his tally: all out for 82 in 15 overs, with a top score of 18 not out.

That innings of Brendon's launched the IPL. It gave the tournament instant credibility by overdelivering on the promise and justifying all the hype. It worked for me as well: if he hadn't smashed it and we hadn't been absolutely pumped, I might not have played a game that season. But desperate times required desperate measures and I was immediately promoted to the starting line-up.

My debut was against the Mumbai Indians, minus Sachin Tendulkar, at Wankhede Stadium. As Shaun Pollock was running in to bowl me my first ball, I was thinking how often I'd watched him on TV. I got bat on it and took off like a startled rabbit, ecstatic that I hadn't got a duck. On the way to 23 off 12 balls, I hit my first IPL six: a slog-sweep off Harbhajan Singh that landed on the grandstand roof. Virat also got 23 and Boucher steered us home with two balls to spare.

I held my place for the next three games, then joined the Black Caps' tour of England. I did reasonably well, particularly in terms of strike rate. Basically, I just tried to whack everything to the leg-side; anything that went through the off side wasn't meant to. The franchise had got some stick for signing a bunch of orthodox batters — Dravid, Kallis, Wasim Jaffer, the Indian opener — plus Shiv Chanderpaul who, while hardly orthodox, was seen, somewhat unfairly, as essentially a red-ball player. I guess I brought a different dimension.

Despite my abbreviated season I hit the most sixes by an RCB player, including a 119-metre effort off Jake Oram against the Chennai Super Kings (CSK), which I think still qualifies as one of the top six IPL sixes. I'm not convinced it actually went 119 metres, but I certainly smoked it. Technically speaking, Bangalore isn't at altitude, but it is 920 metres above sea level so the air is a bit thinner, which probably helped.

No one really knew what to expect of the IPL, but it took off from Brendon's launchpad and it has been onwards and upwards ever since. I enjoyed every moment: the hype and hoopla, playing in front of huge crowds, rubbing shoulders with greats of the game. Facing Shane Warne, who skippered the Rajasthan Royals, the inaugural winners, was a highlight. Even though Victoria and I weren't there for long, India was a mind-blowing experience. It helped that we both enjoy Indian food.

Then my country called. These days Black Caps get to play the whole tournament. Those of us who played in the early years pushed for it, but the fact that New Zealand Cricket now gets paid for providing players to the IPL was a game-changer.

Over the years there have been a few articles and on-air comments on the theme of Taylor needing a rocket because I supposedly didn't care deeply enough about playing for New Zealand. In 2013, I again had to leave the IPL to play two warm-up games — although Brendon and I didn't actually play in the first — and two test matches in England. That meant giving up US$550,000 to earn $15,000. I had no qualms about doing so, but it made the claims that I wasn't committed to playing for my country hard to take. But in those days the Black Caps were losing games and perceived to be overpaid, so we were always in the media's sights. How things have changed: from media punching bags to media favourites.

It was my first tour of England and I was part of a batting line-up with very little experience of English conditions. I played a warm-up game and then we were into the first test at Lord's, something I'd dreamt of since I was a kid.

I got a good-luck text from Stephen Fleming who was embarking on his post-playing career. Brendon and I were with Leanne, but he was pretty tight with Flem and it seemed like just a matter of time before he switched. Flem said he'd be coaching CSK the following year and wanted to recruit me for US$550,000.

I don't know what factors were behind the terms in which Flem framed the offer, but they made me very uneasy. And, given his status as an outstanding Black Caps player and captain, I was taken aback that he'd spring something like that on a young player about to play the biggest game of his career to that point. I looked up to Flem, but that episode troubled me.

Meanwhile, Leanne was talking to Hogan, who was on his way out of RCB, whether of his own volition or not. He said I should ask RCB for US$700,000, adding that, if and when I signed for that amount, I could move to Kohi. I was thinking, 'Why the hell would I want to live in Pukekohe?' The boy from the Bush had never heard of Kohimarama. I probably should have taken his advice: if I'd bought a house in Kohimarama back then, it would be worth a lot more now. I ended up signing with RCB on a two-year deal at US$700,000 pa. It was heady stuff: I'd gone from being a virtual unknown and on more or less the minimum IPL wage for an overseas player to having a profile and a big salary.

IPL 2009 was played in South Africa because of the Indian elections. Jesse Ryder was at RCB that year, the final step in our joint progression from intermediate school teams in Masterton to the world stage. RCB hadn't had a good 2008 tournament so there'd been a shake-up: a new coach in Ray Jennings, an intense ex-wicketkeeper who'd had a short stint in charge of South Africa, and a new captain in Kevin Pietersen. I got on well with KP, who was a big personality and pretty direct but didn't really get a feel for his captaincy because I didn't play many games early on. When he went back to England on test duty, Kumble became captain and a batting spot opened up.

Anil was blessed with a very good cricket brain, but captaining an IPL team can be tricky because of all the different dynamics at play. Anil was big enough and wise enough to consult and seek assistance and interacted wonderfully with both the Indian and overseas players.

The tournament kicked off with a doubleheader in Cape Town: Chennai vs Mumbai and Bangalore vs defending champs, Rajasthan. Snow Patrol performed at the opening ceremony. It was mid-April, quite cold and I felt under some pressure. When you're being paid big bucks, your boss, teammates and fans expect big things. Furthermore, Ray Jennings wasn't saying much to me, so I wasn't sure he wanted me in the team. He'd signed Jesse but had inherited me.

I remember telling Leanne, who was over there, that the coach wouldn't even say hello to me at breakfast. And about the only thing he'd say to me at training was, "Taylor, your left hand is shit." He was talking about my catching ability; presumably my right hand was okay. I assumed it was his way of hardening me up and asserting his dominance. Ray had this routine in pre-game team talks: he'd single out one of the young Indian players and say, "Remember, boys. . ." The guy he'd picked on would have to complete the sentence by shouting, "Don't f--k it up." After a while the Indian lads worked out that it was just a joke and "Don't f--k it up" became our catch-cry.

Jesse opened the batting and made a two-ball duck. He lasted twice as long as I did — bowled around my legs by future Black Caps bowling coach Dimitri Mascarenhas for a golden. The boys from the Bush had got us off to a flyer — 0/2 after three balls. Fortunately, Dravid got runs and Kumble ran through the Royals, taking 5/5.

The next game, against Chennai in Port Elizabeth, was nothing to write home about either: I got off the mark this time but then put one straight up in the air to be caught and bowled by Freddie Flintoff. I bowled an over that went for 13, we got pumped and I got dropped.

I played two of the next eight games, making 31 and 16. At one point, we won three games in a row without me being involved and I was thinking that could be it. But the streak didn't last: we lost a couple and went to Pretoria to play KKR in what was a must-win game if we were to have any chance of making the finals.

My dialogue with Jennings was still minimal, verging on non-existent, so I got to the ground not knowing whether I was going to play or watch. Our bowling coach, Eric Simons, a former South African all-rounder whom I called "Kevin" because he was a dead ringer for Kevin Costner, went to find out. He returned with good and bad news: the good news was that I was playing; the bad news was that the franchise owners hadn't wanted me to play. Anil had gone into bat for me.

Brendon got 84 not out and we chased 174. I played what's certainly my most famous innings if the reaction is anything to go by; people still send me messages about it. I got 81 not out off 33 balls with seven fours and five sixes. Cow corner took a pasting. After that, I played every game with some success and we made the final against the Deccan Chargers at the Wanderers. It was a frustrating day. We restricted them to 143, mainly thanks to Kumble, but I holed out off Andrew Symonds when I was going well and we came up six runs short.

RCB's brand ambassador was the glamorous Bollywood star Katrina Kaif, who's actually British. I knew very little about Bollywood but enjoyed keeping abreast of the showbiz gossip. I did a media Q & A that included the question, "Who's your favourite actress?" Knowing which side my bread was buttered on I said, Katrina Kaif. (I'd never seen any of her movies and, in fact, still haven't.) Katrina came to Johannesburg for the semis and the final and the owners must have asked her if there was an RCB player she'd like to meet. She returned the compliment by nominating Ross Taylor.

I'd just got back to the sheds after hitting the winning runs in our semi-final against CSK. Someone who obviously hadn't spent much time in sports teams' dressing rooms thought then would be a good time to bring the two of us together. They brought Katrina in just as I'd stripped down to my bike pants. She didn't linger. When I was decent, we had a chat but, not surprisingly, the conversation didn't really flow. But, as I've since pointed out more than once, a famous Bollywood actress did ask to meet me.

I had two other memorable experiences in Johannesburg, but only one was memorable in a good way. A week or so before the final, a group of us decided to go to a Super Rugby match at Ellis Park: the Lions against the Waratahs. There was Cameron White, Eric, me and Evan Speechly, the Bangalore physio who was the Springboks' physio when they won the 1995 World Cup. He's one of the best in the business and is still with RCB.

Night was falling. We took a wrong turn on the way to Ellis Park and ended up in Hillbrow. The name didn't mean anything to me, but apparently Hillbrow made Soweto seem like Kohimarama. According to its Wikipedia entry, Hillbrow is known for population density, unemployment, abject poverty, urban decay, prostitution and crime. There was a horrible moment when Cameron and I realised the South African guys weren't concerned or anxious, they were bricking it. "Whatever you do," they told us, "do not get out of the vehicle." I was sitting there quaking, thinking, 'I'm not even that interested in this f---n game.'

The night before we'd flown in late from Durban. Rahul, Eric and I went for a bite to eat at 11.30 pm. We were there till 2.30 in the morning, just talking cricket. I asked Rahul if he thought he would average 50 if he played for New Zealand, given our green wickets. (Kane Williamson has upended the conventional wisdom that no one could do that.) Without a hint of boastfulness, he said

"Yeah." His self-belief was so strong he didn't even have to think about it.

Aside from some sessions with Hogan, the two best cricket conversations I ever had were with Kane before the World Test Championship final and that one at the Montecasino hotel. Dravid's openness and willingness to share his knowledge were inspiring.

One of the great things about cricket is there's so much to talk about and everyone approaches the game in their own way, whether their point of difference is physical, technical or mental. Eric and I kept going back to that conversation for days afterwards. He'd been around the game for a lot longer than I had, had played for and coached South Africa, but he was blown away too.

I used to pick Rahul's brain on playing spin. In New Zealand, you're always told to play *with* the spin so you look to play off-spinners to the on-side. Dravid had the opposite view: he looked to hit offies through the off-side; going leg-side was very much his second option. I found it interesting that the master technician did the exact opposite of what's drummed into Kiwi cricketers from a young age. I followed his lead and came to relish playing off-spin through cover.

In India in 2010 we drew the first test in Ahmedabad — Jesse and Kane, on debut, got hundreds — and the second in Hyderabad where Brendon got a double. We won the toss and batted in the third test in Nagpur but were rolled for 193. Dravid played our vaunted spin attack — Vettori, Williamson, Guptill and Taylor — with ridiculous ease, making 191 to set up a big win for India.

Rahul gave me his shirt after that game. I asked him if he could get me something signed by my boyhood idol Sachin Tendulkar. I was too embarrassed to ask him myself; it wasn't my finest hour on a couple of counts. I doubt many superstars would have taken kindly to that request, but he got Tendulkar to sign his playing top and give it to me. Rahul Dravid is quite simply an exceptionally nice human being.

We had another year together at RCB, then both went to Rajasthan to play under Shane Warne. Rahul is very composed and dignified, but even *he* was on the edge of his seat when Warnie opened up about his eventful life and times on a flight from Hyderabad to Mumbai. It was both riveting and hilarious. The "Sheik of Tweak" was a superb storyteller with an inexhaustible fund of sensational yarns. Sadly, few, if any, can be repeated here. Sadder by far is that we'll never get to hear another Warnie story.

The next year the IPL was back in India and I was probably at the height of my popularity. I think I can claim to have been one of the first overseas players to be embraced by the Indian public. I felt the love every time I went out to bat — the crowds would yell, "Taylor, Taylor, Taylor, we want sixer." When RCB played Otago, who'd won our domestic T20 championship, in the Champions League, the southern men were stunned by the reception I got. Ian Butler bowled the last over. I was taking him for a few when he abruptly told his skipper, Craig Cumming, that he couldn't carry on because he had a sore knee. He then proceeded to jog off the field, an exit that earned him a bit of stick from his teammates afterwards. Warren McSkimming had to finish the over, which went for 25.

In 2010, we were about to play Mumbai at the M. Chinnaswamy Stadium in Bangalore. There was a huge crowd in — as always, thousands more milling around outside the ground — and this big Madras Rubber Factory blimp, like the Goodyear Blimp they have on the US PGA tour, hovering overhead. I was having throwdowns when there was this amazingly loud boom. My first thought was that the blimp had popped. There was no reaction among the crowd so we carried on with throwdowns. Next thing, security guards ran on and shooed us off the field. In the dressing room they told us two bombs had gone off outside the ground. They didn't know how big or sophisticated the bombs were or whether there were casualties.

The Indian guys didn't seem too worried. My concern was that, if they pulled the plug on the game, there could be more bombs as we left the ground. I was young, in a foreign country and in a totally foreign situation, so I took my lead from Boucher and Kallis, the senior overseas players. Eventually the game got under way. I took a good catch to dismiss Tendulkar but didn't score many runs and we got cleaned up.

No one was killed but, sadly, there were some injuries. We heard later that they found an undetonated bomb outside the ground and the perpetrators were a local political group trying to make a name for themselves. We drove through the area on the way to the airport the next day and it was a mess — fences blown over, rubble everywhere. With the benefit of hindsight, the officials really played it down. If it happened today, I very much doubt you could persuade the players to carry on regardless.

Mum loved me playing in the Caribbean League because I'd tell her how much praying we did in the huddle. My attitude towards playing for teams in other countries was always that they had to be open to overseas players, but I had to fit in to their culture. You start by learning a few words of their language: hello, goodbye, thank you. Before long, they're feeding you swear words. I've run stuff I picked up in the IPL past Indian New Zealanders who reckon my vocabulary of profanity is more advanced than theirs. Our local grocer, who hails from the Punjab, keeps telling me, "Ross, I'm going to teach you some *good* words."

Kohli taught me a few zingers and the support staff were always helpful in that regard. Whenever you spent any time with them, you'd come away with some new material. The South African contingent taught me some Afrikaans. "Puss" is an Afrikaans pejorative — it means pretty much what you'd think. Every time I came up against Kallis, he'd bowl me a bouncer first ball. I'd duck it, he'd quietly say "Puss," smile at me and walk back to his mark. Boucher would be laughing away behind the stumps. It probably looked a bit feisty on TV, but it was actually very friendly and all from the IPL days.

Colin Munro emigrated from South Africa when he was a teenager. As the Munros were moving into their house, their next-door neighbours' cat went AWOL so the neighbours were outside calling, "Here puss, puss, puss." Colin's dad was totally perplexed: "What are these Kiwis on about? We've only been in the country one day."

I believe the IPL was a major factor in changing the New Zealand team's mindset. It stripped away much of the aura that surrounded big-name players from other countries. Within the Black Caps the chat was all about what it was like playing with those guys: "Ross, what was it like playing with Kallis and Dravid?" "Jake, what are MS Dhoni and Matthew Hayden really like?"

The big takeaway, the thing that struck us all, was that they weren't superhuman. It sounds silly but, because they were big personalities and legends of the game, we tended to put them on a pedestal. There was a time when the Black Caps were more focused on what the Aussies were doing in their warm-ups than what we were doing in ours. Playing with them took away that aura. Yes, they were world-class players; yes, they were better than us. But not by much.

Chapter 12.
Have Bat, Will Travel

The 2011 IPL auction got under way after stumps on day two of the first test against Pakistan at Seddon Park. The visitors were 235/4 in reply to our first innings of 275. In the changing room, Brendon was following the auction on his phone and providing a running commentary. Early on, Bangalore bought AB de Villiers for US$1.1 million. Then suddenly: "Ross is up to $500,000 . . . he's at $550,000."

When it got to US$650,000, I went outside to ring Victoria. The noise from the changing room was getting louder and had gone from "Woo-hoo" to more like "Whoa". I went back in. Brendon was saying, "$900,000 . . . $950,000." The boys were going off. I was trying to find out which team was doing the bidding — it was good old RCB. Then the Rajasthan Royals came in at US$1 million. I was shaking, thinking, 'Holy shit, what's happening?'

Victoria Taylor: It was mind-blowing. I went to pick him up from Seddon Park. I walked into the ground — there was no one around. Ross came out with Jesse and a few others, looked at me and went "A million bucks!" really loud. My first reaction was to shush him, as if to say "Keep it under wraps." We went home and had a few champagnes and Mum and Dad came around. I don't think we slept much that night. It was like "What the heck just happened?"

Shortly after tea on day three we were 36/0 in our second innings, 56 runs behind. The game didn't go into the fourth day: we were skittled for 110 on what was a decent batting wicket. Pakistan needed fewer than four overs to knock off the required runs and win by 10 wickets. Talking to the media, new coach John Wright called our performance "unacceptable". In the privacy of the changing room, he was more philosophical: "Remember, boys, it's just a cricket match. No one gives a f—k in China."

I spent four months in India that year: two months at the World Cup, two months with Rajasthan. Victoria, who was pregnant, was at home organising the wedding and renovating the house. As much as I like Indian food, I did get to the point of making the odd visit to McDonald's.

While it was amazing to go for a million dollars, in the long run I would've been better off if RCB had got me for US$950,000. If they had, it would have been my fourth year with them. While the IPL is pretty unsentimental, there is loyalty towards long-serving players and I probably would have had a longer IPL career as a one-franchise player. On the other hand, if I'd stayed at RCB, I wouldn't have played with greats such as Virender Sehwag, Shane Warne, Mahela Jayawardene and Yuvraj Singh.

When you fetch that sort of money, you're desperately keen to prove that you're worth it. And those who are paying you that sort of money have high expectations — that's professional sport and human nature. I'd paid my dues at RCB: if I'd had a lean trot, the management would have had faith in me because of what I'd done in the past. When you go to a new team, you don't get that backing. You never feel comfortable because you know that if you go two or three games without a score, you come under cold-eyed scrutiny.

A case in point: Rajasthan played Kings XI Punjab in Mohali.

The chase was 195, I was lbw for a duck and we didn't get close. Afterwards, the team, support staff and management were in the bar on the top floor of the hotel. Liz Hurley was there with Warnie. One of the Royals owners said to me, "Ross, we didn't pay you a million dollars to get a duck" and slapped me across the face three or four times. He was laughing and they weren't hard slaps but I'm not sure that it was entirely play-acting. Under the circumstances I wasn't going to make an issue of it, but I couldn't imagine it happening in many professional sporting environments.

There was never a dull moment with Warnie running the show. After we got humiliated by the Kochi Tuskers — they chased down our miserable total in seven overs — Warnie gave the team an almighty spray. (I didn't feel it was directed at me because I didn't play that game.) One of the coaching staff took him aside to let him know he'd gone over the top and probably upset the younger lads. Warnie took it on board and called the team together to apologise. He concluded with, "After all, it's just a game of cricket. Tomorrow morning the sun will rise and I'll wake up beside Liz Hurley." Something in those mixed messages must have struck a chord because we blew the Mumbai Indians away in our next game.

The expression "living legend" should be used a lot less than it is, but that's exactly what Warnie was. I watched his every move. The fact that he was larger than life — a great performer who was also a showman; a generous-spirited, vibrant personality who was always fun to be around — made his premature death even more shocking. He lived life to the fullest: it could be said that he packed more into his abbreviated existence than many people would manage in several lifetimes. This line from the famous sci-fi movie *Blade Runner* could serve as his epitaph: "The light that burns twice as bright burns half as long and you have burned so very, very brightly."

The South African off-spinner Johan Botha and I were sitting next to Rahul Dravid at breakfast in Jaipur. We asked him if he wanted to go for a coffee; he didn't really, but we twisted his arm. We got a cab to a five-storey mall. We hadn't taken any security with us, which was naive. Within two minutes the mall was packed — there were at least 4000 people — and we had to get mall security to extract us.

I'm sure Rahul saw it coming, but he was too polite to turn us down. "Botes" and I were profusely apologetic on the way back to the hotel. Rahul played it down with his usual class, saying we probably would've been okay in a bigger city like Mumbai but, in the smaller cities, they didn't see big-name cricketers that often. Jaipur's population is around four million. After that, coffee with Dravid was always in the hotel.

There was always a commotion in the hotel lobby when the superstars came down for breakfast. Virat Kohli would often come down wearing headphones — it's hard to buttonhole someone who has got headphones on. One of the things the Indian players enjoy about touring New Zealand is being able to walk from place to place, for instance from Seddon Park back to the hotel. If Sachin Tendulkar had tried that in Mumbai, he never would have got home.

Nayan Doshi, who played county cricket for Surrey and whose father Dilip played for India, was in the Rajasthan squad. Although he was classified as a local, he was born and raised in England and tended to hang out with the overseas players. He was right into photography and had a contact at Ranthambore National Park, a tiger reserve. He was planning a night drive up to the reserve after the game, did I want to go? I was dead keen and knew Dravid was too, but we decided to leave early in the morning.

Nayan and Jake Oram left after the game while Dravid and I headed off about 5.30 the next morning. You don't leave the ground until quite a while after the conclusion of a day–night IPL game, then it takes two or three hours to wind down, so you mightn't get to sleep till 2 or 3 am. The drive to the reserve took several hours. On the back roads, we seemed to bounce from one pothole to the next — it was like driving on judder bars. I tried to sleep but my head just kept banging against the window.

I asked Dravid, "How many times have you seen a tiger?" He said, "I've never seen a tiger. I've been on 21 of these expeditions and haven't seen a single one." I thought, 'What? 21 safaris for zero sightings.' Seriously, if I'd known that, I wouldn't have gone. I would've said, "No thanks, I'll watch the Discovery channel."

Jake had been out in the morning — no joy. There was some baseball game on TV that he wanted to watch so he didn't come with us on the mid-afternoon safari. It wasn't long before our driver got a radio call from a colleague to say they'd found T-17, a famous, tagged tiger. Dravid was thrilled: 21 safaris without seeing as much as a tiger turd, but half an hour into number 22 he'd hit pay dirt.

We pulled up beside the other vehicles, open-top SUVs a bit bigger than Land Rovers. The tiger was on a rock, a good 100 metres away. We were stoked to see a tiger in the wild, but the people in the other vehicles immediately aimed their cameras at Rahul. They were as excited to see him as we were to see the tiger. Maybe more: across the globe there are almost 4000 tigers in the wild, but there's only one Rahul Dravid.

We went out again the next morning and found some tracks. Next thing a tiger was right in front of us, no more than two or three metres away. The driver had barely finished telling us that they'd recently seen this tiger's sister when she appeared: we had two tigers almost within touching distance. We were in an open jeep so quite exposed, but the tigers were obviously used to vehicles. The game wardens with us had guns but said we'd only be at risk if we were threatening the tigers' young ones. It was pretty amazing to have gone two from two — two tiger sightings on two safaris. Rahul was two from 23 but he couldn't have been happier. He had a smile on his face for days afterwards.

Warnie gave me a hospital pass when we played RCB, tossing me the ball when Kohli and Chris Gayle were in full flow. Warnie was a gambler: the game was slipping away from us so he tried to buy a wicket. I managed to bowl five respectable balls but the last one went for six. My only other IPL over followed the same script. It was Bangalore against Chennai in South Africa, with Dhoni and Suresh Raina at the crease. The first five weren't too bad, but then I tried to bowl an arm ball. It came out as a low full toss and Dhoni gave it what it deserved.

In 2012, I was traded to Delhi and my salary went up to US$1.3 million, which worked out at around US$85,000 a game. The way it works is that you get 80 per cent of your sign-on fee whether you're selected or not. If you were signed for $2.8 million for a 14-game competition, that's a match fee of $200,000. If you're not picked, you get $160,000. There's no rhyme or reason to what happens at IPL auctions: the more you try to analyse and understand the decision-making, the more confused you become.

There were games when Sehwag went nuts, so I was surplus to requirements batting-wise. I didn't get a catch, in fact, barely fielded a ball, but I still got paid. You could say it was swings and roundabouts: I had to forego some big paydays to play for New Zealand, but there were also times when I was lavishly rewarded for just turning up. Missing three games with a broken arm cost me more than a quarter of a million, but I would have missed more of the tournament if I hadn't had an operation straightaway. It was definitely money well spent.

We had a memorable night at Sehwag's restaurant. A lot of the guys liked their football so we were watching Manchester City play Queen's Park Rangers on a big screen. It was the final round of the Premier League and Sergio Agüero scored in stoppage time to give City a 3–2 win and their first title for 44 years. The food was fantastic, particularly the prawns. I couldn't stop eating them but didn't realise Sehwag was aware that I was making a pig of myself.

We played the next day. Sehwag was smacking it to all parts, making it look easy. The overseas batters, me included, were struggling. I was feeling nervous because I was on big money and knew I had to deliver. The pressure was on when I went in to bat, but Sehwag was so relaxed: he glove-punched me and said, "Ross, just bat like you're eating prawns." It was like cricket was a hobby and he was just playing for fun. From then on, whenever our paths crossed, he would remind me about the prawns.

We had a fantastic team: as well as Virender, there was Mahela Jayawardene, Morné Morkel, Kevin Pietersen, Andre Russell and David Warner. Aaron Finch and Glenn Maxwell wouldn't even be at the games because you could only take six overseas players to the ground. We were having a few drinks one night and Warner was getting a bit loud. By the time we got into the lift to go up to our rooms, he was being smart and annoying with it. I put him in a headlock and gave him a couple of don't argues. "Oh f--k," he said, "I forgot you Islanders are strong." It's amazing what you can achieve with a headlock and a couple of jabs to the melon: David and I have been good ever since. He developed this routine of walking past me when I was batting and muttering — with a big grin — either that line from *Once Were Warriors*, "Cook the man some f----n eggs," or, "You got something wrong with your eyes, boy?"

When we found out I was going to Delhi, Victoria and I started thinking about the Taj Mahal. Mackenzie was six months old and we um-ed and aah-ed about whether we could take her. When we found out it was a four-hour drive from Delhi to Agra, we shelved the idea. Mother and daughter remained in Hamilton.

As it turned out, a number of players and partners wanted to go to the Taj Mahal, so the team manager asked the franchise owners if there was any chance of putting on a private jet. We had a game coming up and eight hours on what was apparently quite a dangerous road wouldn't have been ideal preparation. Infrastructure conglomerate GMR are joint owners of the Delhi Daredevils (now the Delhi Capitals). Kiran, son of GM Rao, the company's founder, and a very nice, softly spoken guy, agreed to the request. There were 11 of us and the jet could only take nine, so

Kiran provided two of them. The flight took just 22 minutes. There isn't a civil airport at Agra so we flew into a military base: some highly placed person had obviously pulled a few strings. It was stinking hot — mid-40s — but an amazing experience, especially since we had exclusive access to the main tomb.

Victoria was back in Hamilton thinking she and Mackenzie could have gone after all. To rub salt in the wound, the next day the *Times of India* ran a photo of Leanne McGoldrick and me on the seat Diana, Princess of Wales, sat on in that famous shot. The caption was, "Ross Taylor with wife Leanne at the Taj Mahal." The whole episode still annoys Victoria and I just can't help winding her up. Every time we see the Taj on the news or in a brochure or whatever, I wax lyrical about how fabulous it was.

In 2013, I got traded to Pune. I was captain for one game — we beat Chennai, mainly thanks to Steve Smith — which must make me one of the few captains in the IPL's 15-year history to have a 100 per cent winning record. The Pune coach was Allan Donald, the former great South African fast bowler, and a nice guy who was briefly Black Caps bowling coach under Wrighty. He'd wanted me to be captain, but the owners were against it because I was leaving early to join the Black Caps. Quite frankly, I was more than happy not to be captain. We didn't perform all that well and Allan and our skipper, Angelo Mathews, the Sri Lankan all-rounder, were twice summoned to Mumbai to be grilled by the owners.

The following year I went back to Delhi. Jimmy Neesham was there and had the dubious distinction of missing a midday team bus departure after a big night. I can't think of anyone else I've ever played with who has missed a midday leave. Kevin Pietersen was pretty hard-nosed: he just said, "He can find his own f----n way to the airport." His — not unreasonable — rationale was that he'd been up late with Jimmy and still managed to be on the bus. KP had been fantastic in 2012 as part of a very strong playing group. In 2014, the team wasn't as good so, as captain, KP was under some pressure.

One of Kevin's Indian mates was opening a nightclub, so he asked a few of us if we'd put in an appearance. JP Duminy and I decided it would be a good idea to show our faces. We left about 12.30 am. After we'd waited for a taxi for over half an hour, these guys who were hanging around outside the club offered us a ride — basically to anywhere we wanted. They didn't look dodgy so we asked if they could drop us off at our hotel, which was out by the airport, 40 or 50 minutes away. No problem at all. It wasn't till we were under way that we thought about the situation we'd got ourselves into: in a car in the middle of the night with a bunch of randoms who could be taking us anywhere. The reassuring thing was that the driver was phoning around his friends and family saying, "You wouldn't believe who's in the back of my car." He wanted to take us to meet his family — "It's not far out of our way" — but JP wanted to get back to the hotel so we suggested we could meet them there. Only in India.

That was my last year of IPL. I sometimes say that giving up the slog-sweep cost me my IPL career and therefore a lot of money. But I was trying to become a better player and prove to those who dismissed me as an across-the-line slogger that there was more to my game.

Martin Crowe stressed that the key to becoming a more consistent run-scorer was eliminating ways of getting out. For instance, you should strive to get forward to reduce the chances of being bowled or lbw. Hogan didn't tell me to drop the slog-sweep — it was never directly addressed — but I knew that putting it away would eliminate ways of getting out.

It was a conscious decision. As a captain, I wanted to lead from the front by scoring runs consistently. I didn't talk a lot; I tried to do my talking with the bat. And I was conscious of the power of perception: people can live with it if you nick off trying to be technically correct; if you hole out playing a slog-sweep, look out. Ironically, towards the end of my career, commentators started asking, "Where's Taylor's slog-sweep?"

I had a short stint with Victoria in the 2009/10 Big Bash. Back then it was a more modest enterprise, involving just the state teams. I signed before Christmas; Victoria and I flew to Brisbane on the 27th and I played against Queensland in Brisbane on the 28th. Beforehand, I met up with a few of my teammates, including skipper Cameron White, with whom I'd played at Bangalore, and David Hussey. Victoria and I had just got engaged so they were all congratulating me. I was a bit nervous and, just to make conversation, I asked Cameron when he was getting engaged. Everybody laughed at that, but they absolutely cracked up when Hussey said, "When he goes to Japan." It went right over my head. The point was that Whitey had no plans to go to Japan. That would change.

I had a nickname before we even touched down in Brisbane. Clint McKay, a fast bowler who played for Australia, had said to Aaron Finch, "I see we've signed that Kiwi guy, Ross Smith." Finchy said, "It's Ross Taylor, you idiot." But when I turned up, they were all calling me "Smithy". I was wondering if it had something to do with Ian Smith, but then how would they have known about that relationship? As you learn very quickly about Victorians, practically everything can be traced back to the AFL. Ross Smith played for St Kilda and won the Brownlow Medal for best and fairest player in 1967. During that innings of 290 in Perth, the Aussie commentator James Brayshaw, who was quite heavily involved in AFL, also called me Ross Smith, but quickly corrected himself.

We had a really good team — Dwayne Bravo, Finch, Brad Hodge, Hussey, Matthew Wade — but lost the toss and were sent into bat on a green Gabba wicket. As I was waiting to go in, I kept thinking, 'Imagine flying all this way to get a duck.' I got dropped second ball, made 58 off 36 balls and won man of the match.

I played one more game for Victoria, the semi-final which we won. (I couldn't play in the final because of my New Zealand commitments.) The top two teams from Australia qualified for the Champions League so the Vics were happy. My Victorian adventure was short and sweet but very worthwhile. It was hard cricket. Playing alongside those guys provided a good insight into the Australian cricket psyche and diminished, in my mind, the aura surrounding their cricketers.

I actually qualified for the Champions League with three teams: Bangalore, Victoria and Central Districts, who won our competition. Because I wasn't available to play for CD, RCB had to compensate New Zealand Cricket to the tune of US$200,000. Most of that money went to the domestic associations with CD getting a double share.

When I was at Sussex in 2015, I was asked to do some studio work for Sky TV UK which was showing the IPL. I'd never done any television work, but it was potentially an avenue to explore when I finished playing, so I thought why not give it a go? A driver picked me up from where we were staying in Hove and took me up to the Sky studios in London. I was very nervous. They'd told me the main entrance to the studio was shut on a Saturday, but the driver would know where to go and a runner — TV speak for general dogsbody — would take it from there.

Sure enough, the runner was waiting. He started chatting away about football, asking me which club I supported. I said, "Liverpool," and got a strange look. There were lots of people in the room he took me to, some of them familiar faces, but the only one I could put a name to was Michael van Gerwen, the Dutch darts player. Mark Ramprakash, the former England batsman who was my co-panellist, was nowhere to be seen.

As they were putting a microphone on me, the runner and another guy came over. The runner asked me my name; I told him. He looked at the other guy and said, "I told you it's not him." I was about to go on *Soccer AM* masquerading as actor/musician Jacob Anderson aka Raleigh Ritchie — Grey Worm in *Game of Thrones*. Jacob supports Manchester United who were playing Crystal Palace in the FA Cup, hence the strange look I got for being a Liverpool supporter.

We were two minutes away from perpetrating one of the bigger fiascos in the history of live television: "We're delighted to have as our special guest *Game of Thrones* star and long-time Manchester United supporter, Jacob Anderson." Cut to close-up of panic-stricken Kiwi cricketer.

I played for the Trinidad & Tobago Red Steel in my first stint in the Caribbean Premier League. Port of Spain is a bit of a melting pot with a large Indian population. The favourite street food is "doubles" — a flatbread sandwich with curried chickpeas. The other players kept raving about them so I decided I had to try them.

Getting on for midnight, Kevin O'Brien, the Irish all-rounder, our physio, her friend and I went out to sample this delicacy. The famous doubles place was shut, but I was starving so we got some KFC and headed back to the Hilton. We had to go around Queen's Park Savannah, an open space with a road around the circumference that is often described as the world's largest roundabout.

As we were going around it, our driver saw police cars up ahead. She pulled over. Several cop cars came barrelling up and a bunch of guys waving AK47s jumped out. We'd had a few drinks. Kevin might've had had more than a few because he wound down the window and, ignoring the guns in his face, yelled, "What's going on, man? We're Trinidad Red Steel; we just beat Jamaica." In a Caribbean accent. It turned out that we'd stopped at a spot where many a drug deal had gone down.

We went to Saint Kitts to play the St Kitts and Nevis Patriots, Martin Guptill's team at the time. He and I hit the beach the day before the game. Gup had forgotten to bring sunscreen so before long he was complaining about getting burnt and wanting to go for a swim. We were only 10 metres out, up to our waist, but the current dragged us across to some rocks.

Suddenly I couldn't get my feet on the bottom. I didn't want to get cut on the rocks and not be able to play the next day, but that very quickly became the least of my worries. I was fighting the current and starting to take on water. Gup was trying to hold me up but was getting tired. He cut his foot and knee on the coral, so he moved a metre or so but then couldn't reach me because of the current and couldn't touch the bottom either. We were really panicking. I was waving frantically at people on the beach who waved back, no doubt thinking, 'What a friendly chap.'

Then a blond kid, maybe 13 years old, paddled out on his surfboard and dragged us back to the shore. He was from Hawaii — his father ran a timeshare complex — and a very cool little dude: "No problem, guys," he said when we thanked him from the bottom of our hearts. "Yeah, there's a whirlpool by the rocks. I've saved six or seven people there."

I was shaking for a good hour afterwards. Word got around that we'd nearly drowned and when I got on the team bus, our skipper Dwayne Bravo said, "Ross, what were you doing swimming in the Atlantic? No one swims on the Atlantic side of the island. You always swim on the Caribbean side." I said, "That would have been handy to know before I nearly downed." They all laughed their heads off.

That incident aside, I really enjoyed the Caribbean. It was a bit like being in the Pacific Islands: devoutly religious people who laugh a lot and where everything works on island time. Some of the most fun I've had in cricket teams was at the CPL. The Caribbean boys like KFC even more than I do — I'd never seen anyone have it for breakfast before. We had quite a few early-morning flights and you had to see the queue at the Trinidad Airport KFC at 5.30 am to believe it. The cricketers there have all got six packs so they can get away with it.

The big downer is the travel: to get from island A to island B, more often than not you have to go via island C. While Caribbean Airlines were really good, the alternative was LIAT. According to the locals that stands for "Leave Island Any Time." (It actually stands for Leeward Islands Air Transport.) My worst experience involved leaving the hotel in Guyana, on the South American mainland, at 9 am to fly to Antigua. Because the flight left late, we missed our connecting flight to Saint Lucia and ended up going via Barbados. We got there about 8 pm. The food outlets were shut so we had to clear Customs and leave the airport to get something to eat. We didn't get to Antigua till three in the morning, our bags didn't turn up for another hour or so and we were playing the next day. Somehow we managed to win.

In Guyana, we stayed at the Princess Hotel, a newish property next to the new cricket ground. We'd been given bottles of El Dorado rum, a famous local beverage. Samuel Badree and Nicholas Pooran came to my room: Samuel just wanted a chat while Nicholas was on the prowl for another bottle of El Dorado. Badree is very religious, so Pooran and I were vying for his rum. A couple of mice ran out from under my bed and Badree and Pooran completely lost it — they literally jumped onto the bed. Guyana is known for its giant anacondas and here were these guys getting the heebie-jeebies over a couple of mice.

I also played for the Jamaica Tallawahs. When I went to get on the team bus to go to Sabina Park for the first training, there wasn't room for my gear bag. Krishmar Santokie said, "Come with me, Ross." He had a Range Rover Sport, better than a bus any day. The first thing I noticed in his car were the two ammunition magazines in the drink holder. I pointed at them: "What are they for?" He said, "They're for my protection, man." (Violent crime is a major issue for Jamaica.)

Glenn Phillips was at the Tallawahs. Sweetwood, a great jerk chicken joint in Kingston, was just over the road from the Pegasus Hotel. Glenn was nervous about crossing the road, because you got offered every drug under the sun. As we were going over for lunch, Glenn said, "Ross, did you know that today's Jamaica's Emasturbation day?" I said, "It's Emancipation Day. Emasturbation Day is any day you want, mate."

One year we were invited to a party at Chris Gayle's house, which is on top of a steep hill in Kingston. So steep, in fact, that our bus couldn't manage it — we had to walk up. There was a movie theatre, a gym and a dance floor in a mirrored room with a stage and stripper pole. The event was sponsored by Appleton Rum. (After a test in Jamaica in 2012 I treated myself to a shot of 21-year-old Appleton; the hotel barmaid refused to pour Coke into it.) The "Universe Boss" seemed to have invited every Miss Jamaica contestant of the previous decade. About midnight, Dwayne Bravo was up on the stage, duetting with some dude. I thought, 'I know that voice.' It was Shaggy. Apparently, he had a house just down the road.

Chapter 13.
Top Guns

I set myself the challenge of picking a test team from the best players I played with. This is it:

Rahul Dravid (Royal Challengers Bangalore and Rajasthan Royals)
Virender Sehwag (Delhi Daredevils)
Kane Williamson (New Zealand)
Steve Smith (Pune Warriors)
Jacques Kallis (RCB)
Virat Kohli (RCB)
Mark Boucher (RCB)
Shane Warne (Rajasthan)
Dayle Steyn (RCB)
Stuart Broad (Nottinghamshire)
Shane Bond (New Zealand)

Anil Kumble (RCB) would be 12th man and Warnie would be the captain. The boys would be all ears during his team talks, that's for sure.

I played with Steve Smith in 2013. His technique wasn't as radical and I wouldn't have said, on the basis of what I saw then, that he'd be where he is now. He was a good player, but really seen as a leg-spinning all-rounder. No one realised how much drive he had or how mentally strong he was. With all the moving parts in that technique, he'd get crucified if he didn't succeed, but it works for him. It works because he's able to replicate it ad nauseam and it messes with bowlers' minds — they don't know where to bowl to him.

Glenn Phillips, who bats a bit like Smith, made his test debut in Sydney in 2020. When Glenn came out to join me in the middle I was thinking, 'He's going to get some stick here.' Pat Cummins bowled the first ball to him: "Oh, we've got another Smudger here," he said and the rest of them started chirping away. Glenn's pretty unflappable; he ended up making 52, our top score. Nathan Lyon came up and said, "Are you okay, Ross? Are you a bit disappointed no one copies your technique?" I just laughed.

All the very good players have a bit more time, but Smith, like AB de Villiers, can hit a given ball to three or four different areas of the field. With players of that calibre, you have to be even more patient. When you've got a plan for a Steve Smith or Kane Williamson or Virat Kohli, you have to execute for overs on end; it's no good coming up with a plan, then abandoning it if it doesn't work straightaway. And even then, one of the things that makes these guys great players is that they're very quick to work out what the plan is.

It took Smith 40-odd balls to get off the mark in that test at the SCG; when he finally did, he got the biggest ovation of the day. At his press conference, he talked about the big roar when he got off zero. In the previous test at the MCG, with 30,000 Kiwis in the crowd, he was massively booed when he came out to bat but claimed afterwards he hadn't been aware of it. As Tom Latham pointed out, you have to have very selective hearing to hear cheers but not boos.

Other batters in contention were Kevin Pietersen (RCB and Delhi), Shivnarine Chanderpaul (RCB) and Mahela Jayawardene and David Warner (both Delhi). Shiv and I made our IPL debuts together after being overlooked for the very first game in which Brendon put us to the sword. He was a bit like Steve Smith: a difficult guy to bowl to. With unorthodox techniques it's really hard to settle on where the best place to bowl is. Everybody has a theory.

I was off to England where Shiv had a good record, so I asked him how he approached batting there. He said, "You've just got to play tight." He'd set the bowling machine up and hit balls for a couple of hours, just trying to play tight. It was useful advice, although I was never a big indoor bowling machine guy. And I had to bear in mind that my idea of playing tight probably bore little resemblance to Chanderpaul's.

I don't think Joe Root gets the accolades he deserves. He's the least lauded of the fab four. Actually, I'd make it the fab five and chuck in Pakistan's Babar Azam. He's someone I like watching — his back foot punches are unreal. Hashim Amla was another one who didn't get the recognition he deserved.

There are batters you enjoy watching. You don't want them to score runs against you, but you don't really mind them making a few — as long as you win. For me, there are three categories: those I would've paid to watch, a very select group; those I liked to watch and those I could take or leave. The very select group consists of Chris Gayle, AB, Sehwag and Kohli.

Speaking of select groups, there were very few cricketers who got the crowd roaring — at home or away — every time they came out to bat: MS Dhoni, Kohli, Sachin Tendulkar — and Shahid Afridi. (That partly reflects the Indian and Pakistani diasporas because those two teams have fervent supporters in the crowd wherever in the world they play.) Afridi is in that company for one simple reason: as a spectator you could be absolutely certain that he'd try to hit sixes regardless of whether the match situation required it or, indeed, cried out for caution.

(Afridi was quite a personality, but I never had a run-in with him. The subcontinent teams don't sledge as a rule; they say very little. He was renowned for having a crushing handshake, although I can't say that registered with me. As a youngster I was often told to err on the side of firmness when shaking hands. Meeting Ross Taylor senior, and knowing he'd played prop for the Kiwis, I made a point of going in hard. After we'd got to know one another, he remarked on my strong handshake. It was half compliment, half complaint.)

My team is playing at the Basin Reserve, which means you've got to have someone who can truck it up into the wind. Jacques Kallis would draw the short straw. Speaking at the parliamentary reception before the Wellington test in 2012, the Proteas captain, Graeme Smith, said Kallis didn't like bowling at the Basin because he was worried about losing his hairpiece. That got much more of a laugh than anything in my speech.

I know there are lies, damned lies and statistics, but in cricket, over the long haul, the numbers tell the story. Statistically, Jacques mounts a very strong case for being the greatest cricketer of all time. There's no question, therefore, that he's my all-rounder, but Ben Stokes, who I played with at Durham in 2010, deserves a mention.

He was 18 or 19 and very much a Kiwi. Over a Guinness, I asked him if he wanted to come and play in New Zealand. He was keen so I sent a message to New Zealand Cricket CEO Justin Vaughan saying this guy Stokes was a really good young cricketer and interested in playing for New Zealand. Vaughan replied along the lines that he could start playing domestic cricket and we'd see where it went. I went back saying we'd have to offer him more than that because he wouldn't be interested if it meant starting on the bottom rung of the ladder.

Obviously, it didn't come to anything. I think Ben was sincere about playing for New Zealand, but NZC would've had to have acted swiftly and decisively and given him some pretty solid assurances, which Vaughan clearly wasn't prepared to do.

After a T20 in Birmingham, the Durham team bussed to

Nottingham where we stayed overnight. Stokesy, whom I'd sort
of taken under my wing, wanted to go to the casino over the road
from the hotel. A few of us went with him. Admittedly, I might
have been one of the last to go to the bar, but they'd obviously
been planning this for a while: as I went up, they all pulled out
their phones to take a photo of the tight Kiwi finally putting
his hand in his pocket. "About bloody time," they said. "You're
making a fortune in the IPL and you haven't bought us poor
county journeymen a drink." £150 worth of tequila shots and
Jägerbombs later . . .

Now, I pull that stunt on other people. When Trent Boult
bought me the only coffee he has ever shouted me — at a Starbucks
somewhere between Newcastle and Manchester — I said, "Oh,
about time" and whipped out the phone.

In next to no time, Stokesy won several hundred quid, quite
a lot of money for a lad on £18,000. The others, who included
England fast bowler Steve Harmison, said, "You can look after
him, Ross. We've tried, now it's your turn. Good luck." So, Ben kept
winning money and I kept taking it off him for safe keeping. When
we left around 4 am I was carrying close to £700.

Back at the hotel, I said, "You're not going back out, are you?"
Ben said, "Nah, I'm off to bed." I gave him his money and hit the
sack. Next morning, he seemed fine, but someone told me a few
of the boys had gone out again and Stokesy had blown every last
penny of his winnings. I told him he was an idiot; he just laughed.
Good on him. He probably doesn't even remember the night he
blew 700 quid.

I'm choosing my wicketkeeper first and foremost on glove work,
hence I've gone with Boucher. The others in the frame are Brendon
and BJ Watling. Brendon was probably the most agile keeper I've
played with, while BJ was a phenomenally gutsy grafter who saved
us plenty of times.

With the quicks, there's the question of whether you'd opt for
Boulty or Neil Wagner ahead of Shane Bond to add variety to the

attack. Bondy, an exceptional cricketer, played a lot fewer tests than Boulty and Wags. But you've got to consider the opposition's perception and the intimidation factor — everyone was scared of Bondy. You can have a plan for a certain team, but sometimes it boils down to how you combat their key individuals.

In terms of longevity, Stuart Broad is at the other end of the spectrum — 152 tests compared to Shane's 18. Broady had my number until I played with him at Notts. After that, I'm proud to say, I don't think he ever got me out. There's a huge amount of analysis and theorising these days, but Broady's philosophy was to bowl a fourth stump line and let the ball do the work. It sounds absurdly simple but requires great control of line and length, and immense discipline.

You try to read bowlers and work out how they're setting you up, but Broady was a little like those left-arm spinners who just put it in the right area and leave the rest to natural variation: some turn, some don't. That's what made the Sri Lankan, Rangana Herath, such a difficult customer. It's the old story: if the bowler doesn't know what it's going to do, how the hell can the batter?

In England, you try to cover both the outside edge and the inside edge, but if you can handle playing and missing or inside edging, it becomes a simpler process. Sometimes you've just got to play ugly. Broady could swing or seam it back in, so you were always thinking about covering both edges. You'd play and miss, so you'd try to cover the outside edge and he'd bring one back.

After that conversation, I faced him with the mindset of not caring if I played and missed. I tried to stay side on and cover the inside edge more than the outside edge because I'd rather be nicked off than bowled or trapped lbw.

It's really tough to keep coming up against a bowler who has got your number but, generally speaking, if you play against a bowler a lot, you get to know his triggers and tricks. The guys with unique actions — Jasprit Bumrah, Lasith Malinga, Muttiah Muralitharan — are harder to read. Give me a conventional bowler any day, no matter how quick, rather than an unconventional bowler whose action takes a lot of getting used to.

Another quick worthy of consideration is Morné Morkel (Delhi). He probably doesn't have the record of the others, but he created a lot of pressure for Dale Steyn. His natural length was back of a length, a bit like Bondy, so he didn't get as many lbws or bowleds as some. If Kyle Jamieson maintains his performance level for another couple of years, he'll put himself in any Dream Team conversation.

If my team was playing on the subcontinent, I'd have two spinners, maybe three. Anil Kumble would come in for Broad. Anil was such a different type of bowler to Warnie that it really wouldn't be like having two leg-spinners. Sehwag and Kane could bowl some off-spin, but Dan Vettori would definitely come into consideration if I went for a third spinner. Mark Craig, who made a massive contribution to our test win over Pakistan in the UAE in 2014, would be the best specialist off-spinner I've played with.

Murali was hard to get your head around because it went both ways, but he wasn't the only one who could do that. He was the big name, but I thought Saeed Ajmal of Pakistan was just as good. I don't think it was a coincidence that when the ICC clamped down on illegal actions, particularly in relation to the doosra, batters' averages started going up. Suddenly, you were only having to worry about one edge. We lost the first test in Sri Lanka in 2019 with Akila Dananjaya getting a five-for. The match officials raised questions about his action — he'd been suspended the previous year — so he couldn't play in the second test which we won. Would we have won if he'd played? Good question. Did he chuck it? I have no idea.

If I was picking a team for the white-ball formats, the specialists like Dwayne Bravo (Trinidad and Tobago Red Steel) would come into consideration. Vettori did some pretty unbelievable stuff in short-form cricket. When he was on song in an ODI, the Aussies would be happy to take him for 30 off his 10 overs, as long as he didn't take a wicket. The question with Dan is whether he'd get enough wickets. I probably wouldn't pick Steve Smith in my ODI team: Kallis would open and I'd bring in Kevin Pietersen. Kohli would have to bat at three. Martin Guptill and Brendon McCullum would definitely come into contention, as would Shane Watson (Rajasthan). Broad wouldn't make my ODI team, so that could bring in Boulty.

When I think about the best players I played with, two names that don't appear on my team sheet immediately come to mind: Jesse Ryder and Mathew "Skippy" Sinclair. Very different people, but alike in the sense that they were amazingly talented players who would have done fantastic things for New Zealand cricket if they'd been managed better.

Kane is the best New Zealander I played with; Bondy would be a close second. Jesse had more pure, natural talent than both of them. His hand–eye coordination was unbelievable. I feel he should have had at least 15 centuries in both tests and ODIs. He was that good. And he could bowl. I remember him bowling at 137 kph off a few paces against India at Eden Park. I'm not saying he bowled 137 kph all the time, but he was a lot quicker than you thought.

John Wright: When I first came back from India, I threw to Jesse Ryder once. It was like throwing to Tendulkar.

Could he have been managed better? That's the million-dollar question. I'm not saying it would have been easy. Regardless of how you apportion responsibility, though, you'd have to think that, when things got tough, he could have been managed better than he was both by NZC and the various provincial associations he played for.

Ian Smith: Two blokes with the same raw talent and from similar circumstances come out of the same area. One goes to Napier Boys' High, the other goes to Palmerston North Boys' High. One realised just how good he was and was prepared to work on it and got the help. The other probably didn't know how good he was and was lost. If you saw Jesse Ryder fly, with his hands and his timing, there was nothing more beautiful. If you look back over the last 20 or so years of New Zealand cricket, he was probably the single most unrealised talent.

Skippy was the most consistent player on the domestic circuit. It was almost like Kane at international level — you were surprised when they didn't succeed. He still gets talked about a lot in the Central Districts environment, which shows his stature.

I learned a lot from him, notably the importance of being hungry for runs. When I was batting with him once, I took a single off the last ball of three or four overs in a row. Skippy was renowned for doing exactly that, so it was a bit of a master/apprentice situation. He wasn't happy about not getting the strike and eventually told me, "Nah, you stay down there."

I played my first home test with Skippy — against England at Seddon Park in 2008. All told, there were four Palmy Boys old boys in the team, the others being Jamie How and Jake Oram, while Gary Hermansson was the mental skills coach. I got 120 in the first innings and, in the second, watched from the safety of the non-striker's end as their left-arm quick, Ryan Sidebottom, completed a hat-trick — Stephen Fleming and Skippy caught at gully by Alistair Cook and Jake LBW. It was my birthday and the Barmy Army were singing "Happy Birthday".

I suppose you could compare Skippy to England's Graeme Hick and Mark Ramprakash, guys who were absolute run machines at first-class level but, for whatever reason, only showed glimpses of that dominance at international level. Skippy might've had some technical flaws, but so do we all. If anything could be laid at his door it would be that fantastic player though he was, he perhaps could have evolved more over the course of his career.

I was always seeking to get better. If you want to have a long career, you have to embrace continuous improvement. There were times when I tinkered too much and it's sometimes the case that, in the process of correcting one fault, you create a different problem. One of my strengths was that I was really specific about the aspect of my game I was addressing.

There were things about Skippy that I didn't want to imitate, things he probably didn't even realise he was doing. He was an enigmatic personality, a bit different: he just opened his mouth and stuff came out. We used to call them Skippyisms: "Remember boys, it's a war of nutrition"; "We're all just prawns on a chessboard"; "We've got to be really pacific with our plans". He told someone his wife Tina was a barrister. "Oh, so she's a lawyer, eh?" "No, no, she makes coffee." At CD, the senior players would just tell him to pull his head in, but the New Zealand team environment was far less straightforward. When I got in there, I listened and kept my mouth shut.

But when you consider that, in the first 18 months of his test career, Skippy got 214 on debut against the West Indies, 150 against Allan "White Lightning" Donald in Port Elizabeth and 204 not out against Pakistan, you'd have to conclude that, from then on, New Zealand didn't get the best out of him. That definitely wasn't all — or even mostly — his doing. The Aussies really got into him, and perhaps he never quite got over that, but the big issue was closer to home.

Mark Greatbatch: Skippy was badly managed. He's a bit sensitive, but everyone's different in their personality and character. Unfortunately, I don't think he was treated very well. He was in groups during the period that created a difficult culture or a difficult environment and he really suffered for that. Deep down, Skippy's a lovely guy.

The Black Caps team he went into contained some big personalities and the changing room give-and-take would have been pretty robust. Skippy was a soft target for people who didn't miss soft targets. At the same time, some of his teammates were probably worried that he was going to take their spot. In those days, if you saw someone coming for your spot, your job, your livelihood, you weren't going to make things easy for them. In that regard, the "team first" mantra didn't really apply. It was team first once you'd looked after number one, and you knew you were playing next week.

Skippy must've always felt like an outsider. I think it would be different for him now. This current team is welcoming towards new players coming into the environment and would accept Mathew Sinclair much more readily than the teams he and I started out in.

After Skippy retired, he rang me out of the blue: he and Tina had started up the Black Cups café and he asked if I could do a bit of promotional stuff for them — show my face, have some photos taken, sign some shirts and so on. I went along and put my best foot forward; Skippy wandered over and said, "By the way, Ross, the coffee's on me." Classic Skippy.

Chapter 14.
Standing in my Shoes

I only changed my gloves during an innings if I absolutely had to, for instance if I'd ripped them diving to avoid being run out. That was probably superstition, but then at what point does your routine become superstition? The way I looked at it was that, as a batter, there was only so much you can control: you react to and have to deal with what the bowler presents. I could control my mind and my preparation, all the way down to the order in which I put my gear on.

Superstition is all cause and effect. You have such and such for breakfast, you get runs, you keep having such and such for breakfast. If I made runs, I'd try to replicate pretty much everything next time around. And vice versa: if I failed, I did things differently next time.

I went through a phase during which Victoria had to book my haircuts. I'd rung the hairdresser, I'd got a duck, I made a connection. Once you've planted that seed in your mind, it's hard to get rid of. That particular superstition snowballed to the point where I had to pay the hairdresser in cash. Thankfully, I got over it. New socks became my go to: Martin Guptill was the first to notice that, if I didn't make runs, I'd wear brand new socks next time I batted.

Leanne McGoldrick: For Ross, there were always certain things that brought him good luck or bad luck and, the longer he played, the more superstitious he became. Early in his career, I was staying with Ross and Victoria. It was the evening before a game. While they were out, I noticed Ross's playing gear in a pile on the floor; thinking I was being helpful, I put it in the wash. When Ross and Victoria got home, I noticed Ross seemed upset. He was clearly trying to compose himself so I thought it best not to say anything. Sometime later I found out that he had to wash his own gear the night before a game — no sooner. (He actually rewashed the gear that I'd put through the laundry.) Luckily for me, he played well the next day.

The night before my first ever World Cup Game — against England in Saint Lucia in 2007 — Victoria and I went to a Chinese restaurant. I had crispy aromatic duck, one of my favourite meals. Liam Plunkett bowled me a fullish outswinger first ball; I went for the big cover drive, nicked it and Andrew Flintoff took a one-handed diving catch. Rule number one: don't have duck the night before a game.

Mind you, Freddie had an even worse day than I did: he also got a golden duck, didn't take a wicket and England got hammered. About 1.30 am he decided it would be a good idea to have a nightcap with Ian Botham, who was staying on a boat out in the bay. Freddie commandeered a pedalo, put to sea and had to be rescued by hotel staff. He woke up the next morning, still wet and with sand between his toes, to the sound of his irate coach, Duncan Fletcher, pounding on the door.

Years later, we went to a dégustation dinner that included duck. I said I couldn't have the duck because I was playing in two days' time. Our friends persuaded me the rule only applied when I was playing the next day. So, I had some duck and, sure enough, two days later I got a golden.

In late 2019 we were in Mount Maunganui to play England. We were staying in apartments so at 7.30 the night before the game I was in a New World getting Weet-Bix and yoghurt for breakfast. It suddenly hit me that I'd forgotten to pack my batting trousers. We were moving house and, amid the disruption, I'd left home without the two pairs of batting trousers that I'd alternated between over the course of 100 tests. (It was amazing they'd lasted that long given how hard on clothes some hotel laundries are.)

I rang Victoria to explore the possibility of her meeting me halfway. She didn't spend a lot of time thinking about it: I got a very firm "No way", which wound me up massively. I rang Sky commentator Simon Doull, who also lives in Hamilton, but he was already at the Mount. There was no choice but to drive home. I was in the Kaimais when Victoria rang to say the Northern Districts CEO was coming over in the morning and could bring my trousers. But I was halfway there and not receptive to compromises or olive branches so I kept going. I got back to the Mount about 11 pm and was so wide awake I didn't get to sleep till midnight. Then Joe Root won the toss and chose to bat so I didn't even need the trousers.

It shows how mentally all over the place I was during the England series leading into the World Test Championship final that, for the first time in my test career, I didn't wear either of those pairs of batting trousers in the second innings at Lord's. You could call it clutching at straws but that's how desperate my search for runs had become. Having said that, I don't think if I would have had the nerve to do it in the first innings, in case I got a duck and was on a pair.

As I said, there's superstition and there's routine. When the wicket fell and it was my turn to bat, I'd pick up my gloves and my drink bottle, have three sips, put the drink bottle down, put my helmet on, grab my bat and walk out. When Jeff Crowe, Martin's brother and an experienced ICC match referee, came to dinner, he revealed that, when I was going out to bat, the match officials added on a minute to ensure the fielding team didn't get unfairly penalised. Apparently, it was common knowledge that I took longer to get out to the middle than just about anyone else. (Jeff knows his wine: when I offered him a selection to choose from, he picked the best one.)

My next game was at Lord's where it's quite a way from the changing room to the middle. I went through my routine really quickly. Afterwards, I was telling Chris Broad, a former England opening batsman and now an ICC match referee, about the conversation with Jeff. Chris, who is Stuart's father, said, "Yeah, now that you mention it, you actually passed the dismissed batter on the field." If it had been pointed it out to me, I would've done something about it years ago.

When I went out to bat, my focus was on taking deep breaths — in through the nose, down through the diaphragm — and settling my heart rate down. My heart would be pumping, so I had a routine to calm myself down and get into a rhythm. It started with the sips of water. Some days there's a man and his dog; other days you're playing in front of 90,000 people. Some days you walk out to bat past a bunch of six-year-old kids telling you how crap you are — "See you in two minutes, quack, quack." Whatever the setting and circumstances, you have to breathe.

In terms of a pre-first ball routine, I think only England's Jonathan Trott took longer than I did. Crouch, have a look at the sky, do a bit of gardening. If I felt I wasn't as mentally switched on as I needed to be, I'd go through the routine again after a break in play.

Not everyone was a fan. It used to annoy Ricky Ponting who'd be complaining from second slip that, "The bowler's f----n ready." That always made me laugh. In fact, when I played the Aussies, that was my gauge of whether I had my routine down pat. The opera isn't over till the fat lady sings; my pre-first ball routine wasn't over till "Punter" yapped, "The bowler's f----n ready."

Some bowlers would retaliate. When I eventually faced up,

they'd take a few steps, come to a halt and go back to the top of their run-up. They were sending a message: two can play that game. Then I had to decide whether I wanted to take it up a notch and really make a statement by going through my whole routine again.

When I first played for the Black Caps, I had a bat with holes in the rubber grip, but I was too superstitious to put a new grip on. Stephen Fleming was appalled. And if I wasn't scoring runs, I'd definitely swap bats on the scientific basis of change my bat, change my luck. Superstitious yes, but not obsessive about bats as many players are. I didn't mind someone picking up my bat and having a play with it, except when I was next in. I'd happily use a brand-new bat in a game — I'd just have some throwdowns in the morning as I did when I got 290 in Perth — whereas most guys would give it a good workout in the nets first to break it in and get used to it. Guys couldn't believe I'd use a new bat on just a few throwdowns, but I'd always done that. Babar Azam used to say, "Ross, you always look like you're using a new bat."

Bat throwing — as in hurling your bat across the dressing room after getting out — never made sense to me. Your bat's your tool. Besides, unlike some, I usually had only three or four bats in my kit. Don't get me wrong, I've flung my helmet and gloves into my gear bag, but not the bat. There were times when I stomped back into the dressing room absolutely steaming, but carefully placed my bat in my bag. Tim Southee and the other bowlers would be over in the corner laughing because I hadn't chucked it. That made me the odd one.

My bats were made in England. These days, most bats are made in India. I stuck with the same sized bat — 2 lb 10 oz for test cricket, a little heavier for ODIs — and pretty much the same shape. There was a bit of a curve, but they were pretty flat compared to the Indian bats. It puzzled some of my teammates that I stuck with the same shape and size while everyone else's bats got bigger.

When I was playing for Jamaica in the Caribbean Premier League, Andre Russell, the captain, wanted to drop me because he thought my bats were no good. He'd pick my bat up and wonder out loud how I could hit it as far as I did with "this piece of crap". I actually think it was more about me than my bats: Andre wanted to get a local player into the team but first he needed to create a vacancy.

Some guys were obsessed with other people's bats. They'd pick your bat up and, if they liked the feel of it, ask if you had a spare they could have. The current obsession is with Indian bats. The Indian stars have so many bats that it's no wonder the overseas players in the IPL feel free to ask for one. When a batter gives you one of his bats, I wouldn't have thought he's handing over the best in his bag. The opposite, in fact. Maybe the guys doing the asking think the Indian stars' worst bats are better than our best ones. The Indian bats are lighter and bigger because their wood is soft and dry, so they probably do send the ball further. They don't last as long, but who cares when you've got 30 in your kit?

Central Districts' first game of the 2015 season was against Otago at Nelson Park in Napier. I was going to Trinity Hill Wines to taste the Homage Syrah from the barrel; Ben Smith decided to tag along. Ben cheekily asked if I was going to buy him a magnum of one of Trinity Hill's other wines. I said I would if he got a hundred. I don't quite know what possessed me to do it, but I promised to buy him three magnums if he got a double century. (His top score at that stage was 180.)

We bowled first on a green seamer. Josh Clarkson, then a young kid from Nelson, was on debut. Last ball before lunch, Tom Bruce bowled a full toss to Ryan Duffy who clubbed it. Josh was at a catching mid-wicket: the ball burst through his hands and ricocheted off his head, ballooning quite a way up in the air. Tom caught it, Ryan was out caught and bowled, the boys were laughing, as you do when someone cops one, and Josh was a bit tearful — not because he'd been hit in the head, but because he thought he'd dropped a catch. We were saying, "It's okay, mate, you nodded it straight to Tom." Quite an introduction to first-class cricket.

Otago got 352; we made 650 for eight, with Ben Smith scoring 244. He was also sponsored by Gunn & Moore and had borrowed one of my bats — they all thought I got the best ones. The unwritten rule is that, if you get a hundred with someone else's bat, you get to keep it. So not only did I owe Ben three magnums, I also had to give him a bat. Doug Bracewell got a five-for; when he heard about Ben's windfall, he said, "What about me?" I gave him a magnum as well. I'd ordered six magnums and ended up with two, kissed a bat goodbye and made only 48 on a belter. Nice work, Ross.

Will Young went to Gunn & Moore New Zealand to get some bats, but the only top of the line ones available had my signature engraved on the back. He copped a bit of stick for using a Ross Taylor autograph. Early in his international career, Trent Boult had a Ross Taylor autograph bat, but he sandpapered my signature off. Jamie How once made the mistake of going out to bat against Australia with a Ricky Ponting autograph Kookaburra. Adam Gilchrist was carrying on saying, "Hey Punter, you've got a fan here."

Cricket in New Zealand is a pretty white sport. For much of my career I've been an anomaly, a brown face in a vanilla line-up. That has its challenges, many of which aren't readily apparent to your teammates or the cricketing public. Given that the Polynesian community is dramatically under-represented in the game, it's probably no surprise that people sometimes assume I'm Māori or Indian.

Having studied racism in the media at university as part of a sports degree, Victoria probably noticed things that many others didn't. For instance, it used to upset her that my bad shots were often put down to "brain explosions" or "dumb cricket" whereas other players' bad shots were "lapses in concentration" or "poor shot selection", or excused on the basis that, "Well, that's the way he plays."

In many ways, dressing-room banter is the barometer. A teammate used to tell me, "You're half a good guy, Ross, but which half is good? You don't know what I'm referring to." I was pretty sure I did. Other players also had to put up with comments that dwelt on their ethnicity. In all probability, a Pakeha listening to those sorts of comments would think, "Oh, that's okay, it's just a bit of banter." But he's hearing it as white person and it's not directed at people like him. So, there's no pushback; no one corrects them. Then the onus falls on the targets. You wonder if you should pull them up but worry that you'll create a bigger problem or be accused of playing the race card by inflating harmless banter into racism. It's easier to develop a thick skin and let it slide, but is that the right thing to do?

Not long after Mike "Roman" Sandle became Black Caps manager, he said to Victoria that, when he was manager of the Blues rugby team, he'd observed that the Māori and Island boys struggled with managing money, "so if Ross wants to talk about it. . ." Victoria laughed it off and it probably didn't take Mike long to realise that, however well-meaning, he'd been a bit hasty in his assumptions. When I came back into the team after the captaincy drama, I found myself sitting next to Mike Hesson in the Koru Lounge at Dunedin Airport. He'd come straight from his house. "My cleaner's Samoan," he said. "She's a lovely lady, hard-working, very trustworthy." All I could say was, "Oh, cool."

I have no doubt that Roman and Hess and the guys who engaged in the "banter" would be dismayed to learn that their remarks landed with a thud. Let me be clear: I don't think for one minute that they were coming from a racist perspective. I think they were insensitive and lacked the imagination and empathy to put themselves in the other person's shoes. What to them is a bit of harmless banter is actually confronting for the targets because it tells them they're seen as being different. Instead of the message being, "You're one of us, mate," it is, in effect, "You're one of them." In that sense, it's the opposite of colour blindness.

I didn't even have the option of retaliating: when your father is Pakeha, your grandparents were Pakeha and you have Pakeha uncles and cousins, it's hard to call someone a "white bastard" with much conviction. I'm probably one of the few international athletes who have been racially abused from both sides — I've been called a black and a white bastard in cricketing circles.

I was fortunate in being able to draw on the experience and guidance of Murphy Su'a, the first Samoan to play cricket for New Zealand. He was a great sounding board on cricketing matters and, as someone who was active in the Samoan community and Samoan cricket, on Samoan culture. Talking to Murphy, it was clear that the Black Caps environment had become more sensitive and tolerant since he made his international debut in 1992. That trend continued during my time with the Black Caps. When I became a Black Cap in 2006, I couldn't have broached the subject as I've done here. Hopefully, in 16 years' time, it won't need to be broached.

All Blacks hooker Dane Coles and I attended a careers day for a couple of schools at Parliament. I had to tell Dane that Colin de Grandhomme had got a German Shepherd, an ex-police dog, from the Bay of Plenty police, who name their dogs after All Blacks. Colin's dog was called Dane Coles. It couldn't run upstairs and hated concrete floors.

The Pakeha kids from Northland knew who we both were; the Samoan kids from Tawa or Porirua knew Dane, but had no idea who I was. They were asking me, "What's your name? What do you do?" They were blown away to discover there was a Samoan playing cricket for the Black Caps.

In his autobiography, Sonny Bill Williams talked about wanting to be a role model for young Māori and Pasifika who are held back by a lack of confidence and their personal circumstances, and therefore don't fulfil their potential. I know from personal experience how true that is. If I'd been more confident, I would have been a better captain and made a better fist of various situations. But you are who you are — you can't snap your fingers and be transformed. All you can do is strive to ensure that you keep growing.

I wouldn't be comfortable being a poster boy, but I'd hope that one of the takeaways from my career is that good cricketers can emerge from a Polynesian background. Admittedly, I had a few things going for me: a father who was into the game, very supportive grandparents who paid for me to go on rep trips, and a gear sponsorship from the age of 14. In terms of gear, cricket is expensive compared to rugby and rugby league, which probably puts some Polynesian parents off the game. But maybe New Zealand Cricket should be putting more resources into the Polynesian community because there must be more where I came from.

PART FOUR:
THE LONG GOODBYE

Chapter 15.
A Game of Inches

On the morning of our first game at the 2019 ODI World Cup —
against Sri Lanka in Cardiff — I found myself in the unfamiliar
position of being interviewed by Brendon McCullum.

I think he was more nervous than I was, and that's saying
something, since I was acutely aware of my history of
underwhelming starts at World Cups. In 2007 there was the golden
duck after the crispy aromatic duck. I didn't get a bat against Kenya
in 2011 and made 14 against Sri Lanka in 2015. Back then, Baz
may have been a bit out of his comfort zone doing live TV, and
perhaps someone had told him to be more animated because he
boomed out his questions, even though I was only a metre and a
half away. We won by 10 wickets. I didn't get a bat; in fact, I didn't
really do anything. For me, the first games of tournaments were
just a waste of time.

I got 82 against Bangladesh and was pleased with the way I
used my feet to the spinners. The old Taylor–Williamson running
between the wickets issue reared its ugly head once again, but
this time we got lucky. The throw went to the keeper, Mushfiqur
Rahim, who made a meal of it, taking the bails off with his elbows.
During the 2021 T20 World Cup in the UAE, I did some TV work
with former Black Caps fast bowler Mitch McClenaghan. When
Kane was run out against Pakistan, Mitch joked on air that I'd get

the blame, even though I was in a TV studio half a world away.

We beat Afghanistan, shared the points with India when the game was rained off and pipped South Africa in a tight one. The West Indies game in Manchester was a fantastic contest. Kane and I put on 160 after both the openers got ducks — he went on to get 148. They looked dead and buried, but Carlos Braithwaite very nearly took the game away from us. After making 101 off 81 balls, he tried to hit a six that would've won the game, only to be caught right on the boundary by Trent Boult. There was an over left, but he was batting with the number 11. I felt for Carlos because he deserved to be a winner. We were in a huddle, absolutely elated. I saw Carlos on his knees so I went over and told him, "You should be proud of yourself. That was one hell of a knock." He was pretty distraught, so it probably didn't register.

Before that game, news came through that Craig McBride, my old Wairarapa rep coach, had been killed in a plane crash at Hood Aerodrome in Masterton. He picked me for Wairarapa as a 15-year-old and put me at first slip, which isn't where the youngest guy in the team usually fields. We'd stayed in contact — every now and again he'd ask me for a few bats for fundraising events. I was touched to be asked to write a little eulogy which was read out during the wake at the Lansdowne Cricket Club.

After that epic win over the Windies, we lost three in a row — to Pakistan, Australia and England — but were still on course to make the semi-finals because our net run rate was so high. Pakistan needed to win their last pool game — against Bangladesh — by an unfeasible margin.

From the outside, it would have looked like we'd lost momentum, but I always felt that being the underdog worked for us. After we lost to England, I said to coach Gary Stead, "It's the best thing for us." Steady told us to take a few days off to do our own thing and recharge: "Let's just get ready to win," he said. "We're two wins away from the World Cup." It was a good call.

It was an unusual situation, having had three poor games in a row but still being in with a shot at a World Cup. In our defence, the wickets were pretty average. Before the tournament there was an expectation that England, having built a power batting line-up, would roll out belters and teams would be posting 350–400. It certainly didn't play out that way.

The Lord's wicket for the Australia game was one of the worst I'd ever played on in England and the conditions were the hottest I'd ever experienced there. It was one of those games when you knew well before the end of their innings that they'd got too many. The wicket was very dry — Kane bowled seven overs for 25 runs — and deteriorating. That became the trend: captains started bowling part-time spinners who were turning it square. The Riverside Ground in Chester-le-Street, where we played England, was actually a good batting wicket for the first 25 overs, but after that it went downhill fast. We were no chance batting second on that track.

My best mate, Marcus, and his fiancée Michaela, were in Newcastle, as was my second cousin Lome Fa'atau, who played on the wing for the Hurricanes and Chiefs before plying his trade in the UK. I stayed on in Newcastle to hang out with them, which was a great time-out heading into the semi-final. We were expecting to play Australia who we knew would be tough. But South Africa beat the Aussies in the very last pool match, flipping the semi-final match-ups around. It would be fair to say we weren't exactly bullish at the prospect of playing the Aussies, but we quietly fancied our chances against India.

The day before the semi-final at Old Trafford, I copped one smack on the thumb when getting throwdowns from batting coach Craig McMillan. My immediate thought was, 'Oh no, it's broken.' Our physio assured me it wasn't. It was bruised and sore but sometimes that sort of an injury can be a good thing: it deflects some of your focus away from the game and the magnitude of the occasion because you're thinking about how it might affect your batting and whether you need to make adjustments. I got hit on the thumb again before the pink-ball test in Perth later that year and made runs then as well.

One of my strengths was that, regardless of what sort of form I was in, I always backed myself to get to 30 or 40. If you get out, then so be it, but you've scrapped and put the team in a better position. That was my mindset for the semi-final. We won the toss and batted; I joined Kane at 69/2. It was another poor wicket and we were both struggling. I always enjoyed partnerships with Kane, but sometimes he was so into his own batting that it was hard to get his attention. A sport psychologist once told me that "Batting is a metaphor for life: you've got to have empathy for your mate." That was very much the case in this game: Kane was even more reassuring than he usually was. I was scratching around and apologising for the pressure I was putting him under. He just kept saying, "Don't worry, Ross, you're doing fine. We're going well."

I'd suggest that Kane and I were two of the better players of spin, but it was hard to get Ravindra Jadeja and Yuzvendra Chahal away. Australia and South Africa had both got 300-plus on the same ground a few days earlier, so the expectation was that the semi-final would be a high-scoring affair.

But the longer we batted, the more we felt that 240–250 would be competitive. I got some stick from the TV commentators along the lines of, "It's a semi-final, you've got to be aggressive." The only assessment that mattered was the one Kane and I were making about what was a good total.

Kane got out in the 36th over, so my job then was to get to about 45 overs, depending on wickets in hand. If there are five wickets in hand, you go at 45 overs; if there are seven, you go at 43. If the opposition have an amazing death bowler like Jasprit Bumrah or Lasith Malinga, you might have to go earlier to target other bowlers. We were in the power play and I was just starting to go for it when it rained. We went into the reserve day at 211/5 with 3.5 overs remaining.

Competition details — the rules and processes around the

particular format and series or tournament — kicked in. Coping with changes to competition details wasn't one of my strengths, and a one-day game becoming a two-day game amounted to a pretty significant change, especially given that I was not out overnight. I was up till 1 am replying to texts from family and friends. They all said the same thing: "If you can just get to 250. . ." Baz texted: 250 was his number, too. I was texting back saying I thought 240 would be good.

The next morning Kevin Pietersen, who was commentating, came over as I was warming up. He said, "Mate, what were you and Kane doing yesterday? It's a good wicket." I told him we thought it was a 240–250 wicket. He asked, "Can Kane Williamson read a wicket?" I replied, "I guess we'll find out."

The rain had changed the pitch. It had sweated under the covers, so it wasn't as dry and slow; it was a bit tacky, but you could hit through the line. I was in two minds: the fact that you could hit through the line was advantage India, but the tackiness could help our quicks. We got 239/8: we'd given ourselves a chance, but we needed early wickets.

Matt Henry and Trent Boult bowled brilliantly: one ball into the fourth over India were 5/3 with Rohit Sharma, who'd made a ton of runs in the tournament, Virat Kohli and KL Rahul back in the shed. I thought Kohli's lbw was a bit high, but the umpire's call went in our favour. When Jimmy Neesham took a fantastic catch to get Dinesh Karthik India were 24/4.

Rishabh Pant and Hardik Pandya were uncharacteristically circumspect, but they built some sort of platform for MS Dhoni and Jadeja. As that partnership grew, I started to wonder if the hard work we'd put in the day before would be enough because the wicket had changed. Jadeja started to really pump it and there was the Dhoni factor — regardless of the scoreboard, you'd never beaten India until Dhoni was out. Chris Harris used to say that "You've always got more time than you think." Dhoni could operate on that principle because he backed his ability, was so calm under pressure and was an absolute master at pacing an innings.

He was panned by the commentators for batting too slowly, but he'd been in that situation so many times and would have backed himself to win the game for India. It's easy to make categorical pronouncements in the commentary box that skate over or ignore how the wicket is playing and the bowlers are bowling. Furthermore, the new Old Trafford has pretty big boundaries, so you had to be a lot more calculating than on a ground like Eden Park. I'm sure Kohli and coach Ravi Shastri had absolute faith that Dhoni would get the job done.

In those situations, players — me included — can fall into the trap of thinking you have to do it all yourself. Batting is about partnerships: sometimes it's your day, sometimes it's your mate's day. Dhoni would have believed he could get there, but he also knew Jadeja was on fire at the other end. Jadeja got 77 at a strike rate of 130. Only five others made scores of 30-plus in that game; only two had strike rates above 70 — Kane's was 70.5, mine was 82.

When Jadeja went, India needed 32 off 3.1 overs. Straightaway Dhoni blasted Lockie Ferguson over cover for six — and, as I said, they were big boundaries. I was getting a bit twitchy, thinking, 'Here it comes.' It was ours to lose, but it was also the perfect Dhoni scenario.

Dhoni flipped a short one behind square and went for a second run. He came up an inch short. Given what happened in the final, it was ironic that Martin Guptill's throw secured our spot. Guppy is our best fielder and one of the best in the game. He has a rocket arm, but the targeting system wasn't always engaged. This time it was locked on. Although I was pretty good at calling run outs, that one was too close to call. I asked umpire Richard Kettleborough: "I think he might be out," he said.

The boys had assigned me the role of working out the prize money. Before the game, Ish Sodhi said, "Come on boys, let's win this game — if we make the final, it'll go towards my wedding."

When we came off the field I gave Ish a hug and said, "There you go, Ish, there's your wedding sorted."

We shook hands with the Indian players. Virat said, "Go well in the final, mate. Go and have a bucket of KFC and win the final." (When we got to London I googled the closest KFC — it was on Queensway in Bayswater — and made a beeline for it.) KP was about to go to air. I walked over and said, "I told you 240 would be enough." "Well done, mate," he said. "Well done." I had to go for a drugs test, which was just about the last thing I felt like doing. But at least we'd won. I got tested after we lost at the semi-final stage of the 2007 World Cup and that was a lot worse.

Victoria's parents had looked after the kids while she was in the UK for part of the tournament. (She went home after the Australian game.) When the semi-final went into the reserve day, she rang the travel agent to see if there were seats available to London the following night. If we made the final, she'd be flying back to London the next day having barely got over her jet lag so, rather than watch the game, she went to bed early. She was woken up around 4 am by a call from some of the partners who were at the game. Mackenzie had seen the result on her iPad and came running to see Victoria saying, "Mum, Mum, we won. Does this mean we're going to London?"

My parents-in-law, Robyn and Peter, have done so much for us over the years. Robyn didn't know we were in the final but probably feared the worst when Victoria rang her at 6 am: Robyn opened the conversation with "What?" Victoria flew out with Mackenzie and Jonty that night, leaving Adelaide with her parents. Life as it was before Covid.

We asked the kids what they wanted to do for dinner the night before the final. They couldn't make up their minds so we asked the concierge for a recommendation. He said there was a good Italian two blocks away which was perfect because the kids could have pizza. Who should walk into the restaurant but David Warner with his wife and kids? The Aussies had lost their semi-final to England, but the test players were sticking around for the upcoming Ashes series.

My strong view was that we had to approach the final as if it was just another game. When the coaches asked for my opinion at the batting group meeting, I made the point that the 2015 team played some fantastic cricket to get into the final but froze when we got there. For me, it started on the bus: we needed to do exactly the same as we'd been doing since we arrived in the UK.

Throughout the tournament we warmed up by playing a hybrid of soccer and volleyball, one side of the bus versus the other. It got so competitive that all the chat on the way to training or a game was about soccer-volleyball rather than cricket. It's easy to get tunnel vision going into high-stakes games, so building other stuff — cards, music — into your routine helps you relax and makes things more enjoyable. The bus trips to the MCG in 2015 and Lord's in 2019 were chalk and cheese in terms of the guys' demeanour and the noise level.

It was raining on the morning of the game. Steady sent out a text telling us not to come down at 8.30 am, but what he didn't realise was that Lord's drains really quickly. We got to the ground late; the game was starting in 45 minutes which meant we had a condensed warm-up. It probably helped in that we didn't have to think about it too much.

The English guys, who are normally quite upbeat, seemed a bit nervous, but I'd never heard anything like the noise that greeted them when they came out for the anthems. Even the members in the Long Room were going off. I thought, 'Wow, if they don't get up for it after that, they never will.'

I got in in the 22nd over but struggled to get going. Adil Rashid was bowling from the pavilion end with the short downhill boundary on my left. I was thinking, 'I'm going to take Rashid down, I'm going to slog-sweep him.' Then Henry Nicholls got out. The game was finely balanced so I decided to give it another over. They took Rashid off and brought on Mark Wood. His stock ball is the away swinger, but he was coming down the slope. I got my head outside the line and fell over a little bit, was hit on the pads and up they went. I thought 'That's high,' but Marais Erasmus fired me. We'd used up our referral when Henry encouraged Gup to refer one that was smashing middle stump. I walked off thinking maybe it was clipping the top of the stumps — and berating myself for not keeping my balance.

In a test match, I'd block that back-of-a-length delivery, but in white-ball cricket you've got to try to work it to square leg or fine leg because those are the free areas. You've turned a good ball into a single and rotated the strike with a low-risk option. In the middle stages of a 50-over game, that's all you're trying to do. There were times when I misread the length and was plumb, but quite often that back of a length ball is going over the stumps.

The members in the Long Room tell you, "Well played" whether it was or not. I was thinking, 'That's your World Cup done — you'll be remembered for getting 15. Well done, Ross, you hopeless prick.' I took off my gear, watching a replay of the dismissal: ball tracker showed it was missing the stumps. After I was out, it normally took me 10 or 15 minutes to get over it, but for some reason I just thought, 'It is what it is.' It was definitely one of my more subdued post-dismissal reactions. It wasn't until after the game that it really hit home and I got angry over the decision. Apart from everything else, if I'd been given not out, we would've had one leg bye.

I got out that way quite a lot early in my career, then DRS started coming to the rescue. As I said, it felt high. If we'd had a referral, I probably wouldn't have even asked Tom Latham; I would have just gone straight up. There had been times when I thought — rightly, as it turned out — that it was high but had made the mistake of not referring, so by then my attitude was one of being prepared to go with my gut.

Standard practice is to consult your batting partner, but that's not necessarily a straightforward process. He mightn't have been paying close attention. These days, you can't switch off when you're the non-striker, especially when you get only one referral. You've got to focus like an umpire.

DRS can be hard for young players to navigate. It would be a brave call for, say, Rachin Ravindra to tell Kane, "Nah, mate, don't even think about it — that was plumb." He's going to wait and see where Kane's coming from and react accordingly, or at least tactfully: "Yeah, it looked pretty straight but, as you say, maybe height's the issue . . ."

There was a sequel in the Boxing Day test a few months later. James Pattinson hit me on the top of the pad: it felt high, but not as high as the one in the final. Once again Marais Erasmus put the finger up. It was close to stumps and we still had two referrals, so I called it. It was going over the top. After Erasmus changed his signal, I shook my head and, when I got down to his end, I told him, "Marais, you haven't learnt." We didn't get the rub of the green with many umpire's calls in that series.

Our assessment of the batting performance was about the same as the semi-final: we thought we had enough but would've liked 10 more. Jofra Archer bowled a bouncer last ball of the innings: Mitch Santner and Lockie Ferguson didn't try to run a bye; someone in the dressing room said, "What are they doing? That could cost us." It wasn't a joke — we knew it was going to be tight. Afterwards you think about those little moments. I thought quite a lot about my misfield at mid-wicket off Jonny Bairstow that cost us a single.

Boulty swung the first ball of the England innings back in to Jason Roy, hitting him on the pads. I was sure the ball was clipping the stumps, but Erasmus gave it not out. As a rule, I didn't say much to umpires but, under the circumstances, I felt entitled to quietly say to him at the end of the over, "Come on, Marais." If it had been a few balls later, it probably would have been given, but umpires seem very reluctant to give a batter out first ball of the innings. If we'd got Roy first ball, that would have set the tone and given Boulty a real boost. I think his whole performance would have been different. He went for 67 off his 10 after having had an outstanding tournament in terms of economy rate.

It's amazing how this game gives and takes away. Ben Stokes had a golden summer, but rewind to 2017 and Carlos Braithwaite won the T20 World Cup final for the Windies by smashing Stokes for four sixes in the last over. Carlos played unbelievably well against us in the pool game and, if Boulty hadn't caught him right on the rope, we wouldn't have made the final. Ben batted superbly in the final and really won the game for England, but if Boulty hadn't stepped on the rope . . .

And then there was Gup's throw. I was right behind it; when the ball was about 20 metres out, it flashed through my mind that it could hit Ben's bat. Colin de Grandhomme couldn't get near the ricochet and it ran away to the fence. And umpire Kumar Dharmasena awarded six runs instead of five — the rules state that the batsmen had to have crossed before Gup let the ball go for a second run to be added to the tally. It should have been four runs off two balls rather than three off two, and Rashid should have been on strike rather than Stokes. Dharmasena said he had no regrets about the decision because it was made in consultation with the other match officials. Take it from me, Kumar, we had regrets.

I had a chat with Kane just to see where he was and make sure we had the right fielders in the right positions. You probably couldn't have a more high-pressure situation, but he was pretty calm; he knew what he was doing. Everyone remembers Boulty standing on the rope the over before, but who remembers the two runouts he effected off the last two balls. If he'd fumbled one of them, that would have been the game.

I walked over to shake hands with the umpires. They said, "Okay, now we go to super overs." I said, "Really?" That shows you how much we'd looked into the competition details and possible scenarios. In the dressing room, the bowlers were crowded around Kane, giving him their five cents' worth. I didn't join the discussion. I decided he didn't need another opinion; he needed to be as clear as possible.

In hindsight, I should have had my say. I would have suggested that Lockie bowl the super over for two reasons: he'd bowled better than Boulty and the England players had really struggled with his slower ball — they just couldn't hit it. That doesn't mean Kane's decision was wrong. He went to his strike bowler and you respect that because it's a perfectly rational call. Maybe Lockie would've gone for less; maybe not. Those are the "what ifs" that abound in sport.

As we went back into the dressing room between the super overs, I was wondering — nervously — which batters we were going to go with. Nothing was said to me, so I obviously wasn't in the frame. I wished the boys good luck and went and sat on the balcony.

I was thinking Guppy hadn't had the greatest tournament, but this would be his moment: he was going get us over the line. After not facing any of the first five balls, he faced the last ball with us needing two to win and got run out coming back for the second.

We were stunned. No one said anything because no one knew what to say. All we could do was hug each other and shake hands with the England players. Most of them were yahooing with their families as "Sweet Caroline" blared out across the ground. A few of them were a bit sheepish, but the majority were caught up in the moment and the emotion that goes with winning the World Cup.

We were ushered over to the stage for the presentation. A middle-aged man in a grey suit tapped me on the shoulder and said, "Commiserations." My head was down; I shook hands without really looking at him and said, "Thanks, mate". As he walked over to some other players, I got a good look at him. 'Oh shit,' I thought, 'I just called Prince Andrew "mate".' In his remarks, Andrew assured us that the Queen sent her regards and cricket was the winner at the end of the day.

Mackenzie and Jonty were jetlagged, but I took them out to

the middle of the hallowed ground. We took a photo — Jonty was crying — and put it on Instagram. Everyone thought Jonty was crying because we lost, but it was the jetlag. I found out later that, having come all that way to watch what turned out to be the most dramatic World Cup final ever played, Jonty had spent most of it underneath a table with his iPad.

I'm essentially a wine drinker, but it was pretty much beer or champagne which I tend to think of as a celebratory tipple. I'd known Pete, the Lord's dressing room attendant, since I was on the ground staff as an 18-year-old MCC young cricketer. I got him on the case and he foraged some gin for us. I'd never really drunk gin, but I had a few that night.

While we were packing up our gear and drinking away, the partners had been left in limbo. New Zealand Cricket had booked a bar not far from our hotel in Lancaster Gate, so they'd left the ground with that in mind. Eventually they got tired of waiting and returned to Lord's. We had a party in the Long Room: I put the boombox under the portrait of WG Grace. The first song was "Sweet" bloody "Caroline".

We forgot about the result and let our hair down. There was no use dwelling on it: we'd lost the final and that was that. I asked a security guard if any other team had brought a boombox into the Long Room. "Only one," he said. "The New Zealand women's team four or five years ago."

We went back up to the changing room and partied on. Around midnight Mike Sandle decided we needed to get back to the hotel. He said, "Ross, you just take the music and everyone will follow." He reckoned I was like the Pied Piper. There were so many people on the bus — players, partners and parents — that the aisle was packed.

Having flown the family over, I decided we might as well make the most of it. Plus, I wanted to get out of England to avoid the post-mortems. Paris seemed a good option, but there was no escape: wherever we went — on the metro, at Disneyland, at the

Eiffel Tower — people, mainly English and Indian, kept coming up to say "bad luck".

England came to New Zealand the following summer. Before the first test, a few of the boys were out on the field catching up with Joe Root and some of the England players. The subject of the Ashes series came up. "Bloody hell," said Joe, "didn't the Aussies carry on like pork chops when they drew the series?" Tim Southee, who's very quick, went straight back with, "Yeah, a bit like you guys when you drew the World Cup final." Joe just smiled and said, "I think you got me."

Chapter 16.
The Road to the Rose Bowl

Exactly one month after the World Cup final, we began our World Test Championship (WTC) campaign in Sri Lanka. At the first training, it was clear we'd processed that scarcely believable reversal, dealt with it and moved on. We were playing our soccer/ volleyball hybrid warm-up game: when Trent Boult stood on one of the cones marking the touchline, Tim Southee told him, "Just like the World Cup final." The boys laughed; no one said, "Too soon." That told me we'd moved on as a group.

We trained in Colombo, then bussed down to Galle for the first test. It didn't really hit me until I got up to my room that we were staying in the hotel where Mike Hesson dropped the hammer in 2012. I walked around the corner and there was Kane settling into the suite where it all happened. I asked him if I could have a look. Nothing much had changed; I definitely remembered the gothic four-poster bed. Kane had no idea why I was checking out his suite and I didn't enlighten him. Returning to the scene of the crime didn't make me angry. In fact, I went back to my room smiling.

We didn't know how the WTC was going to work, so it wasn't really discussed. As on any tour to the subcontinent or the UAE, the primary focus was: how do we play their spinners? Do you use the crease, try to put pressure on the bowlers or trust your defence? The thing about playing on turning wickets in the subcontinent is that you can't replicate it in training. You can fiddle around, for instance by scuffing up the practice wicket, but nothing can really prepare you for taking guard at 10/2 with four catchers around the bat after baking in 40-degree heat and extreme humidity for 160 overs as the opposition ground their way to 550.

I got 86 in the first innings. I felt as if I had things under control and was headed for a century, but it rained. I was out first ball on day two playing a poor shot — competition details strike again — and we got cleaned up. Akila Dananjaya, who spun it both ways, took five wickets in our first innings, but the umpires raised questions about his action, which meant he couldn't play in the second test. His action was certainly a hot topic in our dressing room.

Although we lost, it was a pleasant change to play Sri Lanka and not have to think about Mahela Jayawardene or Kumar Sangakkara and the prospect of chasing leather for a couple of days. In 2012, we'd had Chaminda Vaas on our coaching staff and, on this tour, Thilan Samaraweera was our batting coach. Having former Sri Lankan players on board was massively beneficial, not so much technically but in terms of reading the conditions, managing the net bowlers and having a relationship with the groundsmen. We always felt the groundsmen would be more forthcoming with Vaas or Samaraweera than they were with us.

The second test was at the P Sara Oval, the scene of the last game of my captaincy. It was nice to go back there and win another one. I didn't do much but, if you're going to have a game to forget, best to do so when some of your teammates have games to remember: Tom Latham got 154, BJ Watling had a big game with bat and gloves, Colin de Grandhomme batted explosively and the bowling unit — pace and spin — got the job done in style.

Even though the WTC final was two years away, we didn't want to come away from that series empty-handed, so we went in with a more aggressive mindset. One of the really good things about the WTC is that every test counts. Previously, Sri Lanka would have approached the second test with a mindset of being 1–0 up in a two-test series, meaning a draw would be a good outcome. But, if they'd won both tests, they would have collected 120 WTC points. As it was, we got 60 points apiece, which was a pretty good result for us.

There's no doubt that Covid worked to our advantage. It forced the cancellation of our series in Bangladesh, a much tougher assignment these days than it was at the start of my career. Even though the Bangladeshis would have been without Shakib Hussain, who was still banned, getting two wins there would have been very hard. Towards the end of the qualifying schedule, Australia opted out of touring South Africa, thereby foregoing the opportunity to bolster their points tally.

Our three-test series in Australia in 2019/20 was a case of coming down to earth with a sickening thud after the World Cup campaign and a run of success in red-ball cricket that propelled us to second in the test rankings. (Australia were fifth going into that series.) The Aussies were formidable, as they generally are in their conditions. We came off the rails in the first test, a day–night pink-ball game at the new Perth Stadium, and never got back on track.

Australia won the toss and batted; test debutant Lockie Ferguson broke down after bowling 11 overs, leaving us a bowler short. It was 40 degrees. They batted for 146 overs, the innings extending till tea on day two. Neil Wagner bowled 37 overs; his four scalps included David Warner, Steve Smith and Marnus Labuschagne, who top-scored with 143.

I was cooked. I sat in the air-conditioned viewing area thinking, 'Come on, openers, let's get through this — I don't want to bat today.' I really hoped the openers would get through at least 10 overs, ideally 20, and then we would have been in nightwatchman territory. Mitchell Starc got Tom Latham in the first over; Josh Hazlewood got Jeet Raval in the second. Ten balls into the innings and I was on my feet.

At the other Australian grounds, you walk out to bat through the members' enclosure. At the new stadium in Perth, you walk out past the punters, ordinary spectators, as opposed to members who tend to be older professional people — polite society if you like. I'd never struck anything like this: there were five and six-year-old kids — and their dads — yelling, "You're f----n shit, Taylor" and "Quack, quack, quack, see you in two minutes." I was knackered, somewhat apprehensive, and getting paid out by kids whose fathers looked on approvingly, if they weren't actually joining in.

I couldn't help but laugh. (Of course, I wouldn't have been laughing if I'd walked off a few balls later and the kids were going, "Quack, quack, Taylor. Told ya.") When I got out to the middle I asked Kane, who'd only faced one ball, "Did you get that reception? Did you have those kids abusing you?" He said, "Shit, yeah." Instead of discussing our dire situation, we were talking about the crowd abuse. It was so unexpected and surreal that it probably relaxed us. We batted for 20-odd overs, putting on 76.

At stumps we were 109/5; I was 66 not out. I'd played 90-odd tests and that was one of the hardest innings to get through. I'd been in that scoreboard situation before — going in in the second over — but never under lights to face a pink ball after fielding for 146 overs in draining heat. And never after being trash-talked by feral kids on the way out to bat.

On my first trip to Australia, Andre Adams gave me some of the best advice I ever received. I was a youngster and pretty quick, so I fielded on the boundary a lot. Andre said, "Whatever do you do, don't bite back — if anything, play along with the crowd. If you bite back, that's you done; there's no coming back." That's what I tried to do from then on. When we went to Australia, South Africa or England, I'd tell the young guys, "Just play along with the crowd."

If you're fielding on the boundary and the crowd tells you to stretch, you stretch; if they want you to come and sign something or have a photo taken with them, you do it. Because I spent so much time at first slip, especially in test cricket, I actually enjoyed the interaction. Admittedly, the older you are and the more you've achieved, the more confident you are about being in that situation, and in your judgement of what you can get away with. Sometimes you'd build such a rapport with the crowd that they'd turn on one of their own if he had a go at you.

Some crowds are notoriously tough, but even with them you'd normally be okay if you could have a laugh at your own expense. It was probably easier for me because I knew what was coming; I knew the first thing they'd target was my huge arse. (As I used to tell people when I was growing up, "A huge arse makes you run fast. It's like pistons.")

Some county cricket crowds are pretty relentless. When I played for Sussex against Essex at Chelmsford, a chunk of the team meeting was devoted to what we could expect from the crowd. By the end of the game, I was getting on with the locals like a house on fire. I just went with the flow and took the piss out of myself. They'd say, "You're going to get your arse kicked," and I'd say: "You know what? I think you're right; I think we're going to lose." They didn't have much of a comeback. You strike some ruthless people up north, at places like Headingley and Old Trafford, particularly if it's a warm day and the students are in the house.

At many county grounds you can actually have a conversation with the spectators who are trying to wind you up. They want to make you bite but, if you engage with them rather than taking the bait, you can end up chatting about where you're going for dinner. The strangest compliment I got over there was, "You're funnier than Doug Bollinger." The former Aussie left-arm quick was known on the circuit as "Doug the Rug" because he wore a hairpiece. Late in his career, he decided to go au naturel and auctioned off the hairpiece for a bushfire appeal.

While we got taken to the cleaners in Australia, we still had three home two-test series — against India, West Indies and Pakistan — in which to rack up points. We won them all 2–0 but we had to work for it.

Everyone produces wickets that suit their strengths in terms of personnel and preferred way of playing the game. We had one of the best seam attacks in the world, so we wanted to play on green wickets that seamed for two or three days. We didn't want to turn up to find wickets that were only slightly green, that seamed for two sessions then flattened out. We needed to win every game to have a chance of making the WTC final, but those sorts of wickets bring the draw into play and draws at home are opportunities squandered.

Hence our surprise over the wicket for the first test against Pakistan at Bay Oval in December 2020, and the intense discussions around the timing of our day four declaration. There were a lot of different numbers being thrown around. Coach Gary Stead and Kane would always ask for my thoughts. Steady was probably the more aggressive of the two, but then it was Kane's neck on the block if he'd declared too early. I felt we needed to pull out before tea to give ourselves two cracks with the new ball — on either side of the break. Secondly, the last thing we wanted was to find ourselves 10 overs short in the last session on day five. If it hadn't been a WTC qualifier, we probably would have set them 400-plus; as it was, we declared before tea, setting them 373, had five overs at them before the break and knocked over both openers.

India winning that amazing series in Australia helped our cause. And when the Aussies pulled out of touring South Africa, we knew that we'd made the final because we had more points than them. It was just a question of who we'd be up against: England, India or Australia. For Australia to make the final, India and England had to cancel each other out in their four-test series in India. That scenario looked possible after England won the first test. Then Ravichandran Ashwin and Axar Patel went to work on wickets that turned from ball one and India took the series 3–1.

No one said it publicly, and it wasn't discussed in-depth but, given the final was going to be in England, we definitely felt that our best shot would be against India. We didn't want to play the host nation because they knew the conditions better than we did. And Australia had played three Ashes series in England in the space of six years, so their seam bowlers knew those conditions better than the Indians.

I wouldn't say we had a mental block about playing the Aussies, but we'd had no joy against them in test cricket since 2011, and that takes its toll. Their quick bowlers are really good and they're just a tough team to play. Playing them on neutral ground would have been less daunting, but our order of preference was India first, England second, Australia third. I suspect most New Zealand cricket followers felt the same way.

Our two tests against England that preceded the final weren't part of the WTC programme. The England and Wales Cricket Board had a gap in their playing schedule that they wanted to fill so New Zealand Cricket CEO David White put the Black Caps forward. We hadn't qualified for the WTC final at that stage, but David was thinking ahead: we had a good chance of making the final and, if that happened, what better preparation than a couple of tests against England? It all came to pass: we made the final; it was against India; and we had the perfect build-up. The Indians had to make do with inter-squad games.

The only thing not going our way was that, with the Delta variant surging and the various Covid protocols and restrictions, it looked as if our IPL contingent wouldn't be able to play the first test. Then the IPL was suspended and the guys went to the Maldives. I was a bit jealous because the Maldives are on my bucket list, but Kane reckoned they weren't a patch on Rarotonga.

I flew to the UK with BJ, Tim and Wags. There weren't enough business-class seats available for all of us so the older guys got an extra day at home. Two days after we got there, it emerged that someone on our flight had Covid so we had to go back into isolation for a couple of days. If the positive case had been cabin crew, we would have gone into a 10-day lockdown.

I'd done my calf muscle a few weeks beforehand, when I was still rehabbing the hamstring I'd torn against Bangladesh. The physio was reassuring me the calf would be okay, but I was nervous. I was only running at quarter speed when it happened, which seemed like a bad sign. I took it really easy at training to give it time to heal, get my confidence up and build enough fitness to be good to go in the final, but I'd never gone into a test without having sprinted beforehand. It was an unsettling time: I didn't have much confidence in my calf and I sensed the coaches didn't have much confidence in me.

Yet another reminder of my age and how long I'd been around was that my last three Black Caps batting coaches were guys I'd played with. I'm sure that coaching someone you played with has its challenges but, frankly, I found it hard with all of them. I guess they thought they didn't have much to offer me, but I still wanted coaching; I still needed another pair of eyes. Shortly before Martin Crowe died, he told me, "You're your own best coach," so perhaps I just wasn't receptive.

The crowd for the first test at Lord's was limited to 25 per cent of capacity. The Long Room was blocked off to the public: we actually had lunch there the day before the game. As well as being the most famous cricket ground, Lord's does the best food. Everyone looks forward to it. You have soup, prawns and get to choose from a range of mains and desserts. But, because of Covid, they were down to a couple of options, one of which was duck. Obviously, there was no way I was having duck the day before a test match. I asked the lady who was serving us if there was any other protein. She said, "Are you halal?" I said, "No, I'll eat it whatever it is." It was chicken. Mitch Santner and Colin had duck and were out in successive overs without troubling the scorers. I did try to warn them.

On the bus to the ground, guys were walking up and down the aisle asking, "Who wants to play golf after the test?" I wasn't sure if it was a good sign or a bad sign. You always go to Lord's

wanting to get on the Honours Board, but I never really got
my head around batting there. At one end your toes are tilting
downhill, at the other end they're pointing uphill. On top of that,
my second test in a series was nearly always better than my first
— it was as if I took one game to get into test mode. There was a
logic to it given warm-up games are pretty much a thing of the
past. I got a less than fluent 14 in the first innings and slogged 33
in the second ahead of a declaration. Neither innings did much
to improve my mental state.

Victoria rang me after the first innings at Lord's. She'd been a
cricketer but, in the 17 years we'd been together, she'd never rung
me to criticise my batting. She sensed my mental state wasn't
great and that if I didn't score runs, my place in the team would
be in jeopardy.

Victoria Taylor: The year leading up to that point had
been quite tough. Between his calf and hamstring injuries
and Covid, Ross hadn't played for three months going
into that game. Retirement was in the back of his mind.
I didn't sleep during that test. I know how Ross operates
and I knew his frame of mind. I felt he had three innings
to secure his spot in the team for the WTC final but
sensed that he was almost reconciled to his fate and
wasn't sure he had the gas in the tank to fight for it. I just
kept thinking he couldn't end his career that way. He'd
dug deep before and I knew he could do it again.
Someone had to give him a talking-to. I took one for the
team — he didn't talk to me for a few days after that.

Between the tests we played golf against the England team at the
Belfry in Birmingham. (We played the Ryder Cup format which
was appropriate since the Cup has been held at the Belfry three
times.) I played off a 16. I hadn't played golf on tour since 2013 in
Bangladesh with Kane — we're both nine-hole golfers. It was the

best time I'd had on a golf course because we each had a caddy and a ball finder: you'd hit it miles off line, two fairways over, then walk around a dogleg right and there would be your ball, just off the fairway on a perfect lie.

Will Young and I played Craig Overton and James Bracey. The England guys were dressed up in matching tops they'd bought at the pro shop so, sartorially, they had it over the Central Stags boys. On each of the first three holes I putted for birdie; one went in, so I was one under par after three holes and we were two up. I could see Craig and James were thinking, 'This guy's a burglar.' It didn't last. The Belfry just had hosted a big tournament so the rough was nightmarish and things went from bad to worse.

We got to the 15th two behind, so still in a chance. I'd lost a few balls and twilight was falling so I switched to an orange highlighter ball. And, being superstitious, I was hoping for a change of luck. I went into the rough again. Five metres in front of me was a stream with a wooden retaining wall. I'd watched a Phil Mickelson video in which he talked about putting the ball back in your stance, and I'd had some success with that. But this time I thinned it. It flew straight into the retaining wall and ballooned back to me. Without missing a beat, I caught it, dropped it and took another swing. I shot 111 and Will and I lost, thus depriving the Kiwis of a clean sweep.

Afterwards the English opener Dom Sibley came up. He said, "Ross, I've had a few beers, but I was on the fairway over from you: did I see what I thought I saw? Because I looked over and could've sworn I saw you catch the ball. I thought, 'I'm losing it.'" The golf sucked, but I had to laugh at the idea of these guys on the next fairway over not sure if they could believe their eyes.

I was in a pretty dark place as I waited to bat on day two at Edgbaston. England had changed their pandemic rules so the ground was at 70 per cent capacity. Under 16s weren't allowed in, so pretty much every single one of the 18,000 spectators was on the turps. On day one, they'd necked 56,000 pints and, by the sound and sight of it, there'd been no let-up. The BBC described it as "the world's biggest stag do".

Devon Conway, who'd got 200 at Lord's on test debut, was on 60-odd; he'd booked his ticket. Will Young, who'd come in for Kane, was on 40-odd and batting really well. I wondered what the coach was thinking. I was pretty sure I knew what the batting coach was thinking, and it wasn't reassuring. I still couldn't run properly. I hadn't had to dig that deep since the ambush in Galle.

Chapter 17.
Handle with Care

I turned 36 on 8 March 2020. A couple of months later I won the Sir Richard Hadlee Medal for Player of the Year in the 2019/20 New Zealand Cricket Awards. However, in the official NZC rankings, determined by coach Gary Stead and selector Gavin Larsen, I was seventh in the test team and second in the ODI team.

When I expressed surprise that I hadn't made the top half of the test team, Steady went on about what the bowlers had achieved. Fair enough, but, as I pointed out, when we played on the subcontinent, some of them didn't make the playing XI. And I was puzzled that I was ranked lower than batters who I'd outperformed and/or had only played a handful of games. It planted the suspicion that my age had become a factor in the selectors' thinking.

That was the backdrop to my player review. I suspected that, having gone hard at Steady over the rankings, they were going to come back hard at me in the review. It was during lockdown, so it was a Zoom meeting. Batting coach Peter Fulton set the tone: "You had a good year, Ross," he said, "but you played a terrible shot against Jadeja in the first innings of the second test [against India at Hagley Oval]." I explained that I was trying to assert some dominance and didn't want to let a left-arm spinner settle on a green seaming wicket that didn't suit him. That was the only aspect of my test performances that Fults deemed worthy of comment.

He then addressed my T20 strike rate, saying I played with more freedom overseas than I did at home. (The comparative strike rates were 160-odd overseas, 130-odd at home.) I pointed out that we were hardly comparing like with like: I'd played 12 games at home whereas the overseas component was two games in Sri Lanka. In the first, I made 48 off 29 balls and won man of the match. I had a sore hip afterwards, the result of bringing out the slog-sweep for the first time in a while, so I missed game two. In the third, I got a golden duck, the fourth of Lasith Malinga's four wickets in consecutive balls, a feat sometimes referred to as a double hat-trick. I didn't have my pads on when Malinga took his second wicket, so I had to rush through my routine to get out to the middle. I knew he was going to bowl the yorker, but I still missed it.

It wasn't a cordial meeting. I was watching the body language: our trainer Chris Donaldson had his head down; Shane Jurgensen, the bowling coach, looked like he'd rather be somewhere else. I was thinking, 'Well, this is remarkable: a review of the season in which I got the Player of the Year award, but there hasn't been a single constructive or positive word.' But Mike Sandle came with a late run, saying I'd been a manager's delight, great with kids and sponsors, always willing to do what was asked of me and, by the way, congratulations on the award.

Having overheard Fults' opening salvo, Victoria stayed in the room to see where things went from there. She was amazed. She couldn't get over the negativity. Schoolteachers are trained to begin those sorts of assessments on a positive note before getting onto the work-ons. When it was over, she said, "If they're saying that to you, I hate to think what they're saying to the younger guys."

I spoke to a few of the boys about their reviews. They'd all been very positive, which was good to hear. It did beg the question though: why was my review so negative?

The best and most beneficial review of my career was around

the time of the eye issue. It was black and white. Hess and batting coach Craig McMillan came armed with stats on my ODI strike rate: these are the top number 4 batters in the world; this is where you sit. It wasn't a vague critique or a matter of opinion — everything flowed from the data.

The first 10 overs weren't an issue because the game situation dictates your approach: if you lose two wickets in that period, preservation of wickets becomes the top priority; strike rate is almost irrelevant unless you're chasing a huge total. In the last 10 overs, only AB de Villiers had a better strike rate than I did. We could all live with that. The problem area was overs 11 to 39. My strike rate was in the mid-70s which put me at the rear of the field, along with Australia's George Bailey.

It wasn't a matter of scoring at 95 to 100 during that middle phase but getting from the mid-70s to the mid-80s. Your immediate reaction is to think, 'Okay, I've got to smack it and hit boundaries', but in fact you're only talking about an extra six to eight runs through that period. It's turning dot balls into ones; it's being busier; it's manipulating the field. I started running balls down to third man a bit more and adopted a more proactive approach to good balls.

Coaches shouldn't assume players at the top level know everything. Just because I'd played more than 400 international games didn't mean I knew it all, as I was only too well aware. The individual has to want to learn and get better, but he or she needs input and information.

I might have been wary, but I wasn't uncoachable; I had my method, but it wasn't entirely set in stone. I would've thought the batting coaches would have tried to get to know me and understand what I was trying to do. If they don't do that, it's going to be hard for them to make their messages relevant I would have thought.

Despite also winning the 2019/20 international Twenty20 Player of the Year award, I was the eighth-placed Black Cap in that format in Steady and Gav's official NZC rankings. The 2020 IPL had been interrupted by Covid: our contingent was just getting back from the UAE so Steady didn't want to rush them straight into the first T20 against the West Indies at Eden Park in late November. When Tim Southee got injured at training the week before the game, Steady rang to ask if I'd be captain, saying, "You're a leader in the team." I said I'd like to think about it.

I agreed to do it. In the end, though, Tim passed his fitness test so I wasn't required to captain. Devon Conway made his New Zealand debut in what turned out to be a crazy game. The Windies sailed past 50 inside three overs, then lost five wickets for one run. As you'd expect, Kieron Pollard found Eden Park to his liking and they posted a competitive score in what became a Duckworth-Lewis game. I was run out for a duck, but Mitch Santner and Jimmy Neesham got us over the line with a few balls to spare.

Games two and three were at the Mount. We won the second easily — I got in with one ball left which I didn't face. The guys in the test team didn't play in the third T20 — which was washed out — because of the short turnaround before the first test in Hamilton. Little did I know that I'd played my last T20 for New Zealand.

Before the second test in Wellington, Steady pulled me aside to tell me I was being dropped from the T20 team. (The team was being announced during the test, so he wanted to alert me beforehand.) He said my performances hadn't been good enough and they had other options, but it didn't necessarily mean my T20 career was over. I guess that gave them the comfort of knowing they had an experienced player in reserve if the young blood they were introducing didn't produce the goods.

I pointed out that I'd had one completed innings, run out for a duck, and was the incumbent T20 player of the year. Steady said, "We don't pick the player of the year." He clearly didn't think I deserved the award. I was flabbergasted, but he had one more shot in his locker: my mobility, he said, was becoming an issue. I thought, 'Wow, where did that come from?' I wasn't as fast or agile as I used to be, but I was a gazelle compared to some notable T20 players, here and overseas.

It seemed as if "mobility" was code and they were tiptoeing around the real issue: my age. Steady and Gav could have been upfront and simply said, "We think your time is running out and we want to go in a different direction." I wouldn't have been happy with that, but I could have accepted both the rationale and their right to do it. In that situation a professional athlete wants reality, however harsh. I wasn't particularly close to Steady, but we'd got along well enough up to that point. The damage done in that conversation was never fully repaired.

I rang Kane to get his take on it. He didn't know what I was talking about. Steady had told him there would be difficult calls to make when picking the T20 team, but Steady had effectively pre-empted the selection discussion, at least as it related to me.

After the second test, Steady flew to Hamilton for a clear-the-air meeting. He apologised for the way it had been handled and stressed that I was still an important member of the team and he didn't want our relationship to sour. I thanked him for coming. I give him a lot of credit for doing that.

About a month later, I was in the car with Victoria and Mackenzie. I was on the phone to Chris Donaldson discussing my training schedule. "We've just got to keep you going, Ross," he said. "You're still one of the fastest guys in the team." Victoria and I looked at each other, both of us confused by what we were hearing. Mackenzie had the last word: "Dad, you're not that fast."

In 2020/21, I was the 10th — out of 20 — contracted player in the country, my lowest ranking since my second year in the Black Caps. Your overall ranking is determined by awarding points based on your rankings in all three formats, with the test ranking having double weighting. It has no direct bearing on selection but determines your NZC income. I didn't get a T20 ranking, which meant I wasn't rated among the top 25 T20 players in the country.

My test ranking was eight; my ODI ranking six. Because of injury I'd played only one ODI, but I'd dropped four places in the ODI rankings. I had the highest ODI average of any New Zealander; I was the third-best ODI batsman in the world, according to the International Cricket Council rankings, but only the sixth-best ODI player in the Black Caps, according to Steady and Gav. It was just two guys' opinion, but they were the two guys who picked the team. The writing was on the wall. As they say, there's not a lot of sentimentality in professional sport.

Gary Hermansson believes that being dumped from the captaincy and the aftermath — the sense of betrayal created by the behaviour towards me on the part of those who pushed for it to happen and those who made it happen — left me with something akin to post-traumatic stress disorder. The nature of that condition is that you are vulnerable to relapses: something triggers you and those feelings and emotions come flooding back. Getting dumped from the T20 team, and the explanation I was given for it, were triggers. I felt unwanted; I sensed the coaches were keen to see the back of me.

The decisions around my rankings were clear indicators that Steady and Gav were starting to implement their plans for life after Taylor. In the absence of any assurances from the coach, I could only assume I was playing for my spot, which is a tough position to be in. That was what I was battling during the two-test series against England before the World Test Championship final. It all came to a head when I was waiting to go out to bat at Edgbaston, which is why I consider the 80 I got that day to be one of my best innings.

Gary Hermansson: Ross was really thrown by his non-selection in the T20 team, both because of his record, in terms of having had a very good season, and because there didn't seem to be any logical reason, other than the fact that Devon Conway was now available. In some ways, that had been looming for a while. But, again, it's the sort of thing that, if it was handled right, it still would have been painful, but explainable and logical. Ross was extremely hurt again, and I think it just reactivated the unresolved pain.

There's no doubt the whole captaincy saga changed me. I found it harder to trust people and take things at face value. I'd like to think I was still respectful when respect was due but, if I felt like I was being badly treated, I'd stand up for myself.

> **Leanne McGoldrick:** The only way up was to work on that mental toughness, that hardness, because he wouldn't have survived otherwise. Ross is still the same person he always was, but he has an armour now. I think that will be discarded as time goes on.

I didn't challenge the process for the sake of it. It was a shame that it wasn't more thoughtful, straightforward and transparent. If that had been the case and I'd known how the last lap was going to unfold, it would have taken the angst out of it: I would've been more relaxed and it would have been easier on all concerned. If only it had been handled with care.

Chapter 18.
The Boys

As an all-format Black Cap, you spend more time with your teammates than your family. You're New Zealand professional cricketers with a common goal — to win — but, beyond that, you mightn't have very much in common. The more time I spent in team environments, the more I came to realise that you don't have to get on with everybody. In fact, that's an unrealistic aspiration. You're going to get on well with some, okay with others and there will be relationships that go up and down. The key is that there's always a level of respect.

The other thing I came to realise was that being in a team for six or seven weeks, as you are in the IPL, the CPL or county cricket, is very different from playing with the same teammates for months on end, year after year. In the former, you're in a slightly artificial environment: you're not there for long enough to really get to know people and it's easy to get along with everyone. It's a bit like being on holiday. The Black Caps and Central Districts were like family with all that entails. When you play with guys for several years, you really get to know them. The relationships are more complex, but the bonds are much deeper.

The environment has changed. The Black Caps squad is increasingly diverse — the side that beat Pakistan in the first test in Abu Dhabi in 2018 contained six players who were born outside

New Zealand. As part of a New Zealand Cricket survey, we were asked to rank the various factors that have contributed to the Black Caps' success over the years. I weighed up whether to put "Immigration" or "World Class Players" at number one. In the end I went with "Immigration", which wasn't entirely tongue-in-cheek — after all, a number of our world-class players were immigrants. The Black Caps are certainly not the only international team to have benefited from immigration.

Having team members who don't drink has changed the dynamics and culture. Not that long ago, non-drinkers would have been cold-shouldered or pressured to go to the bar and sit there with a Diet Coke in the name of team bonding.

The current side is mentally tough by virtue of being highly experienced and having met and overcome adversity. The 2011 victory in Hobart was Dean Brownlie's third test, and I remember some of us saying to him, "Don't get used to this — it doesn't happen very often." It was usually a while between drinks back then whereas recently we've been very competitive, especially at home. You have players who haven't experienced too many defeats, who expect to win more often than not. Before becoming a regular, a guy like Tom Blundell had played a lot of domestic cricket and been in the environment for several years, which equipped him to succeed at international level. When I started, the group hoped that newcomers would play well, whereas now they're expected to play well.

The bottom line in international cricket is that you're not going to win if your players aren't good enough. But, if you've got a good side and you're all going in the same direction and wanting to help each other out, that team is going to get better. And if you've got world-class players, who are also highly professional and hard-working, that new players coming in can watch and learn from, that team is going to get better still. By watching the way Kane Williamson, Trent Boult and Tim Southee go about their business, the younger players learn how to be better cricket players. If the big names in the team are mediocre in an international context and don't have great standards, the new guys aren't going to learn very much and the team isn't going to win very often.

As every cricket follower knows, you need to take 20 wickets to win a test match. The best way of going about that in New Zealand is to produce green seaming pitches. We didn't do that at the start of my career. When John Wright became coach, he made it very clear he wanted green seamers. It just evened things up with the subcontinent teams: they were as much out of their comfort zone on our green tops as we were on their dust bowls.

We back ourselves on our wickets: we feel like our techniques, batting and bowling are better. In recent years, teams from the subcontinent and the West Indies have bowled too short — you've still got to hit the knee roll — and/or haven't been consistent enough. It's no good beating the bat three times in a row then bowling a four-ball, one the batter can put away to the boundary with a low-risk shot. You've got to be patient and disciplined and put together blocks of good overs. I can only imagine how frustrated visiting batters must get when their quicks can't do to us what our quicks are doing to them. Our spinners are under that pressure when we play on the subcontinent or in the UAE: the batting group is looking to them to pose the same sorts of problems as the opposition spinners do to us.

I suspect Gary Stead would like to play a spinner at home for that very reason — so our spinners aren't put in the position of not having played for months on end and then, when we're in Galle or Dubai, it's on them to win the game for us. To their credit, they have done exactly that a number of times; at other times, though, their lack of recent test experience has showed. Kane just wants to win test matches and thinks there's no point playing a spinner if he's hardly going to get a bowl; we might as well have an extra batter. I can understand both points of view.

It was only in the last couple of years that we've had the confidence to play the four-pronged pace attack. Previously, we often played a spinner because we felt we had to. The current quartet just want to keep bowling, so the spinner isn't going to feature until 50 or 60 overs have been bowled. For a captain, there's nothing better than having bowlers who want to bowl all the time. Given the nature of our wickets — apart from Mount Maunganui — and the success of the pace quartet, I sometimes wondered where Dan Vettori would fit into the team now. He became such a good batter that he'd probably play as an all-rounder.

I always had to laugh when I heard our quick bowlers telling interviewers they didn't care which one of them got the wickets and they weren't driven by statistics because it's all about the bowling unit and the overall outcome. None of them liked being the one who hadn't got wickets. I was all for it. It didn't worry me if one of the quicks was grumpy because he hadn't taken any wickets. It showed that they were driven to succeed.

That competition between them made us a better team. Their ambition and desire to succeed, their hunger for wickets, are what makes them outstanding bowlers and a fantastic bowling unit. That's "team first" in my book. The competition within the unit went to another level when Kyle Jamieson came in and made such an impact. There were games within games. Then they'd do an interview and say, "We get on really well" — true — and "We don't care about stats" — not true.

Any top-level cricketer who insists they're not interested in statistics is being economical with the truth, to put it politely. I accept that some cricketers attach less value and significance to statistics than others. But everyone is judged on stats and knows the stats: their own, their teammates' and the opposition players'. And, at the end of the day, the player contracts are based on statistics.

(Peter Fulton had an interesting argument around personal milestones: if a batter goes into his shell in the 90s because he's preoccupied with getting to three figures, the bowlers will criticise him for being selfish. But when a bowler has taken four wickets, he'll keep going till he gets his five-wicket haul, or is too buggered to bowl another over, or the skipper prises the ball out of his hand. It's the same thing. Call it what you want, the point is that, most of the time, both those scenarios work to the team's benefit.)

There was never a dull moment with Boulty and Tim. They've bowled the opposition out, they're stuffed, they have an ice bath, they perk up. Then look out. It's like, "What do we do now? How can we annoy somebody?" They're good friends and they go at people together, but they can also give it to each other. It shows how well they know each other, and it's no coincidence that they're great in harness.

Neil Wagner is unique in a number of ways. Most fast bowlers get slower as the day goes on, so the slips have to adjust by moving closer to the bat. But the longer Wags bowls, the further back the slips go. The standing joke was that we were up closer for Neil's first over than Colin de Grandhomme's. But when Wags was in his 15th, we'd be further back than we were in his fifth. You could end up two metres back from where you were at the start of his spell. That probably says it all. When Tom Blundell first kept to Wags, we had to warn him that, if we moved closer, Waggy would push us back. He's a force of nature, but he's 36 now and starting to complain about being sore after a big shift at the bowling crease. I'm amazed he wasn't saying that 10 years ago.

He has been criticised for bowling what is basically bodyline, the implication being that the umpires shouldn't allow him to bowl so much short stuff. (As far as the batting group is concerned, he doesn't bowl a lot of bouncers in the nets so he can bowl as many as he likes in the middle.) When the wicket is flat, bowlers have to find a way, and Waggy has done that better than anyone. I can understand the argument that you shouldn't bounce tail-enders, but the reality is that everybody does. I guess tail-enders have got to get better at dealing with the short ball.

Wags is a pioneer with plenty of imitators and, as they say, imitation is the sincerest form of flattery. Whenever I played first-class cricket here or county cricket, there would be someone trying to operate like him. What they usually failed to appreciate is that Waggy's method requires total physical commitment and a high level of skill.

All quicks bowl short balls, but most of them can't keep it up for overs on end. Wag bangs in three or four an over for over after over. And there's an art to consistently bowling short deliveries that the umpires don't regard as bouncers: if the umpires start designating them as bouncers, the Wagner-style relentless short-pitched attack becomes unsustainable because of the two bouncers an over rule. You've also got to get the field setting right, but that's easier said than done: in county cricket, for instance, there are quicks who can bowl the Wagner way, but they don't set the right field. Kane has done a great job in that regard. And what's also often overlooked is that it takes a lot of skill and control to bowl to the Wagner field.

The teams that play Waggy the best go one of two ways: you either take him on the whole time or not at all. Where batters get into trouble is when they duck some short balls and attack others. That's when Waggy thinks, 'Here we go.' You've got to decide on your approach and commit to it, but that's very hard to sustain mentally. Ego and bravado come into play. Personally, I think taking it on is the way to go because, if you duck and weave, he's going to keep bouncing you. You just have to get the bat up, play high to low and keep the ball on the ground. Again, easier said than done. I usually did pretty well against him — "Oh, f--k, not you again, Ross," he'd say. Admittedly, he got me for nought the last time I played him, but I'd had duck a couple of nights earlier.

Waggy gets upset when people dismiss him as a one-trick pony. Fair enough, too, given he gets wickets by pitching the ball up and swinging it back in. That's a very handy second string to the bow when the batter is expecting a bouncer barrage. He also has the classic left-arm quick's mode of dismissal: nicking off right-handed batters by slanting the ball across them.

Wrighty always felt Waggy's intensity would rub off on the

other bowlers, and that's exactly what happened — over time, he certainly added some of that hard-nosed South African mentality to the unit. He wasn't an overnight success at test level, but the passion was unmistakable: there's nothing more uplifting for a bowling unit and fielding team than a fast bowler steaming in and giving it everything on a flat track. I have no doubt our opponents talked a lot about Waggy in their team meetings. Whether it did any good is a moot question, because it was obvious that some batters just hated playing against him.

Kyle Jamieson always had eye-catching attributes, but his progress might have been slowed by a perception that he didn't bring a consistent hard edge to his bowling. I never had that impression. Either the perception was wrong or he hardened up in a big hurry once he got into the group. You can put his success down to the fast bowler-friendly New Zealand surfaces, but that ignores a couple of things: first, he has consistently out-bowled his highly experienced, world-class colleagues and, second, he hasn't opened the bowling, and therefore hasn't had the brand-new ball.

He brought another dimension to the bowling attack with his height and control. KJ is 2.0 metres-plus, much the same height as the Windies' Jason Holder. But Holder bowls around 135 kph with the white ball and in the mid-120s with the red ball, although he can ramp it up if he wants to. Kyle has turned himself into a 140-kph bowler with the white ball and consistently hits 135-plus with the red ball. That's a harder bowler to face than a 145-kph bowler of normal height. Because of the bounce he generates, he traps batters on the crease. I used to love watching the great West Indian, Curtly Ambrose, another very tall quick bowler. He would have nicked me off for fun. KJ isn't in that class yet — Ambrose took 405 test wickets at an average of 20.9, so we're talking about an all-time great — but he has some of the same attributes, and he's only going to get better.

KJ just wants to learn and he'll work on something until he gets it right: he came into the Black Caps as an away swing bowler;

now he can swing it both ways. And he's very economical with it. Having Southee and Boult to learn from obviously helped, as did the fact that he came into a confident, successful team. I don't think he would have had such immediate, spectacular success if the team hadn't been where it was.

Perhaps it worked for Kyle to have Tim and Boulty opening up and trying to swing it, in that he may have been the beneficiary of batters just wanting to get through the opening pair and mentally relaxing when he came into the attack. Then he'd have Wags bouncing the daylights out of guys who'd get down the other end with scrambled senses or wanting to play a few shots. Who knows? The point is, it's the most complete bowling line-up we've had because they're so different. With KJ and Devon Conway in the mix, the World Test Championship-winning team was a very complete side. The group has a lot of confidence in Devon. He has a calming presence because of his ability and his mindset — you have to get him out; he doesn't give his wicket away. The only thing missing was a world- class spinner, but we didn't need one on that surface.

It's sometimes overlooked that our bowlers also make a significant contribution with the bat. In our first innings of the WTC final, Kane did the hard work, helped by Colin, but then Kyle, Tim and Boulty made runs that meant India starting their second innings under pressure.

The tail has wagged so often that there's now a confidence within the team that someone will step up. You might be looking down the barrel of 170 all out, but the bowlers will scrap their way to 230. If you get runs out of the tail, it can be the difference between an average batting effort and an okay one. It's not necessarily about someone getting 50 or 60 — often a quick-fire 30 can shift the momentum and get you past the psychological barrier of 200. If you then grab a couple of quick wickets, you've engineered a big momentum shift. An hour earlier you were on the back foot; now you're ahead of the game.

The bowlers have got a little batting group going: they put $50 into the kitty every test match and, if one of them gets a half century or four not outs in a row, he scoops the pool. It's a bit tough on the likes of Matt Henry and Ajaz Patel who are in and out of the playing XI — they have to contribute to the pool when they play but don't get many opportunities to win it. Mark Craig wasn't allowed in because he was getting into the proper batsman category and KJ may be in the same boat.

Tim and Boulty are actually talented batters and could be better if they wanted to. It's a stretch, but it's a little bit like me and bowling: if I'd wanted to, I probably could have been a part-time offie, but I just didn't want to bowl. Boulty's batting aspirations are to get the most runs and hit the most sixes for a test number 11; Tim wants the record for the most sixes in test cricket. That's all they talk about when it comes to batting, but then they're not bad goals to have. Tim had real batting potential and started young enough to have had a lot of upside. He had more raw talent with the bat than Dan Vettori, but Dan wanted to improve.

Martin Guptill had three toes amputated when he was 12 or 13 — his brother ran over his foot with a forklift. Being in a lift with people you don't know can be awkward but try being in a lift with Gup when he's wearing jandals. You get little kids saying, "Mum, look at that man's toes." Gup takes it pretty well.

Gup is one of the best ball strikers and the best ODI opener I played with. His innings of 189 not out against England in Southampton in 2013 and 237 not out against the West Indies in Wellington in 2015 — the highest individual score in a World Cup game — are the best ODI innings by a Black Cap that I've seen. However, I don't think he was an opener in test cricket. Had Gup, with all his natural talent, been given an extended opportunity, he would have been a fantastic five or six for New Zealand for many years.

As an opener in white-ball cricket, you get away with nicking to third slip or gully because there aren't fielders there. That's a single down to the third man and you're off the mark. In test cricket that's out. And a lot of the time in test cricket there's no pressing "game situation" — you've just got to bat. It becomes a mind game because there's no situation dictating how you play. The situation, such as it is, is survival and scoring runs. In one-day or Twenty20 cricket, the situation dictates how you bat: if it's the 45th over and you need 10 an over, it's pretty clear what you need to do.

You've got to be a bit different to be an opening batter in test cricket — that's why Wrighty was so good. I think Guppy's too normal to be a test opener. Tom Latham is probably the exception that proves the rule. One of his strengths, and probably a reason why people see him as a captain, is that if you met Tom just after he'd been dismissed, you couldn't tell if he'd scored runs or not. In fact, an hour later you'd still be none the wiser. I don't know whether it's a subconscious or a conscious thing with Tom, but it seems to be his way of dealing with the ups and downs: not getting euphoric when he succeeds or down in the dumps when he fails. It's a really good trait for an opener to have. All batters have bad days, but openers have more of them.

Cricket isn't like rugby, a game that can be played on emotion. Motivational speeches from the coach or captain are no use to a batter if you win the toss and, as has become the norm in New Zealand, bowl first. The batter mightn't get in till after tea or maybe not even until day two. Or you lose the toss, get sent in on a green wicket and you're on your way out to the middle in the third over. You've got to be able to switch on when called upon. Leanne would ring the night before a game to ask, "How are you feeling? Are you ready?" I used to say, "It's not about being ready now. I have to be ready when I'm needed."

My other job was to take slip catches, which poses a different challenge and requires a different mental skill. As a batter, when you're on strike, you know the ball's coming and you'll have to play it. You can be at slip, concentrating like crazy on every delivery, which you tend to try to do as a young player, but actually have nothing to do all day.

You turn off at your peril when Boulty and Tim are operating with the new ball on a green New Zealand wicket. But if the part-timer was trundling away on a flat deck and everything was hitting the middle of the bat, I'd be starting to talk about what I felt like having for dinner that night. BJ would say, "Bloody hell, Ross, you're talking about food already and it's still the first session."

Or you might be in India: Virender Sehwag is plastering the bowlers to the boundary at will and you're thinking, 'There's no way one's coming to me.' And you switch off, which is obviously dangerous: if you've convinced yourself that you're not going to get a catch, you probably won't take it if you do. There have been times when I've said to the slip cordon or the keeper, "I'm glad he didn't nick that one because I wasn't really concentrating." That happens more than you'd think.

If you're out there all day and 90 overs are bowled, that's 540 deliveries. Just one of those might have your name on it, but that might be the only time you've switched off. On another day, you might switch off a dozen times, but nothing comes your way. You've got to be able to switch on to every ball and stay engaged with the game. What's the bowler trying to do here? What's the captain up to with that field placing? Where's this batter looking to play?

For most of my career I was fortunate to be part of a very proficient cordon. Tom, Guppy, Tim McIntosh, Jamie How, Mark Craig and Tim were all very good slip fielders. BJ Watling was a superb all-round keeper and Brendon had fantastic agility and ability to cover the ground. I enjoyed being at first slip to Brendon because there was no grey area and he liked a big gap. Sometimes I'd be at one and a half which meant I got more catches.

Your depth is the key to fielding in the slips. In New Zealand or Australia, even on a day-four or five wicket, you'd take a very different depth than on the subcontinent. When Wrighty was coach he was always sending out the message that we were standing too deep. The first message would come out after two or three overs. It would get to the stage that the 12th man would only get halfway out to the middle and we'd be saying, "Yes, we know we're too deep, you don't need to come all the way out." The boys still laugh about it.

I can only assume it was a hangover from Wrighty's time coaching India and getting frustrated with nicks dropping short of the slips. You'd much rather it carried and was dropped than have it bounce a metre short. It was only quite recently that I found out Wrighty didn't field in the slips in his playing days, otherwise I would have sent the 12th man back with this message: "What would you know, Wrighty? You were never in there. The guy's bowling at 140 kph and we're only 10 metres from the bat." Easy to say "get closer" from 120 metres away.

After the two-test series in South Africa in 2016 — the first in Durban was rained off and we got thumped at Centurion — we had a joint fine session. In that regard, South Africa were my favourite opponent. They play hard cricket but they're the friendliest team off the field. They were very gracious in defeat after the 2015 World Cup semi-final, which must have been heart-breaking for them.

Chris Morris was making sure no one's glass got anywhere near empty. Mark Craig was running our side of the fines session while Neil McKenzie, who'd done it for South Africa as a player, was still doing it as a member of the support staff, and doing it brilliantly. I'd had a game to forget, run out by Temba Bavuma for one in the first innings and lbw to Dale Steyn for a duck in the second. The ball hit a crack and shot along the ground. I got fined for that, but the South African boys also fined their coach, Russell Domingo, for saying I should have just flicked it off my pads. Not so easy when it scuttles along the ground.

Ish Sodhi and Kagiso Rabada had a very funny rap battle. When I'd played against Rabada in county cricket, he came out to bat with his arm guard on the wrong arm. We asked him afterwards if he'd hurt his other arm and was trying to protect it. No: he simply hadn't realised he had the guard on the wrong arm. In their rap battle, Ish offered to give Kagiso a tutorial on how to wear an arm guard as long as Kagiso pinkie-promised not to bounce him.

Then we heard about what was undoubtedly my favourite sledge. AB de Villiers had quit test cricket, but there was a lot of talk that he was weighing up a comeback. When Bavuma was batting, Wags kept asking him, "What are you going to do when AB comes back?" the implication being that Bavuma would get dumped to make room for AB. Waggy's nothing if not persistent: having asked the question after practically every ball, at the end of the over he waited for Bavuma to walk down the wicket to talk to his batting partner and asked him again. Temba said, "Oh, I'll probably emigrate to New Zealand." Boom. Waggy kept pretty quiet after that. On the bright side he did get a five-for at what had been his home ground before he emigrated to New Zealand.

Chapter 19.
Finishing Touches

The final act of the World Test Championship was the Mace tour — a victory lap around New Zealand with the WTC trophy. Will Young and I went to Whanganui, supposedly for a 20-minute meet and greet with a few dozen invited guests. What we didn't realise was that the event had been more or less advertised in the local paper: there were about 400 schoolchildren and a hundred-odd parents waiting for us in the Community Sports Centre. Willy Nicholls, Henry's brother and the New Zealand Cricket media man, was with us. I told him, "We're not out of here in 20 minutes — there'd be a riot."

The Mayor of Whanganui is Hamish McDouall — Jacinda Ardern's distant cousin, a former TV quiz show star (his specialist subject was David Bowie) and the author of Chris Cairns' biography. Willy usually emceed these gigs, but the mayor wasn't going to be the support act on his own stage. In his introductory remarks he connected Whanganui to the WTC via Harry Cave, a Whanganui man who was one of the heroes of New Zealand's first-ever test victory — over the West Indies at Eden Park in 1956.

Then he launched into a Q&A: "Ross," he said, "how nervous were you and Kane at the end there, knowing that people back home are always worried about your running between the wickets?" I thought, 'Oh great. Here we go again.' I gave a bland non-answer, so he went to Will, asking him what it was like being involved with the Black Caps. Will said, "I love playing with Ross and learnt a lot off him. I mean, Ross has been around a while — he played with Harry Cave." There were 500-odd people in the house, but only two of them laughed: Will and me.

The late 2021 tour of India was a bittersweet experience. As in 2016, the first test was at Green Park in Kanpur. The hotel we stayed at has a tenpin bowling alley and in 2016 the boys got right into it. We were going bowling after the day's play so by the end of the test — which we lost — we were sort of over it. But we had a few beers and decided to have one last roll. There was a device that recorded the bowling ball's speed, so we had a competition to see who could send it the fastest.

I worked out that you got more speed if you launched it aerially rather than along the deck. I was working up a real head of steam, but my thumb got stuck as I went to really let one go. The bowling alley had a very low ceiling. Because my thumb got stuck, there was a delayed release and I absolutely hammered the bowling ball into the ceiling. It was like a bomb had gone off — the lights and all sorts of debris came crashing down.

I apologised profusely to the manager and offered to pay for the damage, but he wouldn't have it. "No, no," he said, "it happens all the time. We've got replacement ceiling panels out the back." I don't know if that was true or he just felt sorry for me. Ish Sodhi, who thought it was the funniest thing of all time, had videoed it and put it out there. So now, if there's a tenpin bowling fiasco anywhere in the world, that's captured on film and posted on Instagram, I get tagged.

Because of the way the wickets in India deteriorate, if you don't win the toss, a draw is a really good outcome. Fortunately, in 2021 the Green Park wicket didn't behave quite as expected. Tim Southee bowled superbly, taking eight wickets in the match and, although we squandered Tom Latham and Will Young's 150-run first innings opening partnership, we managed — just — to salvage a draw. We were nine down on the last evening, but Rachin Ravindra, on debut, and Ajaz Patel held out for nine overs.

Because of Hamilton's extended lockdown and other Covid restrictions and no longer being in the T20 side, I wasn't able to train, let alone play. My only preparation was having Jonty bowl to me in the backyard — no disrespect, Jonty. We didn't have a warm-up game in India because we were in a bubble, so the first delivery I'd faced since hitting the winning runs in the World Test Championship final five months earlier was from Umesh Yadav in Kanpur.

While the wicket in Kanpur wasn't as bad — from our point of view — as expected, the one at Wankhede Stadium in Mumbai was way worse. Once again, India won the toss. After the first session, I said to Gary Stead, "The wicket's a shocker. They shouldn't get past 200 and we're going to struggle to get to 150 if they bowl properly." They got 325 in their first innings; we got 62. It wasn't a 62 wicket, but it wasn't a 325 wicket either.

That's the game of cricket: just because it's a 200–250 wicket doesn't mean they're going to get 225. Someone can bat exceptionally well, as Mayank Agarwal did to get 150 out of his side's total of 325; you can drop catches or have no luck whatsoever. And vice versa: the other side bowls and catches really well and you fall short of the par score.

Ajaz was the only one who looked like getting a wicket, so we were joking about him getting all 10 from quite early on. Tim bowled well, keeping the run rate in check. He was buggered — it was really humid — but he bowled through it; he just kept running in. Tim has matured a lot in the last couple of years and turned himself into a fighter, to use a John Wright expression. Rachin bowled pretty well too but, at this stage of his development, probably hasn't quite got the control to bowl containing spells to batters who play spin well. He'll be all the better for the experience, though.

When Ajaz had got six out of six, we stopped joking about him getting all 10 — it was very much on. He got to nine by having Jayant Yadav caught on the boundary. We were all excited, urging him on in the huddle: "Come on, Ajaz, come on, mate." As we walked back into position I said to Tim, "I haven't been this nervous fielding since you were on fire at the Cake Tin — I didn't want to drop a catch off you then." (Tim took 7/33 against England at the 2015 World Cup.)

Ajaz bowled to their number 11, Mohammed Siraj, who lunged at it; it went off the inside edge for four. I thought, 'Oh no, that could've been it.' Ajaz had a couple of balls left. I was thinking he'd toss one up, trying to buy a wicket. Siraj took an almighty swipe and top edged it miles up in the air. As soon it went skyward, Tim yelled "Yeah!" I was like, 'What?'

Rachin was under it at mid-on. He's a composed young guy and a student of the game — he knows the traditions and the history. This definitely wasn't a case of a naive young kid who didn't appreciate the enormous significance of the moment. It wouldn't have been an easy catch under normal circumstances and these were anything but normal — Rachin must have had a lot going through his head.

Before the game, I saw Ajaz staring at the Wankhede honours board. Of course, everyone wants to get on the honours board but, with Ajaz having grown up in Mumbai, you'd have to say the stars aligned. It was only the third time a bowler had taken all 10 wickets in a test innings and the first time it had been done in the first innings — an amazing achievement that surely sits alongside Richard Hadlee's match haul of 15/123 at the Gabba in 1985 in the annals of New Zealand cricket.

I'd never been part of a changing room where the euphoria was centred exclusively on one player and his achievement. The consensus was that it was the equivalent of scoring 350-plus in a test innings. We were in a weirdly contradictory state of mind because we also knew they'd got too many runs and we weren't in a great position. It must have been tough on our openers trying to clear their minds and focus on the task ahead.

The Indian team's response was very classy and the Indian media and cricket community were happy because it was one of their own who'd done it. The Indians are good at acknowledging significant moments. The hotels always put on a cake for players' milestones or birthdays. When we got to the hotel, the staff and guests lined up all the way from the bus to the reception area to give Ajaz a standing ovation.

We were completely outplayed and I had a poor test match. The silver lining was that we were part of something extraordinary and I'd made a very small contribution to a historic achievement by taking an easy catch.

My performances in India weren't good enough. That forced me to really grapple with a decision that I'd been shadow-boxing with for a while: whether to retire from international cricket. I still loved playing at the top level, but the reality of elite sport is that you live and die on performance. While it was tempting to draw comfort from my longevity and track record and to assume I'd be granted some leeway, my limited interaction with the coaches wasn't particularly reassuring in that regard. I was determined to leave on my terms but acutely aware that, the longer I left it, the greater the likelihood that the decision would be made for me.

The press conference to announce that I'd be retiring at the end of the season was one of the harder things I've had to do in my career. My preferred way of doing it would have been to wait and announce my retirement "with immediate effect", but Gary Hermansson argued strongly that I shouldn't do that. "This is not about you," he said. It was about giving the public the opportunity to say goodbye and involving my family and friends, the people who'd supported me through thick and thin, in the last act of my international career.

The farewell tour got off to a rocky start in Mount Maunganui where Bangladesh recorded their first-ever test win in New Zealand. I thought we took them a little too easily. We got well behind in the game, but Steady was still talking about winning. I don't think that would've been the message if we'd been playing Australia or England. It felt like there was an expectation that Bangladesh would get so far but no further, that they'd roll over at some point. But, whoever the opposition, if they keep you in the field for 176 overs, you're going to be up against it. That takes it out of you physically and mentally.

There was a lot of dissatisfaction with the wicket. The formula that has worked for us is bouncy, green wickets that have something in them for two or three days. The wicket at the Mount had flattened out by lunch on the first day. That said, we didn't score enough runs in the first innings. Once you're 100 runs behind, it becomes hard to catch up: if you're only 40 or 50 runs behind at the halfway point, that's a different ball game.

Because there was no bounce, we couldn't intimidate them. The Bangladeshis must've thought all their Christmases had come at once — if there was ever a New Zealand wicket they didn't mind playing on, that was it. And it doesn't matter who you are, Curtly Ambrose, Pat Cummins or Neil Wagner, when you're 130 or 140 overs deep, it's a tough, hard grind.

Perhaps we should've had lower expectations seeing the two home wins that we had to work the hardest for in recent years were at the Mount — over England and Pakistan. I'll be really interested to see how the wicket plays next time. Trent Boult lives at the Mount and Waggy lives in Papamoa, so the groundsman probably had his ear bashed all winter. The next test there could be all over in two days.

I actually felt pretty good at the crease in that series. From a technical perspective, it was probably the best I'd batted for some time — I just found ways of getting out. There were a couple of soft dismissals, but I hadn't played much cricket and, once I'd made the announcement, things kept taking me by surprise because I simply didn't know what to expect. The emotions aroused by my impending retirement started swirling, within myself and others, at the Mount.

Mackenzie and I presented the players' caps before the second test at Hagley Oval. She added some personal touches, for instance telling Devon Conway that Dad "still hasn't forgiven you for running him out" in Devon's first game for the Black Caps.

Bangladesh won the toss and put us in. When I went into bat the next morning with the score at 363/2, the Bangladesh team formed a guard of honour, which was a lovely gesture. I didn't really know how to react. Should I take my helmet off? Should I take my glove off to shake hands? And the umpires were part of it, which added to my surprise. Tom Latham was on 190 and probably thinking, 'Just get on with it; I don't want to be dealing with this.' Shoriful Islam, the left-arm quick, gave me a pat on the back and, two balls later, a bouncer.

I started well, but on 28 I dragged a ball from Ebadot Hossain and was caught at square leg by Shoriful. There was a hush around the ground and, once the bowler and catcher had celebrated, out in the middle as well. That made us 411/3 and everyone was probably thinking the same thing: that could be it; if we did the business with the ball, I wouldn't get another bat.

We knocked them over for 126 that afternoon. The crowd at both the Mount and Hagley had called for me to have a bowl so, when we were warming up on the third morning, I thought I should roll my arm over just in case. I bowled a couple to Matt Henry, the 12th man. I tried to toss them up, but they were half-trackers; it was ridiculous. Matt was telling me they weren't too bad, which was the nicest possible way of putting it. As we went out to field after lunch, Kyle Jamieson said, "Ross, I just want you to have a bowl." He was quite serious about it. I said, "I hope not."

We were into the last hour of the day's play and it was starting to get dark. When the ninth wicket fell, the crowd started chanting, "Give Ross a bowl." In the group huddle, Tim and a few of the others were telling Tom to give me a bowl. Tom said, "Nah, he's not getting a bowl." The whole team joined in the crowd chant: "Give Ross a bowl, give Ross a bowl." I left the huddle laughing.

Having a Canterbury crowd pulling for me to that extent was a new experience. Victoria and the kids had come down to the tunnel thinking it could be all over at any moment and I'd be walking off for the last time. It was also getting cold so they'd closed the sliding doors to the members' area. Some bloke pulled the doors open, stuck his head out and roared, "Give Ross a bowl." Not what you expect from the members at Hagley.

As he headed for fine leg at the end of his over, KJ said to Tom he had a sore hip and didn't want to bowl another over. He told Tom to give me a bowl, but Tom wouldn't budge. Kyle had taken four wickets and batters nine and 11 were at the crease, so he was spurning a golden opportunity to get a five-wicket bag. Neil Wagner bowled the next over. In the cordon, Tim and Tom Blundell were saying, "Please, Waggy, don't get a wicket." After a couple of balls Tim went over to umpire Chris Gaffaney and said, "Gaff, if you don't say the seamers can't bowl, Ross isn't going to get a bowl." Gaff just smiled.

The umpires conferred at the end of Wags' over. I walked past them slowly to see what was going on. Gaff was telling Tom he could only bowl spinners because of the poor light. (It was that dark I was surprised they hadn't done it two or three overs earlier.) Tom Blundell had bowled in the Melbourne test, but he was keeping. Henry Nicholls isn't a bad bowler but hadn't bowled in test cricket and didn't want to bowl. I was playing along with the crowd, pretending to warm up. Tom relented — he probably felt he had to give the crowd what they wanted. I took my cap off, went to hand it to Gaff and was genuinely perplexed that he wouldn't take it. It shows you how removed from it all I was that I'd forgotten the Covid protocols: bowlers have to give their caps, sweaters and sunglasses to teammates rather than the umpires.

I measured out my run up. Tim was laughing his head off: "Who are you trying to kid, Ross? You don't have a run-up." I had no idea what the field was. I just wanted to get the ball down the other end without making a fool of myself by bowling a head-high full toss or a double-bouncer. The first one was pretty straight, almost a yorker. Gaff had a chuckle. "That wasn't far away," he said. I decided to go around the wicket: the shorter boundary was on the leg-side and it would probably have been easier to hit it there if I was coming over the wicket. By going around the wicket I could push the ball away from the hitting arc.

Tim was telling me to toss it up. I wanted to, but I was hardly brimming with confidence. Tom moved Will Young from 45 to leg slip and brought Trent Boult up from long on, probably thinking that he was wasted back there if I was going to bowl arm balls. I didn't realise Boulty had come almost all the way in. If I had, I probably wouldn't have tossed it up.

The length was okay, but I dragged it across well outside off stump. Ebadot (test batting average 0.88) had a swing but tried to go leg-side, hitting against the angle. It went pretty much straight up, not unlike Mohammad Siraj in Mumbai. I was looking up thinking, 'No way.' Tom made what was actually a pretty good grab because it wasn't his catch — he had to turn and go back for it. It was really Boulty's catch, but he didn't want anything to do with it. Boulty's a very good fielder; he's taken some of the best outfield catches you'll ever see. But he'd dropped a couple and catching is such a confidence thing. It's no different to fielding in the slips: when you drop one and your confidence dips, you start hoping the ball doesn't come to you.

It actually took some of the emotion out of the occasion because I was a bit stunned and amused/bemused that I'd finished my test career that way. If the cricket gods had offered me a choice of scoring a half century or even a century or taking the last wicket, I would have taken the wicket, no question about it. Almost immediately people started sending me far-fetched stats trivia, for instance that I have the best bowling average of guys who have played a minimum of 100 tests and taken a minimum of two wickets. If another criterion was a minimum of 100 balls delivered, I wouldn't qualify because I only bowled 99 in my test career.

New Zealand Cricket, particularly CEO David White and high-performance manager Bryan Stronach, were fantastic in all sorts of ways around that last test and the subsequent ODI series against the Netherlands. We had a great celebration in the changing room — family and friends, teammates and their partners and parents. Steady made a very nice speech when presenting Mum with a framed photographic montage of my career highlights. Everyone in the changing room was on their feet giving her a standing ovation. Kane, who didn't play because of his elbow injury, flew down, which I appreciated enormously. We harked back to the conversation before the World Test Championship final.

Kane was intrigued to have learned — via a TV interview that was shown during the game — that I'm a Samoan chief. I'd told Mum that I didn't want to be a chief, but she didn't listen and accepted on my behalf. When I was in Samoa in 2017, I attended a few dinners where I wasn't introduced as Ross or Luteru. It was title and full name: Leaupepe Luteru Ross Poutoa Lote Taylor. (Whenever I get a message from former All Black Ofisa Tonu'u, a keen cricketer who made his international cricketing debut for Samoa at the age of 49, he calls me "Leaupepe".)

At one of the dinners, I was sitting next to the then Samoan Prime Minister, Susuaga Tuila'epa Sa'ilele Malielegaoi. After I was introduced, he leaned over and said, "Wow, that's a big title." I had no idea that a Samoan prime minister would take an interest in cricket. Maybe I had something to do with that.

Mum's always telling me I'm popular in Samoa, but then she is my mum. I'd like to take the kids to Samoa to show them Mum's village but, when I go, I won't be telling her. If I did, all my extended family — and that's a lot of people given Mum had 13 brothers and sisters — would be coming around to say hello.

Leanne McGoldrick: I first met Ross 19 years ago. He was a shy, humble boy with a warm smile and a huge amount of promise. I get emotional thinking about how far we've come since then and all that he has achieved throughout his career. Through it all, the warm smile and the humility were constant factors and he never lost sight of the important things in life — family, friends, integrity, and empathy. He leaves the game as the same kind and caring man he was at the start of his career.

His journey hasn't always been easy and he was often underestimated. By the end of his career, though, New Zealanders recognised him for what he is: one of our true sporting greats.

Victoria Taylor: Even on a world stage, you look at his numbers and you just think 'Far out.' Those are some pretty good numbers. He just flew under the radar for some reason, I don't know why. I mean, it's not a bad thing and hasn't been a bad thing. And I think he probably preferred it that way. But I would want people to know how resilient this guy actually is and how mentally strong he's had to be to overcome everything that was going on in the background, and walk out there and perform and achieve what he's achieved. I just wonder, 'What was going through your mind? How did you do that?'

The kids and I are immensely proud of Ross and what he has achieved.

Naoupu Taylor: As a mother, it is amazing to see what he has achieved. I'm very proud of Kelu and his wonderful career but, more importantly, of the man he has become. I am grateful for all the people who have supported him and prayed for him throughout his journey.

Fa'afetai i Atua mo Iona alofa ma Iona agalelei, ma le taleni ma foa'iina mo e. Fa'afelai I le tapua'iga ma le nofo tatalo a Samoa ua a'e manuia ai le faiva a le atali'i.

I was determined not to be defined by the captaincy controversy and I think I succeeded in that. I didn't revisit that whole episode with the aim of breathing fresh life into it or settling scores, but simply to tell my side of a drama that turned my life upside down, created divisions within the New Zealand cricket community and left its mark on everyone involved. Time is a great healer and I hold no grudges.

I'm content with my career. I made mistakes, but I also made sacrifices. Of course, there are things I'd do differently if I had my time over again but, when I look at the big picture, I have very few regrets. I believe the various setbacks and challenges made me a better cricketer and a better person. I thank all those who helped me on the journey. There are many of you. I hope I made all of you — and particularly my late and sorely missed friend and mentor Martin "Hogan" Crowe — feel that the time and effort you put into me was a worthwhile investment.

I consider myself blessed to have been part of a great era in New Zealand cricket. It was an enormous honour to represent my country, the Samoan people and the wider Pacific Island community. I look forward to working in that space in the future. And I look forward to watching the Black Caps grow and build on the successes I was fortunate enough to play a part in.

When I played my very last game for the Black Caps, an ODI against the Netherlands in Hamilton, I became the first New Zealand cricketer to play 450 games for their country. A nice note on which to finish. A pretty good achievement for a part-Samoan boy from the Bush.

CAREER RECORD

Statistics compiled by Francis Payne, editor of the
New Zealand Cricket Almanack

Format	Mat	Inns	NO	Runs	HS	Ave	SR	100s	50s	Ct
Test	112	196	24	7683	290	44.66	59	19	35	163
ODI	236	220	39	8607	181*	47.55	83	21	51	142
T20I	102	94	21	1909	63	26.15	122	–	7	46
FC	192	323	27	12369	290	41.78	63	27	65	249
List A	312	296	46	11356	181*	45.42	85	26	74	192
T20	292	275	67	6429	111*	30.90	131	1	32	121

As an occasional off-spin bowler, Ross Taylor took seven wickets in first-class cricket (including three in test matches), three in List A matches and eight in Twenty20 games.

Notable achievements
- Most runs for New Zealand in tests (7683)
- Most runs for New Zealand in one-day internationals (8607)
- Most runs for New Zealand in international cricket (18,199)
- Most centuries for New Zealand in one-day internationals (21)
- Most centuries for New Zealand in international cricket (40)
- Most tests for New Zealand, equal with Daniel Vettori (112)
- Most appearances for New Zealand in international cricket (450)
- On the winning side in test matches on 44 occasions and 216 times in all international games, both New Zealand records
- Most catches for New Zealand by a fielder in international cricket (351)
- First player from any country to make 100 international appearances in each of the three formats

- Holds the record for highest test innings in Australia by any visiting player (290 at Perth 2015/16)
- Shares New Zealand one-day international record partnerships for:
  3rd wicket (206 with Kane Williamson vs England at Southampton 2015)
  4th wicket (200 with Tom Latham vs India at Mumbai 2017/18)
  5th wicket (195 with Kane Williamson vs Zimbabwe at Bulawayo 2011/12)
- Longest first-class career for Central Districts, equal with Mike Shrimpton (19 seasons)
- Fastest century in New Zealand domestic one-day cricket: 49 balls for Central Districts vs Wellington at New Plymouth, 2021/22
- Winner of the Redpath Cup, for New Zealand first-class batting, on four occasions: 2007/08, 2009/10, 2013/14, 2017/18
- Most runs (7690) and most centuries (19) by a number four batsman in one-day internationals (all countries). In all international cricket, only Mahela Jayawardene (16,838) has scored more runs than Taylor (15,613) batting at number four.
- Third most catches by a fielder (351) in international cricket after Mahela Jayawardene (440) and Ricky Ponting (364)
- Test Player of the Year: 2012/13, 2013/14
- Sir Richard Hadlee Medal for Overall Player of the Year: 2012/13, 2013/14, 2019/20
- New Zealand Cricket Almanack Player of the Year: 2009, 2018

Acknowledgement

It may come as a surprise for readers to learn that writer Paul Thomas and I never had a single in-person meeting over the course of this book's production. Instead, all interviews —no fewer than 30 hours' worth — were conducted via Zoom. Such is life in the Covid Age . . .

In fact, the only occasion I ever met Paul face to face was at an introductory lunch with my publishers in Auckland in 2021.

In the end, though, this lack of one-on-one contact proved no obstacle. Throughout the entire interview/writing process, Paul never failed to impress me with his deep understanding of the game of cricket, his warmth, patience and professionalism.

So, Paul, a very big thanks for helping me tell my story. I look forward to sharing a special glass or two with you in the near future . . . let's just hope it's not via Zoom.